BETWEEN THE LINES

BETWEEN THE LINES

A cartoon century of New Zealand political and social history, 1906-2005

Ian F. Grant

Previous books

Bali: Morning of the World (with Hubert Sieben), 1970
Journey Through a Landscape (with Don Neilson), 1976
Inside Down Under (with Bob Brockie), 1976
The Unauthorized Version: A Cartoon History of New Zealand, 1980, revised edition 1987
Out Of The Woods: the Restructuring and Sale of New Zealand's State Forests (with Reg Birchfield), 1993
North of the Waingawa: Masterton Borough and County Councils 1877-1989, 1995
The Smallfarming Revolution: New Beginnings in Rural New Zealand (with Diane Grant), 1998
False Prophets: A Light Roasting of New Zealand's Sacred Cows, 1998
Wairarapa (with Grant Sheehan), 2000
The Other Side Of the Ditch: A Cartoon Century in the New Zealand-Australia Relationship, 2001
Public Lives: New Zealand Premiers and Prime Ministers, 2003
The Look of Greytown (with Chris Slater), 2004

First published by the New Zealand Cartoon Archive,
Alexander Turnbull Library, P O Box 12349,
Wellington, New Zealand.
October 2005

ISBN: 0-9582320-4-0

Cover design: Jan-Michael David, Bravo Design, Auckland
Editor: Diane Grant, Fraser Books
Formatting: Graham Kerrisk, Printcraft, Masterton
Distribution: Nationwide Book Distributors, P O Box 4176,
Christchurch, New Zealand
Printed by Publishing Press Limited, 31 William Pickering Drive,
Albany, Auckland, New Zealand

Front cover cartoon (ATL: DCDL-0000280) and back cover caricature: Murray Webb.

CONTENTS

PREFACE

Traditionally, historical research has relied heavily on official documents and reports and the memoirs and correspondence of participants; more recently newspapers, photographs and cartoons have added different, and sometimes illuminating, perspectives.

There is growing acceptance of the importance of cartoons: they capture the unofficial values and attitudes of the time, providing a street level view of the world, not a high-rise bureaucratic perspective, or a corridors of power slant, and certainly not an ivory tower, academic assessment.

One of the greatest advantages of editorial cartoons is that they can encapsulate quite complicated ideas, get to the nub of an issue. Former prime minister, Sir John Marshall put it well: "A good cartoon can convey, at a glance, a wealth of information; it can epitomise an idea better than a thousand words; it is remembered when words are forgotten; it is instant enlightenment."

At their best, cartoons snatch and preserve the essence of an historical moment. Cartoons are, in a sense, the pulse on the feelings of the day – the quick gut reaction of cartoonists drawing their inspiration from popular sentiment.

Editorial cartoons – present-day ones and from the past – have at least one other significant advantage – they have always been able to make a political point much more robustly than the printed word. As David English wrote, when editor of Britain's *Daily Mail*: "The cartoonist, given that special licence granted over the centuries, can say things others only dare whisper." While New Zealand politicians have regularly sued the print and electronic media for aspersions supposedly cast, much more biting comments in cartoons have not received the attention of defamation lawyers.

Sir Geoffrey Palmer, another former prime minister, said: "History suggests that cartoonists – who often deal savagely with politicians and others – are relatively safe. The Press Council receives a number of complaints about cartoons, but that's usually as far as it goes. A cartoon is, after all, an analogy and cartoonists are generally on safe ground as long as they express genuine opinions."

There is only one New Zealand instance of a court case involving a political cartoon. In 1911, William Massey, then leader of the opposition, sued the *NZ Times* over a cartoon he claimed portrayed him as a liar and responsible for mean and despicable acts. The jury concurred that the cartoon did indeed depict Massey in the way alleged but, being political comment, was not libellous.

Between the Lines is following in the tradition of *The Unauthorized Version*, the country's first cartoon history, published in 1980, then revised and added to in 1987, and which led to the founding of the New Zealand Cartoon Archive in 1992.

The books subsequently published by the Cartoon Archive have had several objectives. The first has been to share with cartoon enthusiasts and those interested in our country's history more of the NZ Cartoon Archive's riches in its substantial and ever-growing collection. The second was to use the cartoons to illuminate and examine that history, especially aspects of it possibly forgotten, glossed over or even deliberately ignored by subsequent generations. The third aim has been to show the 'ordinary' man and woman's view of the events of the time – "the unofficial values and attitudes", "the unauthorised version".

In this book, over 600 cartoons from the Archive's collection are featured – only a handful of which have

What do you think of New Zealand ?
Jim

Jim Gorman, *NZ Listener*, ca 1976. ATL: A-299-193

appeared in previous publications. And while *The Unauthorized Version* covered much of the same political ground, *Between the Lines* examines that ground in more detail, concentrating on the last century – from the year of Richard John Seddon's death – as well as including the 18 fascinating and politically important years from 1987 until 2005, and one of the closest election races for years. Although, of course, history can not be compartmentalised that neatly, the book is divided into decade-bite chapters each of which also gives an over-view of evolving trends in our society as well as cultural milestones.

As we begin a new century a study of the last century underscores the need to know our history to understand the present and have some ability to interpret the future. Wars, unemployment, depressions, outbreaks of prosperity, poverty, health, crime, education, drugs, sex, corruption, political megalomaniacs and nincompoops – all have been in and out of the spotlight during the last century and will continue to be through the next.

While the main focus is on the 1906-2005 period it is not possible, as the setters of social studies and history curricula often seem to think, to view history as a series of unconnected 'themes'. So the introductory chapter traverses – in words and cartoons – the decades up to the beginning of the 20th century to provide the necessary context for what follows.

Readers interested in more information about New Zealand's cartoonists and the publications they cartooned in should refer to the second edition of *The Unauthorized Version* (1987).

Like economy booms and busts and great and lesser public figures, there have been golden and grey cartooning eras. Golden eras in cartooning have been the 1890s, 1930s and 1940s, and the 1970s through to the 1990s.

Sadly, at the beginning of the 21st century, cartooning is in one of its greyer periods. The amalgamation of the *Dominion* and *The Evening Post* in Wellington has reduced further the limited number of cartooning spots and, as the established cartoonists are ageing, younger artists and designers with flair are, it seems, not interested in politics. Instead, several have established international reputations as creators of 'graphic novels'.

Hopefully, the continued work of the New Zealand Cartoon Archive will encourage a new, bright generation of cartoonists to emerge. As this book shows, they have an eclectic and brilliant collection of models to be inspired by.

Acknowledgements

The New Zealand Cartoon Archive appreciates the willingness with which the cartoonists, whose work appears in this book, or their representatives, have given their permission for their cartoons to appear. The same applies to the publications where the cartoons first appeared; we must particularly record our thanks to Solo Syndication, London for permission to use David Low cartoons, APN NZ Ltd and the Minhinnick family for the permission to use Sir Gordon's cartoons and the Lodge family for the inclusion of Nevile Lodge cartoons. Every effort has been made to contact the relatives or descendents of the few cartoonists we do not have information about and, in absentia, thank them as well.

I would particularly like to thank Murray Webb for his post-2005 election cartoon which appears on the book's front cover.

Also, my grateful thanks to all the Alexander Turnbull Library Library staff who helped in so many ways in the production of this book. Particular thanks are due to Margaret Calder, chief librarian; David Adams, Caroline Garratt, Stephen Roucher and Claire Viskovic of Image Services; Heather Mathie of Turnbull Library Pictures; Peter Attwell, Mary Cobeldick, David Retter and the staff of the Research Centre; the staff of the newspaper room; Mary Newman of the Cartoon Archive, Jenny Gailits, and Susan Bartel, Turnbull Library promotions manager.

As always the New Zealand Cartoon Archive is grateful for the support of its sponsors - APN New Zealand Ltd, Fairfax NZ Ltd, Gault Mitchell Lawyers, Grant Thornton, Martin Jarvie P.K.F., Newspaper Publishers Association of New Zealand (Inc.), Norske Skog Tasman Ltd and Profile Publishing.

Most of all I want to thank Rachel Macfarlane and Diane Grant. Without Rachel, my NZ Cartoon Archive colleague, the book would have been an impossibly daunting task. Her assistance in identifying likely cartoons and then ensuring they were all numbered, scanned and assembled was crucial. Diane, my wife and best friend, was, as always, my editor, mentor and confidante. This was a large project researched, written and published in an unrealistically short time. Without Diane's sacrifices, encouragement and optimism when I felt the deadlines unachievable, it simply would not have happened.

Ian F Grant
October 1 2005

1: Introduction

BEGINNINGS OF A SETTLER SOCIETY

While there is migration myth v. DNA arm-wrestling going on about when Maori first arrived in New Zealand and from where, there is no uncertainty at all about when the first European settlers came, or why.

They were largely of English and Scottish stock, frustrated by the lack of opportunity to 'better' themselves in an increasingly callous Britain hell-bent on industralisation, and enterprising and courageous enough to risk a dangerous sea voyage to the bottom of the world, often knowing little more than the lurid stories they had heard about ferocious, tattooed Maori.

Another colony, so small, far away and unpromising made no sense to the Colonial Office mandarins, but their well-manicured hands were forced by New Zealand's proximity to the Australian convict colonies, a growing trans-Tasman trade in timber and 'main chance' rogues, a bevy of soul saving clergy, the effects of traded muskets on Maori inter-tribal warfare, and the campaign of Edward Gibbon Wakefield, the 19th century entrepreneur who did not always let truth get in the way of a good idea.

Captain William Hobson, despatched to take possession of New Zealand in the name of Queen Victoria, persuaded the first Maori chiefs to sign the Treaty of Waitangi, and cede sovereignty, on February 5 1840, just a few days after the first colonists arrived at Wellington more than 500 miles to the south.

The 'great Maori land grab' describes the next 60 years of European settlement in New Zealand succinctly, and with some accuracy. It was a mistake, Wakefield said, to give land away or sell it too cheaply. His core 'sufficient price' theory was designed to keep the necessary equilibrium between capital and labour in the new colony. Assisted labourers would have to work for wages until they could afford to buy land at an artificially high price; their labour would accumulate wealth in the hands of the first landowners, and this would underwrite the colony's development. It was a theory that assumed the ready availability of land, lots of it and when the colonists wanted it.

Despite the Treaty of Waitangi, and Colonial Office instructions to the first governors to safeguard Maori interests, the Wakefield settlers and the others who followed had come, cabin and steerage, to occupy and farm the land. The great debate in the early newspapers, and in later parliaments, was not whether Maori should lose their land but whether the deed should be done militarily, or stealthily with legal finesse.

Under a constitution largely framed by Governor George Grey the two-house General Assembly first met in Auckland in 1854; two years later appointed officials gave way to the first settler ministry. When the central government and provincial councils, in an amiable manner untypical of their later relations, carved up responsibilities and shares of the public purse, the governor retained a firm grip on Maori affairs and 'waste' land purchases.

Anthony Ellison, *Auckland Star*, November 21 1987. J-065-039

Grey bought large tracts of the North Island and most of the South Island from Maori and tried to widen European ownership by significantly lowering the price of Crown land, with the unintended result that huge swathes were snapped up by well-heeled pastoralists. His successor, Gore Browne, flouted Maori tradition, and precipitated the first Taranaki war and later Waikato campaigns, by allowing individual Maori to sell land. In the early 1860s, the incumbent ministries threw out the Crown's pre-emptive Maori land purchase rights and took responsibility for Maori affairs, an unpopular consequence being the gradual withdrawal of British troops who, until then, had been doing most of the settlers' fighting for them.

Generally, Maori had welcomed the settlers in 1840: they saw Queen Victoria's mana as giving them some physical protection and they had a shrewdly calculating eye for trading opportunities and some of the more attractive refinements of European culture. But it had simply not occurred to them that the original trickle of settlers would, in a remarkably short time, make them a weak, sickly minority in their own country, or that the newcomers would be so obsessively preoccupied with by-hook-or-by-crook ownership of land, and then more land. The reaction to the loss of so much land and the weakening of customary Maoritanga was the Maori King movement, a loose tribal confederation which stalled the spread of European settlement into the central North Island.

Meanwhile, the South Island was prospering. Good fortune shone on the Canterbury and Otago settlers. While northerners seethed with frustration, hemmed in by still-stubborn Maori land-owners and a bush-covered landscape, the fire-stick pastoralists opened up Canterbury's hinterland, and goldminers lived in canvas towns thrown up in remote Otago and West Coast valleys. But by the late 1860s the gold fever was subsiding, wool prices had slipped and confidence was on a parallel downward slide. It was not until 1882, when the first shipment of refrigerated sheep and lambs was sent to Britain, that meat, rendered down into tallow, was more than a wool by-product.

It took Julius Vogel, an extraordinary politician-adventurer and a South Islander via London and the Australian goldfields, to convince a sufficient number of his colleagues that New Zealand could spend and grow out of its difficulties. During the 1870s, roads, rail and telegraph wires multiplied prodigiously; thousands of immigrants fuelled the frantic activity and Vogel, instigator of a 'Think Big' scheme that did work, became the first nationally known politician. Pulling strings behind the scenes as he preferred, he was also responsible for abolishing the provincial system in 1876.

In the now all-powerful General Assembly, loose, constantly shifting coalitions of parliamentarians, often with primary provincial loyalties, formed ministries barely distinguishable one from the next well into the 1880s. Despite the well-polished vitriol in debate, these 'oligarchs' had more in common with one another than with the widening electorate which voted for them. They were prosperous and well-educated, and they could afford a part-time occupation that paid a negligible 'honorarium'. Usually they had gravitated to politics out of a sense of duty, sometimes garnished with self-interest. After 1876, with the provinces gone, there was a gradually centralised opposition to the currently ruling clique, with land and its tenure the focal point in the struggles for the treasury benches, and retrenchment the only, paralysing response to deepening depression in the 1880s. There was now virtually universal male suffrage and an increasingly dissatisfied electorate plumped at the next election, in 1890, for the Liberals, the country's first real political party, and for its radical policies.

The Liberals' election-winning manifesto might have been built on the premise of state intervention that left foreign observers breathless, but no great mental leap was required by New Zealanders or their elected representatives; with New Zealand Company paternalism, the control of land sales to Europeans, and Vogel's public works schemes there was a strong tradition of government regulation and involvement.

New Zealand was the world's social and industrial laboratory in the 1890s, but there is little justification for the myth of a sudden flowering of enlightened social and industrial experimentation. Rather, Richard John Seddon, who became premier when John Ballance died in May 1893, was a supremely practical politician who sensibly honoured election promises to open up the country to more and closer settlement and to improve industrial working conditions. Even Seddon's one personal piece of landmark legislation, the 1898 Old Age Pension Act, was mainly a tactical move to secure the electoral support of another sizeable group of voters.

During the first 60 years of organised European settlement, New Zealand might not have been a classless society, but it was a markedly egalitarian one. Like so much of the Wakefield system, its plans for a distinct social hierarchy worked only in part. While a surprising number of the 'gentry' and well educated were attracted to early New Zealand in search of adventure and fortune, birth and learning had limited utility, and respect was earned with artisan skills or hard, physical labour. As well, the enterprising labourers who emigrated to escape the straight-jacket of class, had no intention of doffing their caps to any vestiges of it in the new country. The 'gentry' dominated the shifting coalitions of political power up to 1890 but there was no sense of them exercising a 'natural authority' over fellow colonists. MPs were paid a token honorarium until 1893 and, although parliament rarely met for more than three months a year, this was an insurmountable obstacle for 'working' men.

Regardless of background it took courage and some imagination to leave the familiar for an often harsh, untamed environment so it is not surprising there was a strong, visceral urge to create a 'little England' in the South Seas, with oak trees, gorse and rabbits, with subscriptions to London magazines and the aping of fashionable publications like *Punch*.

New Zealand's distance from the rest of the world and the separation of clusters of colonists from one another has been much remarked upon. During the period of greatest immigration in the 1870s it still took ships about four months to sail to New Zealand; it routinely took 10 months to get a reply to a letter sent to England. The first telegraph cable to Australia, with on-going links to Britain and Europe, was laid in 1876 and, by the 1890s, letters and passengers could make the journey by steamship in about six weeks.

At the end of the 1850s it still took a fortnight to get from Auckland to Dunedin and the 'news' about other centres in the local newspaper would be up to three weeks stale.

This changed rapidly during the next decade with regular steamship services, Cobb and Co coaches with their new and welcome system of suspension and, from 1861, the telegraph. With railway lines snaking out from the main centres in the 1870s, and telephones in the 1880s, an embryonic national network of transport and communications hastened the end of the provincial political

On The War Trail.
Dick the tracker: "Vengeance on the pale-face Opposition slanderer of my good name.
Ha! Ha! I'll spoil his little games. On! On! After his footsteps day and night."

William Blomfield, *NZ Observer and Free Lance*, June 3 1899. ATL:H-723-013

system and travel became much more routine.

During the early years, the use of horses and sprouting of post offices ensured colonists were less isolated than they might have been. From the 1860s, locally-bred horses were cheap and conveniently dual-purpose as they negotiated deeply rutted tracks, carrying people and goods, in town and the country. Unsurprisingly, horse racing – first on beaches and in rough paddocks but soon at race courses – was very popular. By the early 1880s there were six times as many horses per thousand people than in Britain. Women and children – visiting friends and going to school – used horses much more widely than in other countries. There were eight post offices in 1845; by 1875 when every man, woman and child in the country posted a letter at least once a fortnight, on average, there were 647.

From very early on there were two New Zealands: the major towns, on or close to the water that was the principal means of long-distance travel, and the country – rough-hewn townships, isolated from one another, and remote farmhouses, some very grand, on land that was being broken in around them, at the end of barely discernible tracks. Yet from the mid-1850s at least a quarter of the country's population were town dwellers; by the early 1880s, 40 percent of pakeha lived in towns with more than 1,000 residents; and over 50 percent of provincial people lived within 50kms of the main town.

All things considered, the larger towns were surprisingly sophisticated. The first newspaper was produced at Petone in 1840. Libraries were high on the lists of civic priorities. There was a purpose-built theatre in Wellington in 1843; by the 1870s there was a well-established Australasian theatrical circuit with British and American companies touring classical and popular plays.

There was a determination to achieve a degree of civility, even in the most unpromising circumstances. Balls were popular, even if it was a logistical nightmare for women to keep ball dresses unmuddied. Less explicable, apart from the carrying on of 'Old Country' traditions, was a seeming obsession with public dinners to mark an array of events and occasions.

By the 1870s the two biggest cities, Auckland and Dunedin at opposite ends of the country, had about 20,000 inhabitants, Christchurch 12,000 and Wellington 8,000. Where they could they, and much smaller townships, spread themselves over nearby countryside in the not always realised hope that they would thrive and grow. Corrugated iron was already a widely used building material, utilitarian rather than pleasing to the eye.

In the countryside, as well as the towns, there were increasing numbers of grand houses staffed by servants who saw the work as a step along the way, not a lifetime occupation. In the backblocks, it was possible, with a pooling of hard graft, for a family to turn a small plot into a substantial farm in one generation.

There was, of course, another sort of 'frontier' life. A

distinctive male culture developed in the timber, railway and roading camps; 'mateship', and looking out for each other, was the outcome of living in close proximity in cramped conditions and working at dangerous occupations. Contact with women was sometimes restricted to brothel encounters during occasional visits to town. Loneliness and isolation, with large numbers of bachelors marrying late if at all, contributed to the epic levels of alcohol consumption in New Zealand. The extent of liver damage deaths is not known, but a large number of drunken drownings were recorded.

There was certainly a marked disparity in the numbers of men and women in the colony. In 1871 there were 89,000 pakeha men over 20 years of age, and only 46,000 women. At the same time, most men eager for marriage found partners, although practical considerations usually outweighed any romantic notions.

Whether on large landholdings or struggling small farms, wives did a range of household chores, with those previously unaccustomed to such work often taking pride in new-found skills and the degree of independence it gave them.

For many years there was little leisure for most, particularly as the Sabbath was widely and strictly observed. Amusements were often simple and home-made. By the 1870s, rugby was increasingly popular, crossing social boundaries more readily than other sports, and appealing equally to pakeha and Maori. All it required was a paddock, lengths of timber for goal posts, a ball – and the surplus energy of young men eager to test their physical prowess against 'mates' in communities where there were rarely young, single women.

The 1870s were a critical decade in several ways. The steady yeoman farmer was now achieving a predominance that would mould the country's character and give it stability for at least two generations. A number of towns were now of a size that supported growing professional and managerial classes who, along with farmers, would provide the next century's political and community leaders. As well, Julius Vogel's audacious development plan would give New Zealand the economic kick in the pants it needed.

Glimmerings of better times in the 1860s translated into reasonable prosperity in the 1870s, generated by large-scale government spending and the torrent of new, assisted immigrants – 34,000 of them in 1874 alone.

By the beginning of the 1880s New Zealand was poised for rapid growth – over 40 percent of the population was under 15 years of age and refrigeration would soon revolutionise farming – but the grim reality was a long slump, with many of the poor in the growing towns, less able to provide their own food than country dwellers, living in real poverty. The Sweating Commission of 1890 seemed surprised to discover the almost inevitable exploitation of women and child labour in the clothing industry. But while wage-earners found it difficult to survive on weekly pay packets that had not appreciably risen in 40 years, there were financiers and land speculators making – and sometimes losing – large fortunes, their uninhibited commercial dealings unfettered by either restrictive regulations or income tax.

The Liberals, determined not to replicate Britain's poverty, introduced the Old Age Pension, a non-contributory scheme that was also parsimonious and hedged with exceptions. The Workers Dwellings Act early the next century, with the government building houses and renting them to workers, was another breakthrough, and a small dress rehearsal for the state housing initiatives of the 1930s.

Clearly, though, New Zealand egalitarianism stopped short of generosity. Minimum standards, but no more, were important in living conditions, health and education. Primary schooling, free, secular and compulsory from 1877, was designed to produce clerks and shop assistants without complicating aspirations. Secondary schooling, which was not widely available for several decades, was the seed bed for a sprouting professional class.

Through the energetic evangelising of mission schools, it is likely about half the Maori population in the North Island could read by the early 1840s. Strangely, there was not the same enthusiasm among many of the better educated colonists to educate their own sons, such was their preoccupation with breaking in land and stocking it with as many sheep as possible. (In 1861, there were 99,000 colonists and 2.8 million sheep in New Zealand.) It has been estimated that 54 percent of school-age children could read and write in 1858, with an overall literacy rate of 63 percent, which was lower than in Britain.

The nineties were more settled politically and the benefits of refrigeration were now real not imagined. Towns might still be spread out, bedraggled and generally unprepossessing, but homes – which few immigrants had owned back in England or Scotland – were another matter. Austere exteriors were given more character with verandahs and porches and these were dollied up with wooden and metal fretwork; inside, living rooms were purposefully crammed with ornaments, mirrors, pot plants and prints of popular British paintings. It was a suitable, if somewhat cluttered, setting for the 'at homes' that were important in the lives of the wives of the emerging managerial class.

The farm labourer who came to New Zealand in the great tidal wave of 1870s immigration was likely to have transformed his and his family's life in two decades.

Back in England, there was practically no escape from a life of drudgery for parents and children, labouring and 'in service', living a subsistence existence as tenants in old, over-crowded village cottages, a degree of compulsory education only adding to frustrations.

With hard work, a similar New Zealand family would

be living on its own smallholding, in a snug, if rough-hewn home, with plenty of food on the table and, after school, opportunities for children to work in nearby towns, on neighbouring farms or to aspire to a much grander future. There might even be, in pride of place, a piano.

Curiously, the piano symbolised as well as anything the differences between the old and new lives. It was a metaphor for cultural aspirations, a degree of economic achievement, a leisure component to lives, and consideration for girls, who mostly learned and played, beyond being just another pair of working hands. It has been calculated that about 43,000 pianos were shipped to New Zealand from the late 1870s to the end of the century. This equated to one piano – costing up to £40 – in every occupied building in the colony, excluding schools and public buildings.

With some exceptions, it was visitors who had the time and inclination to record their impressions of New Zealand life during the 19th century. George French Angas captured Maori life on canvas before it changed markedly; Charles Heaphy's watercolours traversed more ground geographically, reflecting his surveying work and distinguished land wars service. F E Maning, Lady Barker and Samuel Butler wrote about the early European days with wit, verve and some style.

A long list of animals, fish and plants were brought into New Zealand by acclimatisation societies and others in the early days of European settlement. It was done to add familiarity to the landscape, sport for the leisured and food for the table – all with a blithe disregard of the consequences for New Zealand's wild life and habitats. 'Environment' and 'conservation' were not in common currency, which made Julius Vogel's 1874 NZ Forests Act all the more extraordinary. Vogel, but few of his parliamentary colleagues, recognised the environmental consequences of forest destruction and the need to use the country's timber supplies more carefully. The legislation, greatly weakened, was passed after acrimonious debate, then repealed two years later.

If concern for the environment was still embryonic, there was an increasing enthusiasm for the country's diverse geography, fuelled by more disposable income and better, more varied travel options. The country's small tourist industry, a partnership between government and Te Arawa Maori, had been based at Rotorua, the 'Thermal Wonderland', since the early 1880s. Local and overseas tourists marvelled at the geysers and bubbling mud, 'took the waters' in the restorative hot pools and, until the Tarawera eruption in 1886, inspected the Pink and White Terraces. There were possibly stirrings of a national consciousness as numbers of New Zealanders made 'once in a lifetime' pilgrimages to Rotorua, the Waitomo Caves, West Coast glaciers, Milford Sound, Queenstown, and Mt Cook. A six-in-hand coach service ran between Fairlie and the Hermitage at Mt Cook as early as 1886.

The achievements of the first half century were astonishing, compared to the early colonial periods in other countries. A European population of a sparse few thousand was topping 500,000 by century's end. The colonists had been young – mainly in their twenties and thirties – and behind their personal energy and self-confidence was the mighty, still expanding British Empire. By the mid-1880s, a majority of pakeha in the country were New Zealand born and there was growing pride in their health and vitality. The distressing number of shipboard deaths of children coming to New Zealand in the 1840s was a distant memory; by the end of the century, the death rate of under fives was, impressively, only one third the figure in England and Wales.

Home Away from Home

In the 1830s England and Wales were bursting at the seams, the population doubling since 1750. With the upheaval of the Industrial Revolution, the worrying example of the French Revolution, and the increasingly desperate shortage of work and shelter, successive British governments were not at all averse to shipping the poor, and potentially troublesome, as far away as possible. Canada, America, South Africa and Australia had already absorbed many thousands. James Cook had reported favourably on New Zealand seven decades before, but it was Edward Gibbon Wakefield, with plans to settle this virgin, unspoiled territory, who most focused the minds of politicians and bureaucrats in London and jolted them into action they had been in no hurry to take. Central to Wakefield's ideal – a complete cross-section of British society in New Zealand – was a good sprinkling of settlers of gentle birth. But it was to the poor, virtual serfs in the countryside and semi-starving and brutalised in the cities, that emigration, despite its risks and uncertainties, offered the only hope of a different kind of life.

1. The Industrial Revolution not only turned labour into a low value commodity, but the prodigious output of machines had production outpacing demand. Surplus capital needed to go elsewhere and, as Wakefield theorised, it could be put to work very profitably in a new colony. *Capital And Labour*, Shallabala, *London Punch*, 1843. ATL: J-065-003
2. Scions of some leading county families flirted briefly with the romantic ideal and a number of solid middle-class families saw the opportunities in more matter-of-fact terms, but it was the poor who crowded the emigrant ships to New Zealand during the 1840s and 1850s. *Here And There*, *London Punch*, 1848. ATL: J-065-004
3. New Zealand's founding document, the Treaty of Waitangi, was hastily written following William Hobson's dash to annex the country about the same time the first New Zealand Company settlers arrived – and what it says and means remains hotly debated. *Great Moments in NZ History – Signing the Treaty of Waitangi*, Bob Brockie, *National Business Review*, February 8 1982. ATL: A-314-2-003
4. The problem of finding and keeping servants was a perennial, much commented on, problem in colonial New Zealand. To the gentry they were both a symbol of, and essential to, a genteel lifestyle. To the servants, breathing a more egalitarian air, it was a job until something better turned up. *Colonial Servant-galism*, *Wellington Punch*, 1868. ATL: J-065-001

1

Capital and Labour.

2

HERE and THERE;
or, Emigration a Remedy.

3

4

COLONIAL SERVANT-GALISM.

Lady: "Very well; and what wages do you require?"

Jemima Ann: "Wages! Beg parding, Mim, my *onner-raryum* is Forty Puns per hannum; and I 'lways hattends the Bread and Butter Balls."

A Matter of Inconvenience

By 1500, the identity of the original New Zealanders, the Moa Hunters, had been lost in successive waves of Polynesians who grew the *kumara* or sweet potato and mostly lived on coastal North Island plains where it prospered best. Maori traded widely and raided occasionally when tribal honour was at stake and had extensive congress, trading and sexual, with Europeans, particularly in the Bay of Islands, from early in the 19th century.

When later settlers travelled to the bottom of the world their horizons quickly narrowed again and it was inconvenient, or worse, when Maori slowed the occupation of land they had come to farm or settle on. The clash of cultures and values would come perilously close to destroying Maori society.

1. Maori first arrived in New Zealand 1,200 or more years ago. Unlikely though such a reception committee might have been – except to a cartoonist – the lives of the first human settler hunters and the large flightless birds were closely linked until the moa had been chased, cornered, killed and eaten to extinction. *The Arrival of the Maoris*, Trevor Lloyd, ca 1910. ATL: C-109-003
2. Pre-European celebration of Christmas was a cartoon stock-in-trade of the popular weeklies of the early 20th century. *Chasing the Christmas Moa,* Trevor Lloyd, *Free Lance Christmas Annual*, 1918. ATL: J-065-005
3. By the time the first settler ships arrived, Maori had developed a liking for European tools and consumer goods, understood and profited from the pakeha penchant for potatoes and were soon supplying a wide and essential range of meat, fish, vegetables and fruit to Auckland, Wellington and other new settlements. What they did not realise was that the early settlers were just the advance guard of a continuing migration that would swamp the Maori. *The Landing of the Pioneers*, Trevor Lloyd, ca 1910. ATL: C-109-004
4. Money, grazing animals, guns, individual land ownership and alcohol were all new concepts to Maori. Iron tools, fish-hooks, blankets and Christian values weakened an impressive Maori culture as surely as guns and disease decimated their population. And cash-cropping and land sales undermined the elaborate economic system central to the Maori way of life. *"At Last! Somebody to Blame"*, Garrick Tremain, *Otago Daily Times*, August 31 2000. ATL: H-619-023

1

THE ARRIVAL OF THE MAORIS.

2

CHASING THE CHRISTMAS MOA: A Joyous Old-time Maori Event.

3

THE LANDING OF THE PIONEERS.

4

The Early Settlements

An early Hobson proclamation, declaring all private land purchases void, torpedoed the NZ Company's plans in Wellington, and the Wakefield settlements in Wanganui, New Plymouth (1841) and Nelson (1842). As land-claim hearings dragged on, there was a grim struggle for survival until more adventurous colonists established pastoral runs outside the towns. Ever resourceful, Wakefield now encouraged Presbyterian and Church of England settlements in southern New Zealand. Otago was founded in 1848 and Canterbury two years later – lay associations providing spiritual and temporal leadership; the NZ Company, technical assistance. These settlements were spared disputes with Maori land-owners but, as colonists moved onto plentiful pastoral and agricultural land, the key Wakefield concept of concentrated settlement was ignored. The provincial system, spelled out in the 1852 Constitution Act, was a response to the poor communications between New Zealand's scattered settlements. It also reflected and intensified each community's strongly self-centred interests and aspirations. The provincial councils had considerable political and financial power, particularly after they could profit from crown land sales.

1. Land disputes precipitated the killing of 22 Europeans at Wairau near Nelson in 1842 and sporadic guerrilla raids on isolated Hutt Valley farmhouses until 1846. *Encouragement to Emigrants*, Frank Varley, *Wellington Punch*, 1868. ATL: J-065-002
2. By the time Sir John Hall, Canterbury runholder and long-time provincial councillor, was premier, from 1879-82, the South Island's rail and road systems were much more advanced than the north's. His 'moderate borrowing for moderate growth' policy kept the deficit at bay without disadvantaging his constituents. *The Skeleton in the Cupboard*, CP, *New Zealand Punch* (Wellington), April 24 1880. ATL: J-061-012
3. The discovery of gold underwrote a pastoral boom and consolidated the South Island's economic dominance into the 1880s. But Canterbury's dray road through the Southern Alps was a costly dream rather than a gold bonanza. Even when the road was open, most supplies and gold arrived in and left the West Coast by sea. *Winter – Christchurch, With* No *Road to the West Coast*, *Punch in Canterbury*, August 12 1865. ATL: J-065-006
4. Edward Stafford (centre), premier from 1866-69, as one of *Macbeth s* three witches. Although Nelson's first provincial superintendent, his concerns were national rather than parochial. His centralist policies antagonised the southern provinces: they produced most of the colony's revenue which, it was claimed, was spent on northern problems. *The Witches of the North*, *Otago Punch*, November 10 1866. ATL: J-065-007

1

ENCOURAGEMENT TO EMIGRANTS.
Chorus of loyal Maori subjects.
"Ah! Ah! Pakeha if we kill you it's nothing; but if you kill us, by ____, it's Murder!"

2

THE SKELETON IN THE CUPBOARD.

3

WINTER – CHRISTCHURCH, WITH *NO* ROAD TO THE WEST COAST.

4

THE WITCHES OF THE NORTH.

Punch: "How, now, you false, base, tinkering hags."

The Land Wars

Apart from occasional skirmishes, Maori tolerated and often fed the scattered coastal communities during the early years of European settlement. Governor Grey bought large tracts of both islands in accordance with tribal law, but stubborn resistance to further sales of ancestral land spread out from Taranaki during the 1850s. Most settlers welcomed Governor Gore Browne's 1859 shift in land-purchase policy and his willingness to back it up with military action. The land-sales stalemate led to the Taranaki wars in 1860-61 and 1863 and Waikato fighting in 1863-64, its fanatical Hau Hau by-product terrorising smaller settlements into the 1870s. The British commander, General Cameron, was increasingly concerned that the Waikato campaign – justified on the grounds that the Maori King movement was a threat to sovereignty and security – was simply the quickest way to satisfy the land-hunger of impatient settlers. Isolated acts of defiance aside, notably by Te Kooti who escaped from exile in the Chathams and led bloody raids on East Coast settlements for several years, Maori had lost the land wars by the mid-1860s.

1. The government decision to allow the purchase of the Waitara Block from an individual, against the wishes of chief and tribe, precipitated the first Taranaki war. Maori, with their highly mobile, guerrilla tactics, burned almost all the isolated farm houses in the region; meanwhile, the soldiers were pinned down in their block-houses and behind New Plymouth's fortifications. *Awful Impudence*, *Taranaki Punch*, 1861. ATL: J-065-008
2. About 9,000 colonists were 'on active service', but two-thirds simply attended occasional militia parades. It was particularly galling to General Cameron that while the colonists had the most to gain, they did very little of the fighting. During the Waikato campaign, Cameron's New Zealand contingent consisted of 400 cavalrymen and 100 Forest Rangers. *"Attention! Dress!"*, *Punch in Canterbury*, May 20 1865. ATL: J-065-010
3. Missionaries insisted that Maori, not the settlers, were the victims of the land disputes. The Society was committed to the optimistic view that Christianity and colonisation could work hand in hand, humanely and harmoniously. *Member of the Aboriginal Protection Society*, Frank Varley, *Wellington Punch*, 1868. ATL: J-065-009
4. Te Whiti and his Parihaka *pa* followers responded to European attempts to occupy confiscated south Taranaki land with a remarkable display of passive resistance. John Bryce, the native minister, had the prophet arrested and Parihaka and its fields sacked in November 1881. *For Divers Reasons, Wellington Advertiser*, November 19 1881. ATL: A-095-038

1

AWFUL IMPUDENCE

Maori (loq): "Please when will it be convenient to begin burning the houses in the town, for we have *nearly done* the job outside."

2

"ATTENTION! DRESS!"

Major General Punch: "Volunteers! During the past year your numbers have largely increased, and you have greatly improved in discipline and efficiency. You have devoted much time to drill, and have prepared yourselves to defend your country in time of need. For all this your country is deeply grateful. And the ladies, therefore, hope to see you at the Queen's Birthday Ball, to exhibit *the nice uniforms that your country has promised to supply*."

3

MEMBER OF ABORIGINAL PROTECTION SOCIETY.
"Oh! Really, my Christian Brother, if you continue to indulge in these unseemly eccentricities you will alienate the regard of your most earnest well-wishers."

4

FOR *DIVER S* REASONS.
Support from sugar, blankets, flour all gone;
They've not been left a leg to stand upon.

The Back of Beyond

The first European settlements were tiny, hemmed-in pockets, separated from one another by long distances, their isolation in the North Island intensified by crumpled, bush-covered terrain and in the South by wide, dangerous rivers. Until the 1870s, most travel was by sea, with the early roads and railroads built to service ports. The first explorers were preoccupied with finding more land for settlers. Later, naturalists, surveyors and adventurous colonists searched for gold and nuggets of scientific knowledge. In the Auckland province, the Great South Road pushed into the Waikato with military precision and purpose, and roads followed gold strikes into central Otago and over the Southern Alps. The first railway, a tentative four miles out of Christchurch, was built in 1863 and there were less than 50 miles of track when Julius Vogel's plan for a national rail network was first mooted in the early 1870s.

1. A succession of gold rushes had a growing army of fortune-hunting prospectors and 'new chums' tramping through wild, desolate country to central Otago (1861-63), north to Marlborough's Canvastown in 1864, then south-west to Westland from 1865-67 and finally to Thames, in the North Island, with its rich quartz reefs. After Westland's first payable alluvial gold was found in 1864, prospectors were soon scouring its central creeks, flats and stream terraces. *West Coast Expedition, Dunedin Punch*, 1865. ATL: MNZ 302
2. New Zealand's first steam train rail-line ran from Christchurch to Ferrymead. Provincial superintendent William Rolleston, holding the dray reins, was progressive in many ways, but vigorously opposed to the raising of loans to push the railway south. It reached Rakaia, about 35 miles to the south, in 1873 and Amberley, about 37 miles to the north, three years later. *An Impending Catastrophe!, Punch in Canterbury*, 1865. ATL: MNZ 37
3. In 1865, with Otago feeling the pinch as goldminers left for the newly-discovered Westland goldfields, the Dunedin Chamber of Commerce invited Chinese miners from Victoria to prop up the sagging economy. Any initial enthusiasm waned when further discoveries eased economic concerns. *The Chinese Bubble Burst, Dunedin Punch*, October 28 1865. ATL: J-065-011
4. Despite the jibes, the railways revolutionised life in New Zealand, effectively shrinking the country to a fraction of its previous horse-and-coach size. Nearly half of all public spending in the last three decades of the century was spent on railways. Fastest progress was in Canterbury and Otago; they were the richest provinces and the terrain less demanding. Canterbury's rail tracks were converted to a narrower gauge in 1878. *The Canterbury Snailways*, 1876. ATL: MNZ 1433 (Early Settlers' Museum, Dunedin)

1

WEST COAST EXPEDITION.

2

AN IMPENDING CATASTROPHE!

3

THE CHINESE BUBBLE BURST
Or the flight of the Chinese Ambassador on hearing of the success of the West Coast expedition.

4

THE CANTERBURY SNAILWAYS.
DEFINITION: Reflection - A Train of Thought - A Narrow-Gauge, but not an Arrow Speed.

Coalitions of the Willing

From 1869 until 1890 – with the land wars largely over and the country opening up – a loose coalition of basically conservative, but seldom reactionary, runholders and professional men shuffled and reshuffled subtle cabinet variations of the same faces on the basis of personalities and patronage as much as policies. Aside from the expansive Vogel years and two 'Liberal' ministries, the so-called 'Continuous Ministry' took a hold-the-line stand against land and labour reform and met successive economic recessions with rigid retrenchment.

1. John Hall, Canterbury runholder and 'grid-ironing' pioneer, was opposition leader when Sir George Grey's administration collapsed in 1879. Premier until April 1882, he held together a cabinet of opposing personalities to introduce universal male suffrage and three year parliamentary terms. *The Ministerial Office Bait*, William Hutchison, *Wellington Advertiser*, January 28 1882. ATL: A-095-017
2. Julius Vogel, colonial treasurer by 1869 via Australasian goldfields and part-ownership of the *Otago Daily Times*, turned the conventional depression retrenchment-and-austerity approach on its head with a development plan involving a massive £10 million loan. There were remarkable increases in road, rail and telegraph wire mileages and 100,000 immigrants arrived during the 1870s. Premier twice in the 1870s, Vogel was again treasurer in the Stout-Vogel ministry (1884-87), but was unable to end a lengthy depression. *Leaps and Bounds*, W H R, *Evening Press*, May 18 1887. ATL: C-034-007
3. Harry Atkinson was premier on five occasions and colonial treasurer on several others. His final term was between October 1887 and January 1891. During depression years borrowing had to be curtailed, but not cut off completely. *The Premier s Manifesto*, William Blomfield, *NZ Observer and Free Lance*, November 15 1890. ATL: J-065-022
4. The so-called 'Liberal' opposition, more divided than united by Sir George Grey's radical thinking and autocratic manner, held power for only two brief periods. Grey's 1877-79 ministry had ambitious policies without the support to enact them. Stout's 1884-87 ministry was Liberal in name only. There was very little mantle to pass on when Grey, now a back-bench gadfly and irritant, finally retired in 1894. *The Ascension of the Prophet*, William Blomfield, *NZ Observer and Free Lance*, December 13 1890. ATL: J-065-023
5. In 1890 – a year in which industrial workers had flexed their frustrations in strikes – Ballance's Liberals were able, with some assistance, to form the country's first fully-fledged party government. *After the Battle – A Forecast*, William Blomfield, *NZ Observer and Free Lance*, August 16 1890. ATL: J-065-030

1

THE MINISTERIAL OFFICE BAIT.
Mr H. can confidently recommend this bait to all political anglers. It has been in use several months, and is still as tempting as ever.

2

LEAPS AND BOUNDS.

3

THE PREMIER'S MANIFESTO (A VERY OLD RHYME)
"Who dares this pair of boots displace Must meet Bombastes face to face! Thus do I challenge all of the human race".
Sir George Grey (to Ballance): "Let us go in and win! Don't give him another chance to crush the country ..."

4

THE ASCENSION OF THE PROPHET.
Rush of his would-be Successors to get possession of his Grey Mantle.

5

Young N.Z. (to Labour and Capital, both badly crippled): "I told you before you started how it would be. You have both been punished; and while you were fighting, trade, industry and commerce have been neglected. You will have to shake hands and be friends after all, if either of you mean to succeed. Better shake hands before you begin to fight in future, and then you won't begin at all!"

AFTER THE BATTLE – A FORECAST.

Town and Country in Harness

Small farmers and industrial workers, two critical but politically undervalued groups, voted the Liberals into power at the end of 1890. They were mostly concerned about a fairer sharing of capitalism's spoils, and the Liberals reciprocated by treating the colony's increasingly serious social and economic problems with massive doses of state intervention and control. Trade unions, legal from 1878, grew quickly during the depression of the late 1880s and, after the quick collapse of the Australasian maritime strike in 1890, turned their energies to politics and helping the Liberals win that year's election. There was an early rush of labour-friendly legislation but, as the decade lengthened, there was growing union dissatisfaction with the Liberals' commitment to the country's working class.

1. The raft of reforming legislation the Liberals pushed through the House of Representatives in early 1891 was stonewalled or worse by the conservative, lifetime appointees of the Legislative Council. There is no evidence that Grey, on poor terms with Ballance, was any help and the new premier had to appeal to London before new Liberal members were added to the Legislative Council. *Young New Zealand Sick – The Doctors in Consultation*, William Blomfield, *NZ Observer and Free Lance*, June 27, 1891. ATL: J-065-024
2. The Liberals believed they were elected on a social-justice platform; increasingly agitated conservatives labeled it 'state socialism' and warned about a burgeoning civil service enveloping the country in red tape. It was an exaggeration but, with the level of state intervention, the government was certainly putting 'equality' before 'liberty'. *"Oh, what a tangled web we weave"*, Ashley Hunter,"*NZ Graphic*, 1892. ATL: A-312-8-002
3. John Ballance's ambitious programme with its far-reaching tax, land, labour and electoral legislation was anathema to the business community, the conservative opposition and most of the country's press. William Pember Reeves' compulsory arbitration system would soon strain government-employer relations even further. *New Zealand s Santa Claus*, William Blomfield, *NZ Observer and Free Lance*, December 24 1892. ATL: H-722-140
4. In return for their support of the Liberals, most items on the union movement's lengthy 'shopping list' had been ticked off by 1900 with, left to right, Ballance, Seddon and Reeves playing prominent parts in the process. *A Large Order*, Ashley Hunter, *NZ Graphic*, June 30 1894. ATL: A-312-8-007

1

YOUNG NEW ZEALAND SICK – THE DOCTORS IN CONSULTATION.

Dr Ballance: "I have got the proper medicine to cure the little fellow, but that stupid old nurse persists in dosing him with her own rubbish."

Nurse M.L.C. (nee Hobnails): "You shan't give the little dear anything but what I please."

Dr Grey: "You go ahead, Ballance; I'll find a way of getting that old party out of the way!"

2

"Oh, what a tangled web we weave."

3

NEW ZEALAND'S SANTA CLAUS.

4

A LARGE ORDER.

"Well, my little man, and what can we do for you?"

"Please I want one state bank; one old age pension fund; a coastal marine; something to mend the upper house with; any quantity of cooperative work; a direct veto and an eight hours' day: and would you please look alive because I'm in a hurry!"

Revolutionary Economics

The Liberals' ambitious farm settlement programme involved a mix of property and absentee-owner taxes, low-interest-rate loans and the purchase and subdivision of Cheviot Hills and other large estates. Under the Land for Settlement Act, small farmers could occupy this newly available land on 999-year leases. Between 1891-1911, the number of farms nearly doubled to 74,000 and land privately held in 10,000 acre holdings was halved. The government's small farmer supporters were happy, as were industrial workers, with Reeves' compulsory arbitration system, which had the state resolving disputes not settled voluntarily. Ambitious borrowing was critical to the Liberals' legislative and development agenda, but loan money spent on public works, railways, state advances and compulsory purchase of large estates allowed closer settlement and more intensive farming. Agricultural production lifted as, in tandem, did refrigerated exports and the prices received for them. There were now regular surpluses in the national accounts.

1. Although not obliged to, most unions registered under the Industrial Conciliation and Arbitration Act. At first, decisions favoured unionists and they – particularly skilled workers – found wages rising faster than the cost of living. *Compulsory Conciliation*, Ashley Hunter, *NZ Graphic*, 1893. ATL: A-312-8-005
2. As time went by, the new leasehold farmers, once placid supporters of the Liberals, grew prosperous and more conservative. The Farmers' Union, founded in 1899, challenged the growing influence of trade unions and the government's unwillingness to freehold their properties. *Spineless*, William Blomfield, *NZ Observer*, July 22 1905. ATL: J-065-013
3. Capital investment remained a prerequisite to economic development so there was a certain inevitability about cap-in-hand pilgrimages to the London money market. Treasurer Joseph Ward bolstered the colony's credit and his own career by negotiating, despite opposition doubters, a substantial London loan in 1895 to provide cheap state finance under the Advances to Settlers Act. *Colonial Treasurer Ward Scores One*, William Blomfield, *NZ Observer and Free Lance*, May 11 1895. ATL: J-065-014
4. In June 1894, and again the next year, the government was forced to prop up the Bank of New Zealand, in trouble because it had, like the Colonial Bank, lent too much of its capital and deposits in long-term mortgages secured by unsaleable land. Ward, although personally indebted to the Colonial Bank, promoted its take-over by the BNZ. *Saving a Bank and Averting a Crisis*, Francis West, *NZ Observer and Free Lance*, July 7 1894. ATL: A-295-048

1

COMPULSORY CONCILIATION.
The Hon. Mr Reeves, as the angel of peace, united Labour and Capital in the silken bonds of Industrial Conciliation.

2

SPINELESS.
N.Z. Farmer: "Remember that I am the backbone of the country."

3

COLONIAL TREASURER WARD SCORES ONE.

4

SAVING A BANK AND ADVERTING A CRISIS.

Ward: "One more blow Seddon, and then it will be secure."

Seddon: "Yes. This stay will hold it safely, and only just in time. As soon as this storm is over we must put it on safer foundations. State foundations in fact."

The Ultimate Political Pragmatist

Richard John Seddon, who succeeded John Ballance in May 1893, would be called, if he was practising his trade today, the complete machine politician. He was not a socialist or an idealist. He was – from personal experience and in response to popular demand – a practical humanitarian. Apart from the Old Age Pension Bill, which he bullied through parliament, Seddon showed little personal commitment to the Liberal legislative programme. Yet it was his political pragmatism and dominating personality that kept the Liberals together and in power and ensured the passage of the early, watershed legislation sponsored by more radical colleagues. He eased Reeves out of the government because his minister of labour was likely to upset the knife-edge relationship between unionists and farmers; he needed Ward's advice so welcomed him back to cabinet after indiscretions of, by today's standards, career-ending proportions. Seddon was arrogant, autocratic, dogmatic; he loved power and wielded it arbitrarily, but he never forgot its source.

1. Seddon routinely dispensed patronage. He made little secret of the fact that Liberal supporters were favoured for jobs in the fast-growing civil service – which seemed to have an insatiable need for 'temporary clerks'. *"The Shadow"*, Wal, *The Guardian*, September 29 1899. ATL: A-313-7-007
2. A largely impotent conservative opposition was reduced to personal attacks aimed at Seddon and his colleagues. George Hutchinson attempted to ridicule Seddon with the subsequently discredited claim that the anti-Chinese premier had once been a partner – known as Bun Tuck – in a goldmining claim with a party of Chinese. – *The Great 'Bun Tuck Episode*, Ashley Hunter, *NZ Graphic*, September 3 1898. ATL: A-312-8-023
3. Old-age pensions were introduced on a limited basis, with strict means and residence tests, in 1898. Seddon's advocacy of the Old Age Pension Act, which foreshadowed New Zealand's welfare state, may have stemmed from his concern for ex-miners on the West Coast, but it also won the support of another sizeable group of voters. *The Old Age Pensions*, William Blomfield, *NZ Observer and Free Lance*, October 15 1898. ATL: J-065-018
4. Seddon stamped his personality and authority on parliament, the Liberal Party and the country. He was premier, then prime minister, for 13 years – longer than anyone else, before or after. One reason for his longevity was his unblushing use of patronage, shrewdly rewarding his supporters and 'freezing out' opponents. *Robbing the Hive*, William Blomfield, *NZ Observer*, August 4 1900. ATL: A-312-1-188

1

"THE SHADOW."

2

THE GREAT "BUN TUCK" EPISODE.

3

THE OLD AGE PENSIONS.
Premier Dick: "Here you are, my good friends, here is gold in plenty for your old age. It is a big price to pay for votes, near two hundred thousand, but it is money well spent."

4

ROBBING THE HIVE.

"Emotional creatures who have not .... the logical faculty"

In 1879, when the Hall ministry granted virtually universal suffrage, the degree of discrimination against women was dramatically underlined. But it was not until the mid-1880s that suffragists, many acquiring skills and confidence in the Women's Christian Temperance Union, began campaigning in earnest. Sir John Hall first put up a female franchise bill in 1891, but the Liberals, apprehensive about the political consequences of giving women the vote, blocked legislation until 1893, when the last of three annual, nationwide petitions collected nearly 32,000 names – a quarter of all adult women in the colony. After being passed by the House in 1893, Seddon's complicated manoeuvring to defeat the measure in the Legislative Council so incensed two opposition councillors that they supported the legislation at the critical third reading and tipped the scales.

1. A married woman, while having some social status and respectability, had no legal ability to control her own life and possessions and was, effectively, her husband's chattel until the 1884 Married Women's Property Act recognised married women's legal existence and restored to them the right to acquire, hold and dispose of property in their own right. *Gallantry*, Arthur Palethorpe, *New Zealand Punch* (Wellington), November 22 1879. ATL: H-692-011
2. Divorce was one of the issues debated by the National Council of Women which was formed in 1896 with Kate Sheppard its first president. Before the 1898 Divorce Act, women could not obtain a divorce on the grounds of adultery alone. They had to prove desertion and cruelty. Men, on the other hand, could divorce women for neglect of household duties. *"For Better or for Worse"*, W B, *NZ Observer and Free Lance*, May 14 1887. ATL: J-065-026
3. Sir John Hall, conservative runholder and premier in the early 1880s, was a prominent supporter of the female suffrage movement from personal conviction – and he thought women would vote conservatively. *Women s Suffrage – The Girls Wronged Again*, William Blomfield, *NZ Observer and Free Lance*, September 19 1891. ATL: J-065-028
4. After the 1893 election, oganisations like the Women's Social and Political League of Wellington promoted issues ranging from women governors to dress reform. *News from the Seat of War*, P Izett, *NZ Graphic*, December 1 1894. ATL: 315-3-014
5. Before and after women got the vote critics expressed their doubts. A certain Dr Bakewell wrote in an article: "This is the way we shall be governed now, by emotional creatures, who have not, and never can possess, the logical faculty." *The Doctor Wishes ....*, William Blomfield, *NZ Observer and Free Lance*, February 17 1894. ATL: H-713-117

1

GALLANTRY.

First 'Gentleman': "Oh, come and have a drink, Bob; we haven't had a drink together for a long time."

Second 'Gentleman': "Yes, but, er – how about the – er- lady, eh?"

First 'Gentleman': "Oh, that's all right, it's ONLY my WIFE! Come along!"

2

3

WOMEN'S SUFFRAGE – THE GIRLS WRONGED AGAIN.

4

NEWS FROM THE SEAT OF WAR.

5

THE DOCTOR WISHES HE HAD NOT WRITTEN THAT ARTICLE FOR THE 'NINETEENTH CENTURY.'

"This is the way we shall be governed now, by emotional creatures, who have not, and can never possess, the logical facility." – Dr Bakewell.

Colour Blinded

Prominent Liberal politicians – notably Seddon and Reeves – were unabashed racists, as were many of their fellow countrymen. The Chinese, lured to New Zealand by gold, were feared irrationally because of their different culture and, more prosaically, their frugality which might force down wages. Seddon stubbornly refused to believe official statistics showing the small Chinese community was declining further and introduced harsher immigration rules. Conveniently, the new regulations snared Japanese and Indians as well. To some degree, European attitudes to Maori were tempered by treaty obligations and respect for their fighting ability, but Seddon needed to open up idle Maori land for the Liberals' farm settlement programme. At the time, conventional wisdom had it that Maori, still officially 'natives', were dying out. In fact, Maori were showing remarkable resilience and their population decline had been reversed by 1896.

1. Such was the prejudice, Chinese were considered pests like weasels and stoats. There were about 5,000 Chinese in New Zealand in 1881 with each immigrant paying a poll tax of £10. By 1896 there were just over 3,700 Chinese, yet the poll tax was raised to £100. *Imported Pests*, W B, *NZ Observer and Free Lance*, April 16 1887. ATL: J-065-019
2. When, in 1888, Australian authorities refused entry to Chinese passengers, they made the Tasman crossing in another ship. There was considerable anger when they were allowed to land, with some New Zealanders expressing the view that the time had come for them to emigrate to Australia. *Fair Exchange is no Robbery*, R M S, *New Zealand Punch*, May 12 1888. ATL: J-065-033
3. In the 1890s, the government bought three million acres of Maori land and the King Country's era as a separate fiefdom was over. *The Native Difficulty is Defunct*, William Blomfield, *NZ Observer and Free Lance*, March 24, 1894. ATL: J-065-031
4. When the gold ran out, Chinese in New Zealand turned to market gardening. Their dominance by the 1890s, supplying restaurants and shops and hawking door-to-door, was perhaps a more rational fear as European market gardeners could not compete on cost. *The Chinaman on Top Again*, William Blomfield, *NZ Observer and Free Lance,* August 6 1892. ATL: A-312-6-006

1

Imported Pests
THE STURDY BRITISH COLONIST, AND THE NEW ZEALAND RABBIT
PROTEST THAT THE REMEDY WILL BE WORSE THAN THE DISEASE.

2

FAIR EXCHANGE IS NO ROBBERY.

Labourer: "Well, John! We've all got to clear out, I believe, and allow you the freedom of the colony."

Ah Sly: "You no savee, Mlister, we all you fliends! You savee, Mlister Atkinson say, 'All will comey back from Vlictoria and bling fliends with them!' We fliends! We do eelyding, anyding! We want plotection allee same you."

3

THE NATIVE DIFFICULTY IS DEFUNCT.
Time was when we feared the natives, then we respected them, but now – look!

4

THE CHINAMAN ON TOP AGAIN.

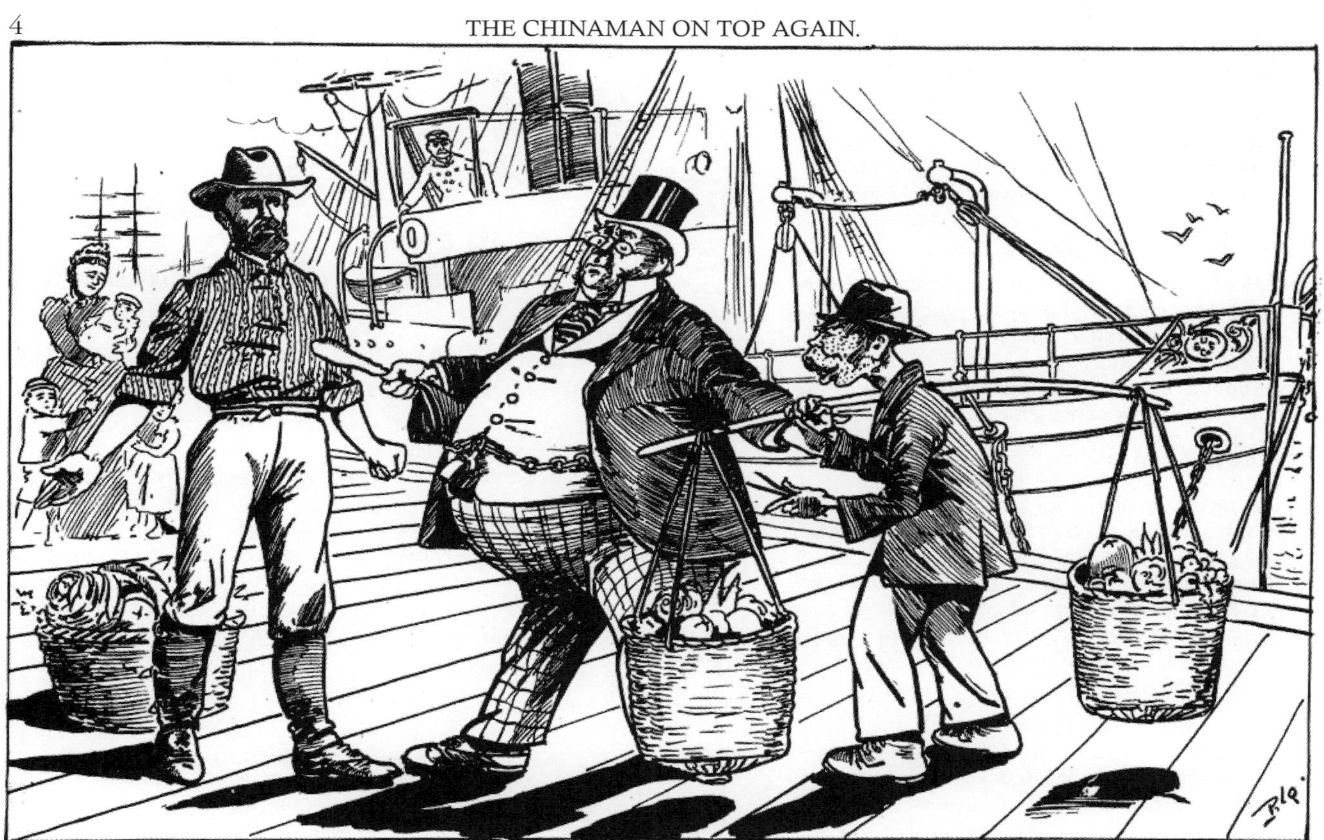

Director Steamship Company: "We take the Chinese vegetables in future; he is so much cheaper than you."
European gardener: "But I have a wife and family to keep, and cannot compete with him."
Chinese gardener: "Choppee stick allee Johnee Chinaman's furniture; me live welly cheap."
Steamship captain: "They'll have a measly Chinese crew on board next."

A Frontier Society

Early colonial life was not all hard work and rough living conditions. There were times to enjoy an inventive blending of 'Old Country' customs and new country attractions. Early on in the port towns, an important occasion was the arrival of a ship – bringing relatives or friends, mail, goods ordered a year or more ago. Anniversaries or, possibly, a royal wedding were ready excuses for a public dinner, with an interminable toast list, a ball or a reception. There were bands to listen to; regattas to sail in or watch. In the country, isolated families made their own fun. Eel-fishing and pig shooting, two favourites, had their utilitarian aspect as well. Riding picnics in the bush – tablecloths spread on the ground – were popular. Children, boys in particular, revelled in games like 'bushrangers' among the tangled log remains of felled and fired bush. Race meetings, along a beach or in a flat paddock, were early attractions, as were agricultural shows. Townspeople shared New Year's Day picnics; sheep station families rode long distances to the grand houses of neighbours for weekends of tennis, dancing and 'networking' that ensured a high level of inter-marriage among the 'squattocracy' on the east coasts of both islands.

1. Fashionably dressed women wore full length skirts, heaped with drapery, ruffles and pleats and worn over bustles – even cooped up in a fortified New Plymouth while Maori, avenging some doubtful land dealings, burnt outlying farmhouses. *Gentleman At The Gate*, *Taranaki Punch*, December 5 1860. ATL: H-685-002
2. Marriage was important for young, ambitious male colonists. Wives contributed much more to the pioneering life than they had 'at home' – all the more so if there was a substantial dowry involved. So, with men substantially outnumbering women, romance and 'love' were often secondary considerations. *Two Sides to a Question – No 2*, *Auckland Punch*, February 20 1869. ATL: H-685-012
3. The difficulty of finding and keeping domestic servants was of considerable concern among the well-to-do. A degree of leisure and the niceties of social etiquette necessitated a servant to welcome guests at the front door and perform a long list of other more physical chores. *Two Sides to a Question – No 4*, C D, *Auckland Punch*, March 13 1869. ATL: H-685-015
4. There was a degree of rough-and-ready egalitarianism within colonial society but, at a time when women had few rights, the pecking order within families remained as it had for centuries. *The Rising Generation*, C D, *Auckland Punch*, April 3 1869. ATL: H-685-017

1

Clara: "Who is that gentleman at the gate?"
Julia: "Gentleman, indeed! I think that if he had the least bit of the *gentleman* in him, he would not have let us squeeze through *that* narrow place! *Gentleman!* My word!"

2

TWO SIDES TO A QUESTION – NO. II.

Miss Snooks (who weighs fourteen stone, but thinks herself as light as a zephyr, has been doing a galop with young Hard-up):
"Oh, Maria, dear, I have had such a delightful galop! And Mr Hard-up is such a capital dancer. I declare that when he was whirling me round the room I felt just like a little bird."

Hard-up (groaning): "Oh, my poor arm, it's nearly off."
Tomkins: "Well, my dear fellow, if she's too much for you, why dance with her?"
Hard-up: "Hang it, man, don't you know she's property in Queen Street, and any amount of money out of mortgages."

3

TWO SIDES TO A QUESTION – NO. 4.

Mrs Brown (loq.): "Yes, the colonial servants are, as a rule, unbearable, but *now* I have a perfect *treasure* of a girl, recently arrived from Home, and therefore cannot possibly have any followers. Think what a comfort that reflection is?"

This is the Treasure entertaining a few of her fellow-passengers in the kitchen, whilst her Mistress is prematurely eulogising her in the parlour.

4

THE RISING GENERATION.

Little Brother: "As Papa and all the other men are out but me, I have just brought this up to keep you girls in order."

5. For some, there was still slavish adoption of fashion dictates from Britain and Europe – over-tight bodices to accentuate shoulders and breasts, corsets to achieve 'wasp waists', heavy full-length skirts, fussily decorated head-gear, gloves and high-heeled shoes or boots – regardless of how much they restricted and hampered women in their much more active, physically demanding lives in New Zealand. *"Here s Miss Smith",* Arthur Palethorpe, *NZ Punch* (Wellington), September 13 1879. ATL: H-692-003

6. Men were heavy – cigarette, pipe and cigar – smokers, but to their womenfolk smoking was more a social dilemma than a health problem. *Miss Lawley on Smoking,* Arthur Palethorpe, *NZ Punch* (Wellington), October 11 1879. ATL: H-692-007

7. The first generation of settlers found it difficult to adjust to the somersaulting of seasons. Christmas was, after all, the time for roaring fires and walks in the snow. *December, 1879*, Arthur Palethorpe, *NZ Punch* (Wellington), January 3 1880. ATL: H-692-014

8. There had been a thriving sex industry in New Zealand from the first contact between Maori and sealers and whalers. With the continuing imbalance between men and women, no amount of Victorian moralising could close down 'red light' districts. *The Betterment of Life*, William Blomfield, *NZ Observer and Free Lance*, January 11 1890. ATL: J-065-027

5

Clara: "Oh, here's Miss Smith coming along; shall we speak to her?"
Amelia: "No, dear! Mama says she can't be a lady, because she wears a stuff dress."

6

MISS LAWLEY ON SMOKING.
"You know dear, if we object to smoking, we should have to object to the society of smokers: and we could never do without the men, the dear creatures."

7

DECEMBER, 1879.

Old England. New Zealand.

8

TO SHEOL

THE WORLD

BLO.

THE BETTERMENT OF LIFE.

2: 1900-1909

KING DICK'S LONG SHADOW

Tracing the beginnings of national identity is a popular parlour game among historians with factors as varied as the victorious 1905 All Blacks and the spilling of blood on foreign battlefields widely mooted. But the influence of Richard John Seddon, the man who dominated New Zealand life at the beginning of the 20th century, should not be under-estimated.

'King Dick' – the sneer became an affectionate nickname in time – increasingly ran the country as a personal fiefdom. Liberal supporters were routinely favoured for jobs in the fast-expanding civil service, and he was genuinely puzzled when he was criticised for saying that electorates returning government members were more likely to prosper.

Seddon stumped the country endlessly, election year or not, unblushingly dispensing patronage, and sniffing out shifts in the political breeze. He never forgot or underestimated the popular basis of his support, all the more so as the Liberals ran out of reforming puff, and a growing pride in New Zealand-ness came from his trumpeting, as a one-man Tourism Board, of 'God's Own Country'.

If New Zealand was, in fact, 'God's Own Country', there was little doubt that Seddon occupied the right-hand seat. He dominated parliaments, cabinets, conversations and the cartoons of the period. In cartoons, he invariably appeared with pouter-pigeon chest – the all-purpose visual swipe at a man whose physical size, presence and power were matched by a massive pride, self-satisfaction and relish for good living.

By the beginning of the new century, and with growing and sustained prosperity, there was much less public enthusiasm for constant change. While the Liberals could parade an impressive list of hugely significant tax, land, labour, social and electoral legislation, they were now more concerned with the mechanics of staying in power. The New Zealand trade union movement, which had backed the Liberals through the 1890s, was unhappy with the drop off in reforming zeal and, in 1904, the annual Trades Conference voted for an independent Labour Party.

In time-honoured tradition, Seddon now turned much of his seemingly indefatigable energy to the wider world. From this distance, and to some cartoonists at the time, he often seems to be a Gilbert-and-Sullivan sort of imperialist. But again, Seddon had caught the spirit of the times. New Zealand, in its South Pacific remoteness, was both smug about its achievements and uneasy about its isolation. Troops were despatched to the South African War, federation with Australia was rejected and there was heady talk of a South Pacific federation based on New Zealand.

Never one to stint food or drink, Seddon's weight ballooned to nearly 20 stone in later life. It was perhaps surprising he lived as long as he did, yet he was only 60 when he died of a massive heart attack in early June 1906, returning home after a punishing 24 day visit to Australia. It was still a great shock to the country, and one the government never really recovered from as it had been largely the force of Seddon's personality and larger-than-life reputation that kept the shaky Liberal-Labour coalition from crumbling completely.

Seddon's anointed successor Sir Joseph Ward, very much the model of the dapper capitalist entrepreneur, provided scarcely needed confirmation that very little of the old Liberal commitment to the working man remained, and that at least tacit approval was given to increasingly pro-employer Arbitration Court decisions.

Ward was a 20th century man; a communications visionary. Knighted in1901 for introducing the world's first universal penny postage, he was an enthusiastic and knowledgeable advocate of new telegraph cable technology and the growing international links it provided.

His credibility bruised by financial conflicts of interest and a personal bankruptcy that kept him from the cabinet table for two years, Ward's 'legislative holiday' promise was a successful 1908 election tactic, but only temporarily disguised his lack of any meaningful domestic policies. Overseas forays as a champion of imperial federation and trade preferences, and the offer of a battleship to the British navy to bolster the empire's defence, were little more than sideshows as the once great Liberal Party crumbled. But there was probably little Ward could have done to save it, now the victim of its own earlier successes.

Small farmers and industrial workers, the two important, previously neglected sections of the community which voted the Liberals into power, now had their own divergent agendas. The Labour movement's messy internal squabbling kept it quiescent through the rest of the decade, but farming interests were beginning to organise more effectively inside and out of parliament.

With dairying's increasing export earning importance, 'cow cockies' were prominent in the recently formed Farmers' Union which hammered away at the twin themes of freeholding leased land and cutting import tariffs that comfortably protected town dwellers. In parallel, a comatose parliamentary opposition was stirring – the loose 1890s groupings of National Associations were united and, in 1904, were re-christened the Political Reform League. William Fergusson Massey, who had served a stolid but lengthy apprenticeship in the House, became leader of a party that owed a primary and uncomplicated allegiance to the fast-swelling number of newly-prosperous, increasingly conservative small farmers.

By decade's end, it was only a matter of time before he would lead the Reform Party to electoral victory.

By 1900, there was a sense of buoyancy and confidence throughout New Zealand. The most rugged pioneering days were over and if the time when pakeha and Maori would live next to each other in suburban streets was still in the future they were increasingly playing against each other on rugby fields. Although, by 1896, the numbers of Maori had dropped 60 percent since 1840 to about 42,000, with the new century numbers began to increase, each census recording rises. With the Maori here to stay, there were extraordinary efforts to 'whiten' them, based on spurious claims of a shared Aryan past with Europeans, so New Zealand could claim, despite obvious evidence to the contrary, a basically British homogeneity. Less perplexing was the growing use of Maori words and symbols to emphasise New Zealand's distinctiveness.

Life had settled down, the shape of the future could be more easily discerned. The gold rush- fuelled explosion of the South Island's population had passed and the 1901 census showed that, for the first time since 1858, there were marginally more people in the North Island, Wellington had superseded Dunedin as the country's third largest city after Auckland and Christchurch, and nearly half the country's 770,000 population now lived in urban centres. By the end of the decade there was gas lighting in the main streets of cities and larger towns and gas and water piped into many homes. A number of inland towns were now thriving, communications aided by better roads, penny postage, and the gradual spread of the telephone. New Zealand had been linked to Britain and Europe by telegraph cable from the mid-1870s, although there was no direct link to North America until 1902.

Railway lines were, in fits and starts, pushing their way through some of the world's most challenging terrain with the main trunk line between Auckland and Wellington finally completed in 1908. William McLean, a Wellington businessman and politician, had imported the first motor car in 1898, the same year his parliamentary colleagues passed the McLean Motor-car Act to allow him to venture out onto the road. Bicycling had become a popular pastime and now the motor car was about to expand picnicking and weekend rambling horizons even more.

So, during the first decade of the new century New Zealanders could, perhaps, be excused a little smugness. They might have tried to replicate a 'little Britain' deep in the southern oceans in some ways, but they had also firmly rejected the home country's institutionalised poverty and rigid class system. There was certainly a class system, and some with a vested interest in the traditional version, but there were now new, more important indicators of status. An impressive number of sheep or significant acreage of pasture, with a crofter lineage that disappeared in Scottish mists a generation or two ago, was now more meaningful than an English county lineage that marched back in orderly procession several hundreds of years.

There was a kind of schizophrenia – proud to be British, yet out of a later, more superior mould – that no one thought about at the time, but has perplexed historians subsequently. Troops were promptly despatched to help the British during the Boer War of 1899-1902, yet there were soon claims that, with their horse-riding skills, marksmanship and toughness, the New Zealanders were altogether better soldiers. And there was considerable satisfaction in handing out thumpings on British rugby grounds in 1905.

A number of stray, and sometimes connected, strands were giving more meaning to being a New Zealander. The abolition of the provinces had weakened regionalism, by 1900 a significant majority of pakeha were locally born, and the country's young men had shown their prowess on battle and sporting fields. It was one thing for Seddon to go on about 'God's Own Country', but it became more meaningful when a number of distinguished overseas visitors – Sidney and Beatrice Webb, Tom Mann, Andre Siegfried and others – talked and wrote glowingly about the world's 'social laboratory'.

New Zealand has had a long-established fascination with showing off: it could no more resist a small display at the great Crystal Palace exhibition of 1851 than a more ambitious involvement at the 1884 International Health Exhibition in London or the elaborate pavilions at world trade fairs in the late 20th century. Local exhibitions celebrating 'New Zealand-ness' were also popular; one in Christchurch in 1906-07 attracted, presumably with many repeat attendees, two million visitors.

However, when New Zealand did not join with the other southern ocean colonies to become part of the Australian federation in 1901, the rejection of previously close 'Australasian' links had less to do with any sense of independence than with a growing, not lessening, dependence on Britain. The sum total of a number of decisions and events in the late 19th century was New Zealand's wholesale, and voluntary, sale to Britain of its economic future, for more than half a century.

The Liberal government's breaking up of large estates and supply of credit through its Advances to Settlers programme had allowed smaller, family farms to take root successfully; refrigeration provided British markets expansive enough to test the ingenuity and enterprise of farmers; and the financier offshoots of a declining colonial gentry, and their British connections, saw the profit in providing the 'infrastructure', freezing works and the increasingly larger and faster ships to complete the farm to London market transaction. Industry which had shown surprising variety and versatility up until the 1890s now narrowed, and became part of the British industrial economy, part processing farm produce to be 'finished' 12,000 miles away.

THE CHURCH HAS GOT ITS SHARE.

CLARKE (at the Anglican Synod): If something is not done to prevent the reckless sale of land by the Maoris, in less than a generation they will be landless and a burden to the colonists.
THE LANDLESS MAORI: Taihoa! But where has the best of our land gone? How much of it have the missionaries got? How much has the Church got? You people have done your share, too, to make us landless.

William Blomfield, *NZ Observer and Free Lance*, December 11 1897. ATL: A-312-6-025

Achieving Dominion status in 1907 was a one-week phenomenon, celebrated with a photograph of politicians on parliament's steps and flag-waving rallies at sports grounds around the country, but then promptly forgotten.

In the new political and economic climate, the remaining great estates and their gentry owners were less relevant than the hard-working families on smaller properties better suited to intensive meat and dairy production. Some did not recover from the pressure to freehold great acreages, either to hold onto them or, as others hoped, sell profitably to the government or private buyers. Many scions of surviving gentry families, eager volunteers at the outbreak of the First World War, literally signed their own death warrants as junior infantry officers.

A new middle class was emerging strongly in cities and towns. If the colonial gentry had been distinguished by their social leadership and serious devotion to leisure pursuits, the expanding group of 'professional' occupations, manufacturers and business managers were strongly committed to their callings and a rigorous work ethic that left little time for leisure. 'White-collar' occupations – creating a lower middle class – were growing apace. Early technology, the increasing availability of consumer goods, the growth of the public service and the private expansion of insurance, banking and other services into the wider market created a surge of jobs in offices and shops after 1900.

Secondary schooling, once the preserve of a few 'private' schools, was gradually more accessible. But ambitious working class parents, who saw at least some post-primary education as the best route to 'white collar' work for their children, badgered schools to add 'standard sevens', which a number did.

They might now vote, and have the ability to do a great deal more besides, but women in the upper reaches of the middle class were expected, despite their smaller families, to stay at home. However, some, who had trained as teachers and nurses, didn't, and overall, the number of women in the paid workforce rose sharply in the first decade of the new century. Tedious, poorly paid jobs in clothing factories were gradually superseded by better paid ones as office clerical workers and shop assistants. In 1911, 28 percent of women were in paid employment, a rate not exceeded until the 1960s.

This was not really surprising, on two counts at least. Possibly because of a strong Scottish influence, girls and young women were extraordinarily well educated. In the 1890s nearly half of public primary school pupils were girls as, in 1900, were 45 percent of secondary school students, and in 1893 more than half the country's university students were women. Secondly, New Zealand women were no longer permanently pregnant. There was a dramatic drop in the rate of child-bearing, more than halving between

1881 and 1926. Possibly the most persuasive of a number of reasons is that an impressive decline in infant mortality removed the need for 'replacement' children.

A whiff of morality in the air also separated the new century from the more roistering earlier colonial decades. While attendance at most established churches was already on a downward slide there was considerable community concern about 'demon drink', with a huge number of regulations getting in the way of the enjoyment of a quiet pint, any loosely defined impropriety, including the reading of Balzac and Zola, prostitution, and even aspects of motherhood. Dr Truby King, celebrated founder of the Plunket Society, was a control freak who promoted a domesticity cult with rigid rules about mothering and child-raising that made military regulations look positively flaccid.

By 1900, literacy was almost universal and every town had its own newspaper and library. From the early 1890s, and taking advantage of new, efficient lithography techniques, a new group of weeklies – *The Observer, NZ Graphic, New Zealand Free Lance* and *Auckland Weekly News* – were particularly popular, concentrating on social, sporting and cultural coverage and, for the first time, making lavish use of photographs and cartoons.

The character-building aspects of rugby were underlined by the 1905 All Black tour to Britain, the 829 points to 39 tally showing that New Zealand bred an altogether superior specimen of young manhood. Rugby was clearly the national game, now played in schools and by all classes throughout the country. To Seddon, dubbed 'Minister of Football', rugby was a convenient symbol for emerging nationhood.

But there was also room for more genteel sports and pursuits. Tennis, a feature of weekend house parties at country mansions, was much more widely played after the success of Anthony Wilding, who won the doubles championship at Wimbledon in 1907 and 1908 with Norman Brookes, and teamed with his Australian friend to win the Davis Cup for 'Australasia' three times between 1907-09. Before he died on a battlefield in Belgium in 1915, Wilding also won the Wimbledon singles title four times from 1910. In the 1890s 'lady cyclists' were gentlewomen engaged in a fashionable pastime; in the early 1900s prices came down, cycling became popular and gave young women much more practical emancipation than the vote.

With New Zealand profitably preoccupied with exporting meat, dairy produce and wool to London, it was happy to import culture, and most of everything else, from London. In 1903, for example, Dame Nellie Melba and Percy Grainger, the composer and pianist, appeared in New Zealand concert halls and the next year the renowned pianist Ignace Paderewski performed in the main centres and Invercargill.

Touring theatre companies, and even circuses, were increasingly common in larger towns; imported township entertainment was on a smaller scale, but the mesmerists, conjurers or vaudevillians of various stripe were welcomed with as much enthusiasm.

During the first decade of the new century, a new form of entertainment arrived, bewitching audiences in the smallest country halls as well as the grandest city auditoriums. The first motion picture show toured in 1902, and it was common for an evening's entertainment to include film, lantern slides and the musical phonograph; the first permanent picture show was established at His Majesty's Theatre in Wellington in 1908.

There were also the first stirrings of concern about the New Zealand environment. After decades of slash and burn, the Egmont National Park was established in 1900; four years later the Scenery Preservation Commission was appointed. Tongariro National Park was formally gazetted in 1907, the same year the last known huia was sighted – and promptly shot.

The Reign of King Dick

By the beginning of the 20th century, Seddon had won three elections in a row, but behind this seeming impregnability the Liberals were beginning a slow process of disintegration. Seddon had long anticipated this. The Liberal and Labour Federation he forged the previous decade gave the first Labour politicians and their concerns a carefully controlled place in the government's plans. It was an arrangement that extended the Liberals' hold on power; it was not until 1904 that a separate Political Labour League was formed. Seddon was equally shrewd with his handling of the wider Liberal Party, ensuring that its more radical views did not dispute his cautious consolidation of the government's gains.

1. Following the 1902 election, which introduced the first-past-the-post system with only one member per electorate, the title of premier was replaced by 'prime minister'; and Seddon lived the role to the hilt. *The Shadow in the Grass*, E Frederick Hiscocks, *NZ Graphic*, December 6 1902. ATL: A-315-001
2. A controversy in Australia about whether the primate or cardinal should have religious precedence, revived memories of the intense rivalry between Seddon, and Robert Stout who might have succeeded Ballance in 1893 had he been an MP at the time. Back in the House, Stout was Seddon's sternest critic until the premier appointed him chief justice in 1898. *A Way out of the Difficulty*, William Blomfied, *NZ Observer*, July 18, 1903. ATL: B-034-006
3. He was increasingly 'King Dick' to his 'subjects', but Seddon had a remarkable ability to reach out to ordinary New Zealanders and to be, uniquely in the colony's history, a 'man of the people'. He steadfastly refused the knighthood that might have weakened his political support. *Richard Seddon Leads a Procession of his Subjects*, E Frederick Hiscocks, ca 1900. ATL: C-034-012
4. Seddon concentrated as much power as possible in his office. He became minister of labour when Reeves retired in 1896 and colonial treasurer when Ward resigned the same year. He held these positions, plus the education and immigration portfolios, acquired in mid-1903, until his death. *A Grand Old Grabber!,* Frederick Rayner, *The Sketcher*, 1905. ATL: A-225-030
5. Seddon was a popular and well-known figure in Australia, but in 1902 an Australian newspaper warned that he was trying to 'march' the new Commonwealth government in the wrong direction. *The Lone Drum-Major*, E V B, *NZ Graphic*, April 5 1902. ATL: A-315-3-030

1

The Shadow in the Grass.

2

A WAY OUT OF THE DIFFICULTY

Sir Robert: "Now then, Dick, you are putting on too much front, and you ve one foot over the line. That s not fair."

3

RICHARD SEDDON LEADS A PROCESSION OF HIS SUBJECTS

5

The Lone Drum-Major.
It is the manifest disposition of Mr Seddon to grip a general sway. His hand needs careful Australian watching. It seems to be his aim in taking the lead in larger Australian affairs to call the tune for the Commonwealth Government on all questions.

4

A GRAND OLD GRABBER!

A SEDDONISM!
Appropriate all the important portfolios for yourself, and take care you also virtually sway the remainder. Whatever happens, BE BOSS!

Far-Flung Ambitions

As his confidence and domination of New Zealand politics grew, Seddon's horizons broadened, although his and New Zealand's curious blend of nationalistic chest-thumping and imperialistic fervour are not easily explained. But a growing feeling of national identity, rooted in a smug sense of destiny and increasingly uneasy awareness of South Pacific isolation, was further stimulated by the South African war and rejection of federation with Australia. There was talk of a South Pacific federation based on New Zealand: the colony felt isolated enough without foreign powers partitioning the Pacific; coaling stations were vital to the North American steamer mail service; a federation would help balance the increased Antipodean sway of united Australia. But the Colonial Office thought differently. Fiji remained a crown colony, New Guinea, Samoa and the New Hebrides were carved up for the convenience of European powers. In the end, annexation of the Cook Islands in 1901 was some small consolation.

1. Seddon never tired of claiming that, with a South Seas perspective and Maori population, New Zealand was best qualified to administer Pacific island groups. *Fills the Bill*, Scatz, *NZ Graphic*, October 18 1900. ATL: H-723-014

2. New Zealand sent delegations to early conferences debating federation of the Australasian colonies, but there were no delegates at the final, bargaining sessions in the late 1890s. Seddon had little interest in any weakening of New Zealand's sovereignty and the findings of a royal commission concurred. New Zealanders plainly preferred Australians as cousins rather than brothers. *The Ruling Passion is Strong in Seddon*, E Frederick Hiscocks, *The Free Lance*, November 17 1900. ATL: PUBL-0096-1900-11-17-007

3. Cartoonists habitually depicted Seddon, imperious at home and abroad, as a royal intimate. In fact, he did attend the 1901 coronation as a royal guest, with the Australian premiers – to their chagrin – only 'distinguished persons'. *King Dick to King Edward*, E Frederick Hiscocks, *The Free Lance,* February 16 1901. ATL: J-065-042

4. New Zealand entered the South African War with jingoistic fervour, but pride in the exploits of the mounted contingents became a significant first blooding in nationalism. Seddon accepted Lord Kitchener's invitation to visit South Africa just as hostilities ended in 1902. *"Kitchener s School" – The Master*, E V B, *NZ Graphic*, January 25 1902. ATL: A-315-3-027

5. Outwardly, New Zealand accepted Dominion status in 1907 with very little apparent enthusiasm. The ties with Britain remained strong, but there were now clear signs of a separate New Zealand identity. *The Surprise Packet*, William Blomfield, *NZ Observer*, September 21 1907. ATL: J-065-040

1

FILLS THE BILL

2

THE RULING PASSION IS STRONG IN SEDDON.

N.S. Wales: "You are a Federationist in heart and spirit, Mr Seddon, so you might just as well dismount from that hobby-horse, and take your seat behind me without any further nonsense. Besides, it is better to be a live ass than a dead lion."

The Only Seddon: "Not I, my lord. My mount may be a small one now, but he will grow apace, and, in the meantime, I prefer to be a ruler even in this modest way to taking the back seat you offer me."

3

KING DICK TO KING EDWARD.

"Now, Ted, old man, you re feeling a bit shy, of course, in your new role as king, and you re likely to make some mistakes. But don t let that worry you. I m an old hand at the business, and whenever you are in want of a wrinkle don t be afraid to ring up your friend Dick. Trust me for pulling you through. Why, over in Australia the other day they said I ought to have been czar of Russia."

4

"KITCHENER'S SCHOOL" – THE MASTER.

Generalissimo Seddon to Lord K[itchener]: "Now, mind you, my Lord, I want my men brigaded together, so that any little service they may do may rebound to the honour of New Zealand and the glory of Seddon, for ever and ever,. Ake! ake! ake!"

5

THE SURPRISE PACKET.

Canada: "Rather large for him, is it not?"
Australia: "Oh, his head is swelling rapidly. The hat will soon fit."

Here to Stay

By the beginning of the new century, the Maori population was growing. With greater immunity to European diseases and a naturally high fertility rate, births were outpacing deaths. Of greater concern now was that Maori would soon be landless. A 1907 royal commission spelled out how decades of land legislation had single-mindedly sought formulae allowing individual Maori to sell, while those who wanted to keep their land to farm and develop were endlessly frustrated by the genealogical complexities of ownership. These difficulties, coupled with persistent ready-cash and hard-liquor sales propositions, encouraged many Maori, already bitter about doubtful confiscations after the land wars, to squander what remained of their birthright in flamboyant binges or sullen idleness. During the 1890s Maori land was sold at the frightening rate of about 360,000 acres a year. Subsequent legislation did not help and the attempt to consolidate scattered kin-group holdings into economic units and farm them as incorporations was only partly successful.

1. A degree of Maori autonomy remained longer in the far north than elsewhere. The 'Dog Tax War' followed the refusal of Northland Maori to pay this tax and local body rates. A pitched battle between troops and 'rebels', that could have resulted in considerable bloodshed, was averted at the last moment. *Strained Relations: Or "Dogged" Resistance*, Ashley Hunter, *NZ Graphic*, May 14 1898. ATL: PUBL-0163- 1898-001
2. James Carroll, minister of native affairs through the decade, slowed the sale of Maori land to about 50,000 acres a year. He also promoted the 'taihoa' policy which encouraged leasing instead of sale of Maori land. *A New Era in View for the Maori*, E Frederick Hiscocks, *NZ Graphic*, February 9 1907. ATL: A-315-1-018
3. The Maori population decline had ended in the 1890s but it remained a popular pakeha myth as late as the 1930s. *The Passing of the Maori – What We re Coming To*, J C Blomfield, *The Free Lance*, December 15 1906. ATL: J 065-037
4. Maui Pomare, Carroll's successor in Massey's Reform government from 1912, did not stop the last major land grab – about 230,000 acres a year until 1920. By the late 1930s total Maori land left was a miniscule 400,000 acres. *Timi s Joy Ride*, Tom Glover, *Truth*, July 25 1914. ATL: J-065-043

1

STRAINED RELATIONS: OR "DOGGED" RESISTANCE.

2

A NEW ERA IN VIEW FOR THE MAORI.
YOUNG NEW ZEALAND: "Now, Granny, you just run away; for I am going to take him in hand."

3

THE PASSING OF THE MAORI.—WHAT WE'RE COMING TO.

4

Timi's Joy Ride.

Oh, for a joy-ride in a grand motah car;
Reform's legislation's removed the old bar;
While Timi and wahine are riding in front,
Their Guardian Angels are smiling quite sweet.

Ah, when they've parted with their native land,
The wiles of such saints they'll then understand;
We sigh for the faith of Timi and Cis –
And wait for their bump into the abyss!

The King is Dead, Long Live Sir Joe

After a fifth consecutive election victory – winning 55 of the 80 seats – at the end of 1905, and with pressure from his back-benchers to promote more able people, Seddon dangled the carrot of his retirement, after another Colonial Conference in 1907. In May he travelled to Australia and kept up his usual punishing schedule for nearly a month. Boarding the *Oswestry Grange* for the return voyage he telegraphed the Victorian premier: "Just leaving for God's own country", but he died from a massive heart attack shortly after the ship sailed. Seddon's deputy, Sir Joseph Ward, was at a postal conference in Rome so acting prime minister William Hall-Jones reluctantly formed a new ministry, but only after King Dick's state funeral 11 days later. The short-lived ministry – 45 days – marked time while Ward returned to New Zealand as fast as available sea transport allowed.

1. With another election comfortably won, Seddon was ready to strut a larger stage again. His May 1906 trip across the Tasman involved an exhausting round of talks on trade and other issues – and he could seldom resist the temptation to suggest to Australian politicians the wisdom of adopting his administration's policies. *Sighing for New Worlds to Conquer*, William Blomfield, *NZ Observer*, April 28 1906. ATL: A-312-1-034
2. An able minister, Hall-Jones became acting prime minister when Seddon left for Australia. In fact, he had no prime ministerial ambitions and, after Seddon's death, made it clear that his would be a caretaker ministry and he would resign as soon as Ward returned. *Trying it On*, E Frederick Hiscocks, *NZ Graphic*, May 26 1906. ATL: A-315-1-015
3. Ward's long record of deviousness, while invaluable to Seddon, did not make him a popular figure. He was responsible for the second ballot system first used at the 1908 election. If no-one polled more than 50 percent, there was a second election between the two highest polling candidates. An attempt to minimise harmful split voting among pro-government candidates, it favoured Labour and was abandoned before the 1914 election. *When Knights were Bold – the Plot that Failed*, Trevor Lloyd, *NZ Herald*, 1903. ATL: C-109-025
4. In this prophetic cartoon, published before the 1905 election, an 'angelic' Seddon shows his consummate skill – not shared by his colleagues – in finding common ground among increasingly disparate groups. *That Parliament of Labour*, J C Blomfield, *The Free Lance*, October 14, 1905. ATL: J-065-017

1

SIGHING FOR NEW WORLDS TO CONQUER.

King Dick: "This country s too small. There s not enough scope for my genius. As my own house is in order, I ll run across to the Commonwealth, and show them how to manage their affairs; after that, America."

2

TRYING IT ON.

The Acting Premier Mr Hall-Jones (loq.): "H-m! The malicious might hint that it's a bit big for me, but I'll show 'em how I'll grow into it."

3

When knights were bold – the plot that failed.

4

THAT PARLIAMENT OF LABOUR.

The Angel of Peace: "Now then, boys, all together to my music. Ah-h-h! that s the style".

The Model of a Modern Wheeler-Dealer

Joseph Ward's beginnings – a poor, Catholic single-parent household in Bluff – could not have been less promising. But, with the risk-taking brand of optimism he inherited from his mother, his chequered business and political careers had more highs than lows. Ward was genial, polite, socially adept, and frequently enigmatic. It was abundantly clear what Seddon thought, sometimes uncomfortably so; with Ward an outpouring of words often obscured any real meaning, and he carefully maintained an impenetrable façade. Ward's concern was survival rather than policy or principle and his clever 'legislative holiday' campaign temporarily disguised the Liberal predicament at the 1908 elections. It was the party's biggest winning margin during nearly 23 years in power, yet there was snowballing dissatisfaction with Ward's do-nothing approach.

1. Ward was colonial treasurer when severely reprimanded in the Supreme Court for persistent attempts to cover up his company's indebtedness to the Colonial Bank. He resigned from parliament in 1896, was declared bankrupt, regained his seat the same year and, because Seddon wanted his astute lieutenant back, was in cabinet again in 1899. *The Colonial Treasurer is Torn by the Financial Wolves*, William Blomfield, *NZ Observer and Free Lance*, June 13 1896. ATL: H-722-197
2. Knighted for introducing the first universal penny postage, Ward is deservedly remembered for the reforms and innovations of his 18 years as postmaster-general. But he was widely lampooned for accepting a baronetcy in 1911. *Joe Ward as the Angel of Light*, William Blomfield, *NZ Observer*, September 22 1900. ATL: A-312-1-004
3. While it meant little to his fellow New Zealanders at the time, Ward believed that 'Dominion' status in 1907 gave more weight to his imperialist ambitions. He was a strong advocate of imperial federation and trade preferences and later, in a display of enthusiastic largesse, offered a battleship to the British Navy to bolster the empire's defences. *Kiwi: "I think I would look better without it"*, Trevor Lloyd, 1907. ATL: C-109-023
4. Not only had unionists grown distrustful of the Liberal-Labour alliance, with its do-as-little-as-possible approach, but farmers saw Ward as an unsympathetic businessman-banker. For Ward, though, there were exciting challenges in the wider world. *Times have Changed*, William Blomfield, *NZ Observer*, November 3 1906. ATL: A-312-1-031
5. Ward had little rapport with unions. There were strikes – the first for many years – in the freezing and mining industries. Ward was losing patience with increasingly militant unionists and the Liberals were losing the support of the Labour movement. *Exit the Skeleton in the Cupboard*, Trevor Lloyd, ca 1910. ATL: C-100-011

1

The Colonial Treasurer is torn by the financial wolves.

2

JOE WARD AS THE ANGEL OF LIGHT.

3

Kiwi: "I think I would look better without it."

4

TIMES HAVE CHANGED.

Trade unionist: "Surely you haven t closed parliament already, Sir Joseph? Why, you haven t given us trade unionists one single labour law to bump the capitalists with. How we do miss good Old Dick."

5

Exit the Skeleton in the Cupboard.

The Liberals Fade Away

Joseph Ward had neither Seddon's prestige nor his charisma – the mortar that had been holding the crumbling Liberal Party together for several years. Now the co-operation between its farming and labour wings had turned to economic competition. By 1900 court awards were failing to keep pace with cost-of-living increases. In 1906, the first strike for more than a decade underlined the fact that real wages were lower than in 1894, when the compulsory arbitration legislation was passed. Unions belonging to the more militant Federation of Labour, formed in 1909, were committed to forcing better working conditions and wages through direct industrial action. After 1899, the Farmers' Union, begun by dairy farmers in Taranaki and the far north, quickly became a political force. Initial support for the Liberals was shifting to the opposition by the 1908 election.

1. Ward 'weathered' growing labour movement dissatisfaction mainly because of its own lengthy period of messy, internal squabbling. A confusing succession of socialist and Labour groupings made practically no electoral impact until 1911. *Labour, Liberalism, Conservatism*, David Low, ca 1908. ATL: B-025-037
2. Ward's 'legislative holiday' policy was really a camouflage for no policies at all. The reality increasingly frustrated farmers, employers and unionists. *Sir Joseph Defines the Government Policy*, William Blomfield, *NZ Observer*, February 15 1908. ATL: A-312-1-032
3. The Liberals' continuing allegiance to 'leasehold' lost the government seats in farming areas at the 1908 election, the opposition's William Massey making 'freehold' his rallying call. *Not for Joe*, William Blomfield, *NZ Observer*, August 1 1908. ATL: A-312-1-038
4. Naval defence was a major topic of discussion at the Imperial Conference in London in 1909. Australia wanted its own naval force and Ward sought to maintain the British Navy's south Pacific presence. His sweetener: the offer of a battle cruiser, to be called *HMS New Zealand*, to Britain. *The Skipper s Return*, E Frederick Hiscocks, *The Citizen*, October 8 1909. ATL: A-315-1-040
5. By the end of the decade, 'freehold' was the overriding preoccupation of the increasingly numerous, smaller leasehold farmers. Ward tried to mix his party's leasehold traditions with freehold concessions – but to no-one's satisfaction. *United – Under One Flag*, William Blomfield, *NZ Observer*, November 27, 1909. ATL: A-312-1-042

1

LABOUR, LIBERALISM, CONSERVATISM.

2

SIR JOSEPH WARD DEFINES THE GOVERNMENT POLICY.

Joseph Ward: "The Government are not extremists. On the one hand, they have no sympathy with the hide-bound individualist who looks upon State action and enterprise as hateful and pernicious. On the other hand, they are not revolutionary Socialists."

3

NOT FOR JOE.

Sir Joseph: "Ah, Mr Massey, you ll have to try again, You cannot frighten me with that bogey of yours; it is anything but natural. Just place it with your other Socialist effigies."

4

THE SKIPPER'S RETURN

5

UNITED – UNDER ONE FLAG.

Government General Ward: "Hullo! General Massey – you re fighting in my camp? Why, I thought you were the enemy."

Opposition General Massey: "Enemy? No. I ve been fighting under this flag all along."

The War on 'Demon Drink'

Drunkenness was a serious problem in New Zealand and other frontier societies from the earliest days of European settlement. After 1886, when diverse prohibitionist groups – with Protestant churches and the women's movement prominent – formed a national organisation, the New Zealand Alliance, there was increased agitation for local, popular-vote, 'wet' or 'dry' decisions. Robert Stout, combining his dislike of Seddon and liquor, forced the government to sponsor a local-option bill in 1894. Stout proposed a simple majority vote to close down all licensed premises in a district; cannily, Seddon's legislation required a three-fifths majority of 'no licence' voters – a crucial difference. The propaganda war intensified now that electors would decide every three years whether licences should be continued, reduced or abolished. Prohibition gained a simple majority of votes at the elections between 1902-11, but not by a sufficient margin for a wholesale move to abolition. In 1908, 12 licensing districts voted for local prohibition.

1. Barmaids were targets for prohibitionists ('wowsers' to imbibers), seen by them as dubious women who encouraged men to drink. They were finally banned, several years after Seddon's death, in 1911 – and were not seen again in New Zealand pubs until 1961. *The Barmaid Wins the Day*, William Blomfield, *NZ Observer*, September 12 1903. ATL: A-312-1-021
2. Between 1880 and 1920 the prohibition movement could point proudly to about 50 laws controlling liquor consumption. Some raised the age at which the young could drink in pubs; others progressively lowered the alcohol content of beer. *"Are You Over Eighteen?"*, E Frederick Hiscocks, *NZ Graphic*, February 4 1905. ATL: A-315-1-009
3. Consumption of alcohol was on an astonishing scale; there were about 500 drink-related deaths yearly during the 1870s, many of them from drowning. 'Demon drink' was also the cause of domestic violence and severe financial difficulties for families. *"Don t Forget to Order a Ton of Coal …"*, David Low, *Spectator*, December 31 1909. ATL: B-025-038

1

THE BARMAID WINS THE DAY.

King Dick: "Well, ladies, if I must choose between you, give me the barmaid."

2

"Are You Over Eighteen?"

SKETCH IN THE BAR PARLOUR OF A BONIFACE WHO IS ANXIOUS NOT TO INFRINGE THE CLAUSE IN THE NEW LICENSING ACT PROVIDING A MINIMUM AGE OF 18 YEARS FOR HIS WOULD-BE PATRONS.

3

"Don't forget to order a ton of coal, dear. Here are two pound notes to pay for it. We are right out."
PEACE PERFECT PEACE
1
"Dear" goes in to "change" the notes and comes out about five bob short.
2
PRIVATE BAR
"Dear" meets a friend and another five bob breaks loose.
3
4
"Lemme (hic) shee now. Half a (hic) ton 'll do."
5 Another friend.
6
"Dear":–"S'all ri'. Quarrer ton'sh plenty. Comeanaveanother!"
7
the balance rapidly shrinks to eighteen-pence
8
COAL & FI
But "Dear" is equal to the occasion.
He brings home a bushel and fondly murmers:
"Here y'are m' dear–
brought it home m'shelf
–save expensh."
9
DAVID LOW

Getting the Country On Track

Rail opened up New Zealand's awkward topography, particularly in the North Island, like nothing else. Rail was the basis of a national communications system, a significant industry in itself and it also symbolised, without much subtlety, the march of progress. Although the first track was built in 1863, there were only 47 miles of public railway line in New Zealand in 1870, at the beginning of Julius Vogel's frenetic and financially challenging public works decade. By 1879 a further 1,100 miles had been added. Christchurch and Dunedin were linked by 1879, but it would be another three decades before the Auckland to Wellington rail journey could be made. The government spent £10 million on rail during the decade. It reinforced the dominance of the four main centres, but it also spawned or grew townships along the way as agriculture and timber milling followed the rail tracks. At the beginning of the 1880s, railway construction stopped as quickly as it had begun, financial difficulties and stringency now dictating government policy. It would be another 25 years before there was another doubling of the country's railway lines.

1. Railway building prospered again, in tandem with the country, in the 1890s. The government took over the Midland Railway Co, a private London company, which had started to build a line linking Canterbury to Westland and Nelson. Gaps in the North Island system were plugged, the Auckland-Rotorua line opening in 1894. *The Hon. R_____ S_____, as "The Colossus of (Rail)roads",* Ashley Hunter, *NZ Graphic*, 1893. ATL: A-312-8-006
2. New Zealand had come out of a long depression by the mid 1890s, but a short downturn in trade at the beginning of the new century again slowed progress on the North Island main trunk line. Work accelerated again, with the economy, from 1904. *Danger on the Track*, William Blomfield, *NZ Observer*, September 8 1900. ATL: A-312-1-006
3. In fact, the last spike was driven to complete the North Island main trunk line in November 1908, with regular services beginning the next February. The first trains took 19 hours and 25 minutes, passengers whiling away the time in sleeper or day carriages and restaurant car. *In Days to Come*, E Frederick Hiscocks, *NZ Graphic*, November 21 1903. ATL: A-315-1-004
4. William Hall-Jones oversaw the completion of the North Island main trunk line after practically no progress was made during the 1880s. In May 1908 he claimed the Wellington-Auckland trip would be possible by Christmas. While regular services did not begin until early in 1909 a train dubbed the 'Parliamentary Special' carried MPs north in early August 1906 to visit the US Great White Fleet in Auckland harbour on a goodwill mission. *The Evolution of a Snail*, J C Blomfield, *The Free Lance*, May 9 1908. ATL: A-313-4-038

1

THE HON. R[ICHARD] S[EDDON] as "The Colossus of (rail)roads."

2

DANGER ON THE TRACK.

3

IN DAYS TO COME.

DISTINGUISHED AUCKLAND NONAGENARIAN (somewhere about the year 1990): "Yes, sir, I can remember way back in the year 1903 my poor father taking me to hear Hall-Jones promise to have the Main Trunk railway completed in a year or so. And here we are celebrating the first run at last. Glorious and progressive country!"

4

THE EVOLUTION OF A SNAIL.

A Better Breed of British

By 1900 the frontier society was in retreat. Within and without the country, communications were improving rapidly. European New Zealanders were the 'British of the South Seas', but British with differences created by distance and circumstances. Sport was becoming one of New Zealand's defining characteristics and rugby was emerging from the ruck as the 'national game', possibly because it was relatively egalitarian, community-based and defined 'masculinity' in the post-frontier era. Co-inciding with the growing belief that it was healthy, civilising and generated the sort of team spirit that might even have military utility, rugby was soon more formally organised and of increasing importance in the secondary schools that grew rapidly after the introduction of 'free places' in 1903. Despite the vote and various legal protections, women were not sufficiently emancipated from domestic and child-rearing roles to have the necessary leisure for much sport. However, this was given its positive spin. The proselytising of Truby King, more a moral evangelist than the saint of mythology, gave respectability to the confining roles of expert mothers and home managers.

1. Despite South African war excitement and Seddon's offer of troops for the Boxer uprising in China, New Zealanders kept their sense of perspective during the rugby season. *The 'Bloke of the Hour*, Scatz, *NZ Graphic*, September 15 1900. ATL: J-065-041
2. The triumphant All Blacks tour of Britain in 1905 – with the final tally 829 points for and 39 against – was more than rugby success; it symbolised a country doing things right. *The Moa and the Lion*, Trevor Lloyd, 1905. ATL: Eph-A-RUGBY-1905-1
3. Turn of the century talk about a baby bonus for parents with large families was premature. The material aspirations of a growing middle class, improved health care and contraceptive practices were beginning to cut a swathe through birth rates. *The Royal Road to Wealth*, EVB, *NZ Graphic*, August 31 1901. ATL: H-711-017
4. As part of the drive for a healthier nation, legislation was passed in 1903 prohibiting children from smoking. *Hope was Lost*, Leonard Booth, *The Exhibition Sketcher*, 1904. ATL: A-350-032
5. Dr Truby King was on the staff of the Seacliff Asylum in Dunedin, and responsible for treatments later considered barbaric, before founding the Plunket Society in 1907. *Rough on the Doctor*, Leonard Booth, *The Exhibition Sketcher*, December 15 1906. ATL: A-350-027

1

THE "BLOKE" OF THE HOUR.

2

THE ROYAL ROAD TO WEALTH.
Mrs Smith (the modern Cornelia): "H'as H'i allus say, 'These are our jewels'. Where would we be without them?"
Mr Smith (the father of twelve): "Most like breakin' stones."

3

4

HOPE WAS LOST

Cyril *(gloomily): "Yes, Maud, my girl, I know it IS a vile habit. I wish I could give it up. But it s too late. I am a slave to tobacco."*

5

Rough on the doctor

DOTTYONE: (at Sunnyside, to other just up from Seacliff): "Is Dr Truby King still at Seacliff?"
DOTTYTOO: "Oh yes, he'll never get better!"

3: 1910-1919

STRIFE ON TWO FRONTS

Sir Joseph Ward hung on at the 1908 election, in part because he had, the year before, bowed to farmer pressure and abolished lease-in-perpetuity, allowing tenants to buy the land they occupied at current prices.

The Reform Party, as yet completely untested and jittery about the outcome of the 1911 election, adopted a more accommodating freehold policy and the crucial, North Island dairy-farmer vote lined up solidly behind the party. However, although outright victory was beyond his grasp, Massey was finally a political figure of some national substance. As well, a distinctive moustache had replaced the previous beard and his middle-aged frame had filled out to something like Seddonian proportions.

Reform won six more seats than the Liberals in 1911, with the ultimate balance of power resting with a quixotic collection of independents, Labour members, as yet without a party caucus, and Maori MPs. When parliament met early in 1912 the Liberals survived, but only with the Speaker's casting vote. Ward resigned and Thomas Mackenzie began his short and limping three month prime ministership before another confidence vote toppled his ministry in July, and Massey was installed at the head of the country's first avowedly conservative government for a generation.

Eighteen long years in opposition had given Massey something of a reputation for cautious reasonableness, but he soon dominated his caucus and party organisation, and events were to cast him in a rigid, right-wing mould. Defined by a restricted political and stern Presbyterian outlook, his policies were quickly in place: no quarter for industrial militants, elimination of political and religious cronyism from the public service, and the freeholding of crown leases.

Just a few years earlier, farmers and unionists had been uneasy partners in a political alliance. But now Massey's reaction to the direct-action, passionately socialist 'Red' Federation of Labour was unequivocating. His tough, uncompromising response to the Waihi miners' strike in 1912 and to the waterfront and general strikes a year later won him the enduring support of the farming community. But the use of special constables, 'Massey's Cossacks', largely recruited from rural areas to keep the wharves working, earned the equally enduring hatred of urban workers and helped convince an indecisive labour movement that a united political approach was essential.

Not surprisingly, given the divisiveness of some of his policies, Massey fell a seat short of a working majority at the December 1914 election, with the resulting parliamentary deadlock and the prospect of a lengthy world war inevitably resulting in a coalition government. Massey and Ward, who was finance minister again and effectively de facto joint head of the government, were now colleagues. But the national government, from August 1915 to August 1919, was largely paralysed by the personal, political and religious antipathy between the two leaders and the unworkable decision to legislate only when both parties were in agreement.

The national government used war-time patriotism and paranoia to justify restrictive 'war legislation' that curtailed personal liberties and branded dissident or embarrassing minorities as the 'enemies' at home. There was an hysterical reaction to anyone or anything remotely German; many local residents of German origin were stripped of their British citizenship and interned; and some were deported in 1919. Opposition to the war effort, such as the refusal of Waikato and Urewera Maori to contribute troops, was considered treasonable. Labour and trade union activists were labeled fellow-travellers of the Germans when they opposed conscription and censorship.

While the politicians at home occupied a kind of uneasy no man's land, over 100,000 young New Zealanders served overseas, over half the men of eligible age and about half of them volunteers. Just over 58,000 were killed or wounded, the highest per capita casualty rate among the allied forces. Later, there was considerable anger at the pointless slaughter and stubborn stupidity of the British generals. In future wars, the New Zealand government would, the theory went, have the final say about the deployment of its troops.

If Massey and Ward agreed about anything, it was the conduct of the country's foreign policy. It was something of a conundrum: balancing the desire to hold tightly to Mother England's apron strings while there was a strong sense of a separate New Zealand identity emerging.

Politicians and business leaders were no longer expatriates safeguarding and exploiting their farming and commercial interests before retiring back to Britain. People were no longer settlers; most had been born locally and felt a growing affinity for the new, hybrid landscape and culture. There was pride too in the social and economic progress achieved in what, by European standards, was a blink in time.

When Massey, the Ulster Orangeman, and Ward, the devout Irish Catholic, travelled to Imperial Conferences like suspicious Siamese twins the purgatory of the long sea voyages together can only be imagined. The two enemies-in-arms had, in fact, returned from another Imperial Conference just as the war ended, celebrations muted by the vicious, world-wide influenza epidemic that struck down New Zealanders in battlefield numbers.

In 1919, when the national government was blamed

David Low, *Bill Massey (Franklin) and Joe Ward (Awarua)*, ca 1911. ATL: A-279-011

for everything from the very high war casualties, to profiteering and the epidemic, Ward, ever the opportunist and sniffing political advantage, withdrew from the coalition with unseemly haste. The country was more divided than it had been for many years: employer versus worker; farmer versus town dweller; conservative versus radical; Protestant versus Roman Catholic. In the end, a battered and weary electorate preferred Massey's reliability and predictability. The Liberals lost further ground and the New Zealand Labour Party, formed in 1916, began to flex its political muscles, but not in time to rob Massey of the one clear majority of his career.

There has been some subsequent puzzlement about why so many young New Zealand men volunteered during the First World War. Nation-building myths have blurred the facts a little. Most of the volunteering happened when the expectation was of a Boer War sort of enterprise. When the horror stories and casualty figures filtered back from France, and it was clear that the previous war had been little more than a romp on the high veldt, the volunteering tailed off and conscription took over. Propaganda is often thought of as a more modern device, but the young men of New Zealand had, by 1914, been subjected to a sustained barrage of imperial and patriotic indoctrination in the Boy Scouts, school cadets and territorials. Nor should the social pressures be under-estimated. Young single men who did not enlist were cold-bloodedly persecuted, often by middle-class women who would, after a domesticated morning topping up the biscuit tins, take to the streets for an afternoon of White Feather League harassment.

The influenza epidemic in 1918 was the second part of a double whammy that took New Zealand a long time to recover from, physically and psychologically. Parents, wives, children and fiancées were struggling to come to terms with their war-time losses when the pandemic struck. Of the 8,600 who died, a disproportionate number were more young men and Maori. In Samoa, recently occupied by New Zealand, one fifth of the population succumbed.

William Blomfield, *NZ Observer*, November 19 1910.
ATL: A-312-1-046

By the end of the war, farmers were very definitely the 'backbone of the country', an image and idea that was to linger on into the closing decades of the century when it was just as definitely not true. By the early 1900s the sharp divisions between the great wool-producing sheep runs and struggling 'cow cockie' properties had blurred. Much smaller sheep-meat farms and increasingly successful dairy farms now had more closely aligned political and economic interests: they supported, and were significant in, the Reform and then the National Party; they created strong national producer and lobby groups, separately and in tandem. Farmers convinced politicians, townies, manufacturers and, most of the time, trade unionists that they were the engine-room of the economy and needed to be treated accordingly. And if sheep still had more social cache than dairy cows, the gap was narrowing.

'Farmer Bill' Massey played a major role in moulding farmer solidarity and, while he had no affection for militant workers, he was more than happy to broaden his support base by nudging workers up the prosperity ladder. The two things workers wanted for their families above all else he was happy to give them. Secondary education, with the opportunities it provided, and home ownership expanded spectacularly, with workers the major beneficiaries.

During the war, and for the first time since 1840, there were more women than men in the country and there was a sharp rise in the number in full-time employment. Many of them were in non-traditional occupations, filling in for men serving overseas, and the new-found confidence in tackling a wide variety of jobs resulted in a steady growth in women's paid employment after war's end.

Middle class wives were cooking with gas before the war and with electricity in the 1920s. The gas companies ran cooking lessons highlighting the much greater versatility of their stoves and the first edition of the perennially popular Edmonds cookbook was published in 1908. In poorer households – particularly if the husband had a steady job and the wife had paid work as well – there would be a coal range or stove, probably a Shacklock, the company in business since the mid-1870s. There might be a bicycle in the shed too, and a short holiday in the planning stages. Just a generation ago, the memory of children who died young would have faded quickly; now there was likely to be a stiffly posed studio portrait of the family in pride of place on the wall.

The growing enthusiasm for motoring was further boosted by stirrings stories of pioneering journeys, like the 8½ day marathon by Model T Ford from Wellington to Auckland in 1912 through the central highlands and King Country, a route never attempted by car before. But while some adventurers had their eyes firmly fixed on the muddy, potholed tracks that served as early roads, others were gazing upwards, dreaming even bigger dreams. Ballooning was popular in New Zealand from the 1890s and a Mr Mahoney, known professionally as Captain Lorraine, had in 1899 the doubtful distinction of being the country's first air fatality when his balloon crashed into the sea near Christchurch and he drowned. More positively, Vivian Walsh made the first controlled powered flight in a heavier-than-air machine in February 1911 at Papakura, near Auckland. Although by 1919 aeroplanes were approved to carry airmail, flying was still considered too risky for passengers – and registered mail.

Despite the expanding telephone network, for most New Zealanders, letter writing was still the most popular way of keeping in touch. In 1915 there were post offices – 2,402 of them – in even the smallest settlements.

In most communities musical and dramatic societies were popular, with the continuing presence of overseas professional companies a yardstick for local standards. It was the era of vaudeville, but there were also tours by dramatic headliners like Marie Tempest and Ellen Terry who lectured, rather than acted, during a 1914 visit. John Philip Sousa toured with his band in 1911 and Irish tenor John McCormack in 1913.

The Elam School of Art and Design in Auckland had taught its first students in 1890, and several major galleries opened over the next 20 years. Yet, during the first decades of the twentieth century, many of the country's most promising artists, including Frances Hodgkins and Raymond McIntyre, went overseas, some permanently. For those remaining, international art styles were still of defining importance, Art Nouveau influences apparent in the work of artists like Margaret Stoddart and Nugent Welch prior to the First World War.

However, writers were not much appreciated, or even understood. Katherine Mansfield, recognised as a great short-story writer long after her early death, had finally left for London in 1908, with signal relief. Yet, time after time, her stories were evocations of middle class family life in New Zealand. Jane Mander lived in London and New York from 1912, and *The Story of a New Zealand River* was much more favourably received internationally than at home.

Films were, during this decade, less of a novelty, but the first faltering steps of the country's film industry certainly were. It might now seem embarrassingly patronising, but *Hinemoa: The Legend of the Pretty Maori Maiden*, screening in 1914, was New Zealand's first feature film. Two years later an Australian filmmaker shot *A Maori Maid's Love* in New Zealand but there was no enthusiasm for showing it locally; the same year most of *The Mutiny of the Bounty* was shot on location in Rotorua, predating the first of four other films about Captain Bligh by 17 years.

The Christmas Spirit chases away gloom, malice and general selfishness, Quick March, January 1919. ATL: A-313-13-001

Ever since the early days of settlement, the wealthy had regularly travelled back to Britain on business trips and for extended holidays and had thought nothing of sending sons to English public schools and universities for their education. In the first decades of the new century a growing middle class, prompted by better traveling conditions and modes of travel, were exploring their own country with enthusiasm. And with the rapidly increasing number of motor cars – 17,000 registered in 1915 – the building of holiday cottages, baches or cribs, or camping by the sea, lakes, rivers or mountains began holidaying traditions that some families would honour for generations.

The End of the Liberals

Ward had introduced the second ballot, as a sort of security blanket, at the 1911 election. In theory, where Massey's Reform candidate was ahead but short of an outright majority, the combined vote of second and third-placed Liberal and Labour candidates would swing the vote the government's way. Joseph Ward was devastated, but should not have been, when there was no clear winner at the December 11 election. Parliament next met in March 1912, when he resigned as prime minister before the inevitable no-confidence motion. Thomas MacKenzie, his minister of agriculture, briefly succeeded him before Massey's Reform Party occupied the treasury benches in July. The Liberals lost more ground at the 1914 election and then in 1919, after four years as partners in the national coalition, lost further seats, including Ward's. The Liberals were finished but Ward and remnants of the party were to later make a brief, bizarre appearance under another name.

1. 'Freehold' was the buzz word at the 1911 election. Ward loosened the shackles of the Liberals' long-time 'leasehold' philosophy, but it was too little, too late. *Sir Joseph Serves Up the Land Bill Pie*, William Blomfield, *NZ Observer*, May 18 1912. ATL: A-312-1-047
2. The farmers were responding to William Massey's firm position on land ownership; a succession of Labour and socialist groupings were fielding election candidates and gaining a following. *Will She Weather It?,* Trevor Lloyd, *Auckland Weekly News*, September 14 1911. ATL: B-034-007
3. Reform won six more seats than the Liberals, with the ultimate balance of power resting with a quixotic collection of six independents, four Labour members, elected on Ward's second ballot, and four Maori MPs. *The Wreck*, Trevor Lloyd, *Auckland Weekly News*, December 21 1911. ATL: A-315-2-017
4. Ward had resigned in March 1912 before the confidence vote was taken, the Liberals subsequently winning this on the Speaker's casting vote. Although Thomas MacKenzie was prime minister, Ward's brooding presence was hard to ignore. *The Sleeping Partner*, William Blomfield, *NZ Observer*, March 30 1912. ATL: A-312-1-054
5. Although an able administrator, MacKenzie was no fire-in-the-belly politician or shrewd political tactician. His three month minority government, which tried to make a virtue of inactivity, collapsed when four Liberals defected to Massey. The plum London high commissionership was MacKenzie's reward for going quietly. *Can He Whip Up the Old Horse?,* William Blomfield, *NZ Observer*, May 18 1912. ATL: A-312-1-055

1

SIR JOSEPH SERVES UP THE LAND BILL PIE.

Sir Joe: "Now, Mister Freeholder, I can recommend the beautiful crust; and you, Mister Leaseholder, will find the fruit lovely and filling."

2

WILL SHE WEATHER IT?

3

THE WRECK.

4

THE SLEEPING PARTNER.

Sir J.G. Ward (at the Government lunch in Wellington): "Whatever I might be doing, I will always find it a pleasurable duty to assist the Liberal Party, with which I have been connected for so many years."

5

CAN HE WHIP UP THE OLD HORSE?

'Farmer Bill' at Last

William Fergusson Massey, son of an Irish tenant farmer and a small landowner himself, became leader of a weak, formless conservative opposition in 1903. Massey and his colleagues built the Reform Party principally by championing the rights of North Island dairy farmers and by taking up the Farmers Union demand for freehold tenure. Farmers feared that the Labour movement would use its increasing political influence to raise crown leasehold rents and increase the land tax. Massey's blunt, authoritarian approach was vital; only briefly over the next 13 years did he hold a clear majority (1919-22) in a constant three-cornered parliamentary contest against the fading Liberals and the coming Labourites.

1. There was plenty of name-calling at the 1911 election, Massey's enemies christening him 'Bismarck Bill'. To his friends, he was 'Farmer Bill', although it was a long time since he had spent more than holidays at his Mangere farm. *Opposition Tactics*, William Blomfield, *NZ Observer*, November 18 1911. ATL: A-312-1-035
2. In power, Massey promptly gave the holders of the old lease-in-perpetuity the opportunity to freehold their land. *The Death of Leasehold*, Trevor Lloyd, *NZ Herald*, August 31 1912. ATL: A-315-2-023
3. A month later, in December 1914, Massey won the general election so narrowly that a joint wartime administration was inevitable. *Trophies*, William Blomfield, *NZ Observer*, November 21 1914. ATL: A-312-1-079
4. The two old political foes traded punches for the last time in 1919. At last, Reform had a clear majority – 49 seats to 24 for the Liberals. After 32 years, Ward lost his Awarua seat. One of eight successful Labour candidates was Michael Joseph Savage. *1919 – at it again*, Trevor Lloyd, *Auckland Weekly News*, 1919. ATL: A-315-2-186

1

OPPOSITION TACTICS.

Young Dominion: "Say, Mr Massey, throwing mud won t get you into parliamentary land. It only stops your moke s pace."

2

THE DEATH OF LEASEHOLD

3

TROPHIES

4

1919 – AT IT AGAIN.

A Wartime Truce

With Reform falling short of a working majority at the December 1914 election, there was soon agitation for a national government. Although there was very little but political habit separating the two conservative parties, the deep-seated antipathy between Massey and Ward delayed it happening until August 1915. The six Labour members became the official opposition. During the war, the bulk purchase for guaranteed prices of all farm produce did not stop the coalition from taking a heavy hand with civil liberties in the name of the war effort. The government extended its own life twice, in 1917 and 1918.

The 1919 election was bitterly fought, the Liberals having scuttled the national administration as soon as the war finished. Ward sensed, but misjudged, the chance of winning power again and, when the votes were counted, only Labour had gained.

1. One of the very few things Massey and Ward had in common was the recurring nightmare of Labour increasing its parliamentary strength, winning seats like Auckland East, held by the minister of munitions and supplies in the wartime coalition. *Ward and Massey s Labour Nightmare*, David Low, ca1910. ATL: B-025-039
2. After considerable haggling over coalition representation, the governor-general stepped in and hastened the formation of a national cabinet with equal numbers of Reform and Liberal members. *That National Cabinet at Last – His Excellency Takes a Hand*, K M Ballantyne, *The Free Lance*, August 6 1915. ATL: A-313-6-020
3. In the national administration, Massey remained prime minister and Ward, who preferred government to opposition, was minister of finance again. Despite regulation of the internal economy by a board of trade, high inflation and pegged incomes lowered living standards. This, plus considerable war profiteering, would boost Labour support at the next election. *Coalition*, William Blomfield, *NZ Observer*, 1915. ATL: B-055-019
4. The coalition leaders returned to New Zealand with some 'perks', but they had been bought at a high cost in lives and the heavy burden of £70 million in war loans. Within two months the uneasy Massey/Ward partnership had ended and it was back to unrestrained party politics. *Our Returning Leaders*, Tom Ellis, *The Free Lance*, June 25 1919. ATL: A-313-3-007

1

WARD AND MASSEY'S NIGHTMARE
– AUCKLAND EAST GOES TO LABOUR

2

THAT NATIONAL CABINET AT LAST
– HIS EXCELLENCY TAKES A HAND.

Governor Liverpool: "Now then, Bill and Joe, this is not a time for slogging each other. Here, clasp hands and work and fight together against the common enemy outside. Our soldiers are risking their lives, and everyone else is making sacrifices. Why not you?"

3

COALITION.
Reform, Liberal and Labour join ranks against a common enemy.

4

OUR RETURNING LEADERS.
Bill: "Well, Joe, have we got everything?"
Joe: "Yes, but where s our War Indemnity?"
Bill: "Hang it all! We ve overlooked that and there ll be devil to pay when we get back."

Ballot-Box Socialism

The Labour movement was divided by different philosophies and tactics during the Liberals' final years in power. Although increasingly in favour of an independent Labour Party, the weaker craft unions worked through the Liberals to reform the arbitration system. The passionately socialist Federation of Labour unions, or 'Red Feds', favoured direct industrial action, but also supported working-class candidates at general elections and by-elections. However, after the crushing strike defeats of 1912 and 1913, even the most militant unionists accepted that the Labour movement had to work through the political system, and the New Zealand Labour Party was formed in July 1916. There was, though, little early public support for Labour: the first Labour MPs owed their seats to Liberal second ballot manoeuvring; and the party's eight seats in 1919 were as much a reflection of the wartime coalition's unpopularity as any upsurge in left-leaning support.

1. If the Labour movement had difficulty agreeing what approach to take, the government-approved violence meted out by police during the 1912 Waihi miners' strike must have been chilling for those committed to direct action. *The Pitiful Plight of Labor in New Zealand*, Will Hope, *NZ Truth*, April 20 1912. ATL: J-044-002
2. The 'Red Feds', who rejected industrial arbitration, were largely drawn from unions – including miners, watersiders, labourers and brewery workers – strong enough to challenge the Arbitration Court. They were not, though, strong enough to stand up to a tough, uncompromising government. *A Stick the Boss Can t Break*, *The Maoriland Worker*, May 3 1912. ATL: A-313-10-016
3. In 1913, when a Wellington wharf strike spread to other ports and unions, the government called in young farmers as special constables and to work on the wharves. Known as 'Massey's Cossack's' after violent street brawls, they kept wharves open and operating. In a situation close to martial law, the strike collapsed after 58 days. *Brave Deeds, Rewarded*, H Mann, *The Maoriland Worker*, April 29 1914. ATL: 313-10-010
4. For some years, the 'Red Feds' had spread, with evangelical zeal, gospels of industrial unionism and the syndicalist doctrine of the American-based Industrial Workers of the World. But most 'Red Fed' leaders now turned from industrial action; two of them, Peter Fraser and Bob Semple, became Labour Party MPs at 1918 by-elections. *The Gentleman from Russia and His Sponsor*, Tom Ellis, *The Free Lance*, March 13 1919. ATL: A-313-3-025
5. With more prescience than most others, New Zealand's Labour movement condemned the terms of the 'peace treaty' following the First World War. *The One Discordant Voice*, Tom Ellis, *The Free Lance*, July 16 1919. ATL: A-313-3-026

1

THE PITIFUL PLIGHT OF LABOR IN NEW ZEALAND.

2

A STICK THE BOSS CAN'T BREAK.

3

BRAVE DEEDS, REWARDED

Special Constables, in various districts, have been presented with medals in honour of their services during the recent strike. The Worker offers the above suitable design, free of charge, for any further medals which may be required.

4

THE GENTLEMAN FROM RUSSIA AND HIS SPONSOR.

Social Democrat: "Ladies, my friend, M. Bolshevik, from Russia. I hope you will be nice to him."

Miss Australia and Miss Zealandia: "Ugh!"

5

THE ONE DISCORDANT VOICE.

The Biggest Sacrifice

In company with the rest of a far-flung empire, New Zealand was automatically committed when Britain went to war following Germany's August 1914 invasion of Belgium. Government and people accepted their filial responsibilities seriously and with enthusiasm. There had been compulsory military training since 1909, and with it the makings of a reasonably trained and equipped expeditionary force. Thousands of territorials queued to volunteer for overseas service; days later an advance party sailed for German Samoa which was occupied without incident. In another two months the main body of the expeditionary force left for Egypt. It was absorbed into the ANZAC Corp and spectacularly blooded at Gallipoli during 1915. The pattern was set for a succession of costly battles and campaigns fought by the reformed New Zealand Division up and down the Western Front in Europe between 1916 and 1918 and names like the Somme, Messines, Passchendaelle and Ypres are still remembered with a curious mixture of horror and pride.

1. Nearly 100,500 New Zealanders served overseas, 42 percent of men aged between 19-45. An appalling 58,000 were killed or wounded, the 58 per cent casualty rate nearly three times higher than in the Second World War. No other allied country made a greater sacrifice on a per capita basis. *It s a Long Way to Tipperary*, E H Thompson, *Light Diet*, 1918. ATL: J-065-049
2. The purported idea was to clear the commanding Turkish positions from the Gallipoli Peninsula to open up Constantinople from the sea. In nine months, 87 percent of the 8,556 New Zealanders who landed at Gallipoli were casualties – and 2,721 of them dead. Ironically, after so much slaughter, the withdrawal from Anzac Cove in December was made without a single loss of life. *Making the Feathers Fly*, Trevor Lloyd, *Auckland Weekly News*, May 6 1915. ATL: A-315-2-002
3. After Maori fought bravely at Gallipoli, the Maori Battalion was formed in October 1917. Oddly, Gallipoli is commemorated as the country's most famous military campaign when it was a futile exercise with little point and small chance of success. *The Spirit of his Fathers*, William Blomfield, *NZ Observer*, December 1915. ATL: A-312-1-088
4. On the Western Front, in September 1916 and as part of the Somme offensive, a total of 1,560 New Zealand troops were killed and 5,440 wounded during one 23-day battle. By now there was a strangely passive front-line fatalism about surviving the next barrage let alone the war. *"Anxiety"*, Jack Gilmour, *Chronicles of the NZEF*, August 30 1916. ATL: J-065-047

1

It's a long way to Tipperary.

2

MAKING THE FEATHERS FLY.

3

THE SPIRIT OF HIS FATHERS.

4

"ANXIETY."

The Home Front

With the heavy Gallipoli and Western Front losses, there was growing doubt that volunteer enlistment could provide the necessary replacements. The government acted in 1916, the year Britain imposed – and Australia rejected – conscription. Reinforcements were selected by ballot from a register of national reservists. The militant wing of the Labour movement wanted wealth conscripted before people, as a more or less logical extension of the belief that the war was being fought primarily in the economic interests of a capitalist ruling class. The government decided that all anti-conscription activity was seditious and promptly imprisoned several Labour leaders including Peter Fraser and Robert Semple. Many New Zealanders of German origin were stripped of their British citizenship and interned. Conscripted Waikato Maori, still smarting at past injustices, were arrested when they refused to serve. Conscientious objectors received similarly harsh treatment. Some early pacifists were forced onto troop-ships, a few frog-marched to the front-line in France.

1. As the casualty rate rose alarmingly, conscription was needed to regularly rebuild the seriously depleted New Zealand Division. Despite the White Feather Leagues and other social pressures, 'shirkers' avoided military service by fleeing the country or going 'bush', by quickly arranging marriages, or claiming 'essential industry' work. *When Johnnie Comes Wounded Home*, William Blomfield, *NZ Observer*, January 29 1916. ATL: A-312-1-089
2. There was clearly war profiteering, particularly with staple commodities like wheat, but the excess-war-profit tax, introduced in 1916, proved unworkable. *Oh £!,* William Blomfield, *NZ Observer*, March 13 1915. ATL: A-312-1-080
3. In August 1915, national registration legislation directed men aged 17-60 to provide personal information and indicate their willingness to serve in the armed forces. Next year the Military Services Act introduced conscription, with all European males between 20-46 liable for military service. *The National Reservist*, W G Harding, *The Free Lance*, August 6 1915. ATL: A-313-6-023

1

WHEN JOHNNIE COMES WOUNDED HOME, HURRAH! HURRAH! THE SHIRKER AND THE SOLDIER.
A Drink. – A Curse. – A Relief.

2

OH £!

3

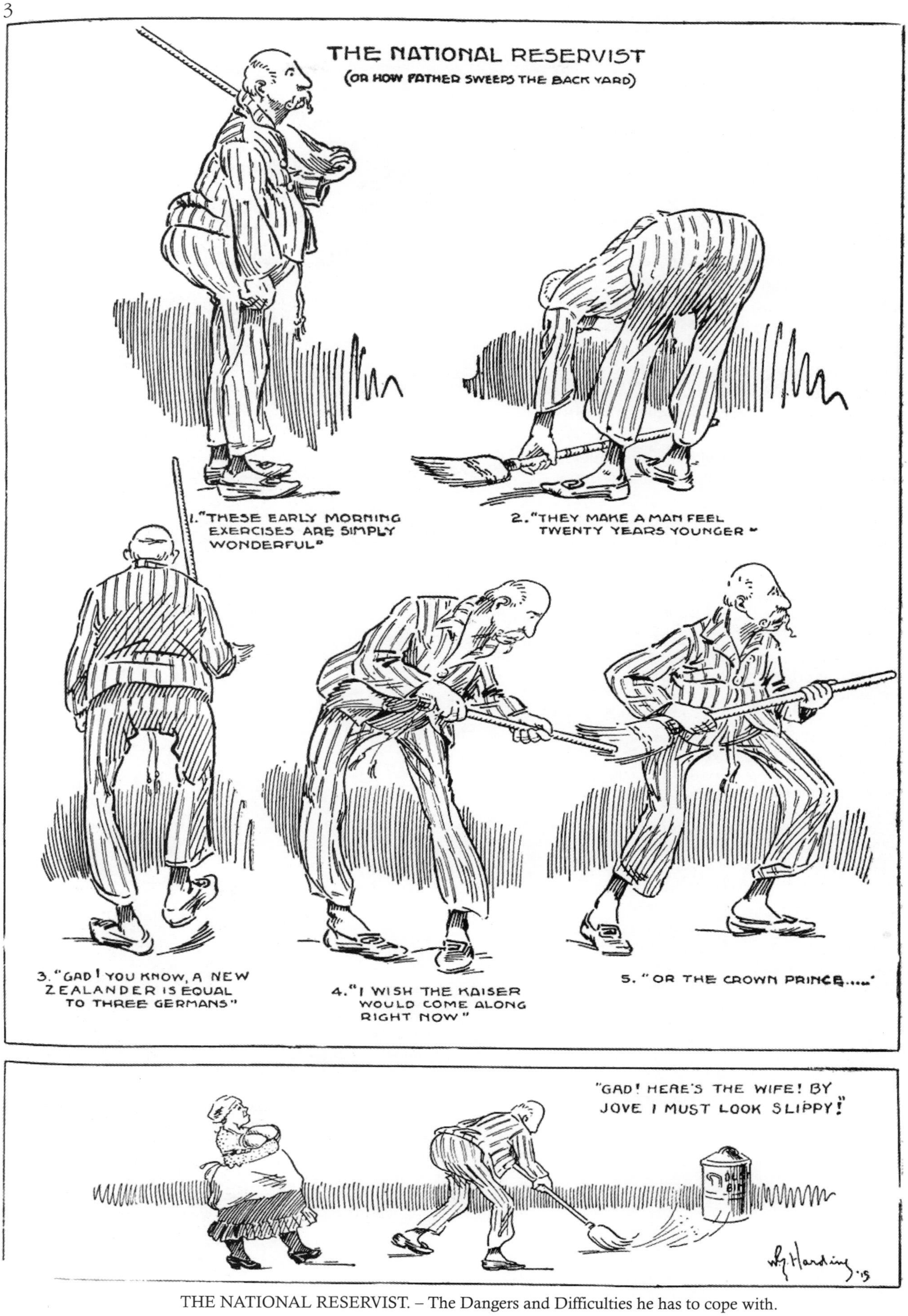

THE NATIONAL RESERVIST

(OR HOW FATHER SWEEPS THE BACK YARD)

1. "THESE EARLY MORNING EXERCISES ARE SIMPLY WONDERFUL"

2. "THEY MAKE A MAN FEEL TWENTY YEARS YOUNGER"

3. "GAD! YOU KNOW, A NEW ZEALANDER IS EQUAL TO THREE GERMANS"

4. "I WISH THE KAISER WOULD COME ALONG RIGHT NOW"

5. "OR THE CROWN PRINCE....."

THE NATIONAL RESERVIST. – The Dangers and Difficulties he has to cope with.

Wowserism's Last Stand

The prohibitionists thought they were winning, even if slowly. At the 1902 and 1905 elections, more than half of the New Zealand electorate had voted 'no licence' locally. The New Zealand Alliance was then jubilant when a majority of successful 1908 election candidates agreed to support a bare majority national prohibition versus continuance poll. But victory was more elusive than that: brewery interests exerted well-heeled pressure, parliamentary minds were swayed, and the prohibitionist vote of 55.8 percent fell well short of the three-fifths majority required at the first national poll in 1911. The three-fifths rule was abolished during the war and the New Zealand Alliance was confident of finally winning the simple majority prohibition-continuance vote at the special 1919 referendum. It was certainly the closest New Zealand ever came to abolition of the liquor trade.

1. Over half the leaders of the prohibition movement during its two particularly active decades, on either side of the new century, were Protestant ministers, usually evangelical and rarely Anglican. *The Wowser s Dream*, Eve, *NZ Truth*, November 25 1911. ATL: A-313-1-032
2. Six o'clock closing was adopted, for no very cogent reason, as a 'wartime measure' in 1917. It remained in force until 1967. *The Prohibitionist on the Rampage*, Bryce Hart, *The Free Lance*, October 5 1917. ATL: A-313-6-030
3. The Women's Christian Temperance Union was formed following a visit, in 1885, of Mary Leavitt, an American feminist and prohibitionist. To many women, including WCTU leaders like Kate Sheppard, the banning of liquor was as vital to the emancipation of women as gaining the vote. *When the Middle Road is Closed*, *NZ Truth*, September 30 1911. ATL: A-313-1-032
4. At the April 10 1919 referendum, prohibition had a narrow victory among resident voters – 246,104 votes to continuance's 232,208. But soldiers in the New Zealand Division, still overseas, made their presence felt, tipping the balance with their 31,981 to 7,723 support for continuance and a 'wet' return home. *The Tantalising Tenth*, Tom Glover, *NZ Truth*, April 19 1919. ATL: A-313-3-029

1

THE WOWSER'S DREAM.

2

THE PROHIBITIONIST ON THE RAMPAGE.

3

WHEN THE MIDDLE ROAD IS CLOSED TO THE MEN OF NEW ZEALAND.

4

THE TANTALISING TENTH.
SOLDIERS HOLD THE SITUATION – SAINTS AND SINNERS IN SUSPENSE.

4: 1920-1929
THE SEE-SAW YEARS

In 1918, the allies had won the 'war to end all wars', with New Zealand paying a particularly heavy and bloody price. It had been a righteous war and God was on the side of the righteous, yet the deity had a funny way of acknowledging this in the post-war years. New Zealand might have at least expected a decade of peace and prosperity. Instead, there were two depressions and a period of worrying political instability.

With the Reform Party dominant, the Liberals fading and Labour now firmly committed to achieving change through the ballot box, it was a messily transitional period in the country's political history. Support for the three political parties see-sawed as an increasingly frustrated electorate kept changing its mind.

The first depression, in 1920-21, could be blamed as much on sentimental generosity to returning soldiers as to a less than grateful British government's slashing of the prices it paid for agricultural products. Financed onto farms with borrowed money by an uncharacteristically generous government, the heroes of Gallipoli and France set off a speculative, land-buying-and-selling spree, further fuelled by two decades of steadily rising prices for farm produce. It was quickly boom to bust when those prices tumbled and Massey cut public service salaries in an unpopular budget-balancing ploy to counter the ballooning costs of war pensions and the national debt.

As the country slid into recession, Massey set up meat and dairy producer boards in an attempt to give some stability to agricultural prices. It helped Reform scrape back into power at the 1922 election, with Massey in the familiar but stressful position of having to rely on the uncertain support of independents.

The next two years, as he prepared the ground for the 1925 election, were Massey's most successful in office. He won kudos and support by pushing ahead with the sorely needed improvement of North Island roads, particularly in Northland, even if it meant more overseas borrowing. His government also clamped down on inflation and interest rates, put money into pensioners' pockets, cut taxes and set up agricultural banks to assist with the farming recovery as export prices improved.

It was a successful strategy, but Massey died some months before the election showed just how effective it had been. He was one of New Zealand's most important political figures; with stubborn patience, hard work and generally sound political judgment he turned a tattered opposition rump into a powerful political party that gave the country considerable stability during two difficult decades.

After the 16 day caretakership of Francis Dillon Bell, Gordon Coates was elected party leader and prime minister. A decorated war hero, Coates' reputation had been enhanced by his appetite for work, grasp of practical problems and willingness to grapple with priorities. While previous ministers had dithered, he finished three main trunk railway lines, centralised hydro-electric construction and set up a main highways roading system.

He approached the 1925 election with the same vigour, and some imagination. The campaign was the first in New Zealand to sell politicians as products. Coates was a tall debonair man with, as it is now called, 'charisma' and Reform promoted the man rather than policies, with slogans like 'Coates off with Coates' and 'Coates and Confidence'.

Reform swept to a memorable election victory, winning 70 percent of the seats. Then, ironically, Coates faltered. Perhaps it was because he had no strong political philosophy – like Massey's passionate commitment to the freehold – or patience with party politics or parliamentary procedures. Whatever the reason, he seemed paralysed by indecision and the government and country drifted. Worse, farm produce prices dipped alarmingly again as the British economy went into recession. When the government did

ANOTHER INSULT TO AIR-LAND
"What on earth is that infernal draught?"
"Just got Wellington on the Loud Speaker!"

Gordon Minhinnick, *NZ Artists Annual*, 1928. ATL: A-311-1-006 act – attempting to license urban public transport, introducing town planning regulations and paying special allowances to larger families – these decisions generally exasperated the Reform government's natural constituency.

Coates was so indifferent to the NZ Political Reform League, the organisation behind the party, that its head, A E Davy, who had devised the ground-breaking 1925 election campaign, decided to take his talents, and membership lists, elsewhere. He had much more in common with Sir Joseph Ward who, although in declining health, dreamed of another tilt at the political windmill. A deal was done and Ward became, miraculously, leader of a new party, a motley patchwork of groups including the remnants of the old Liberal Party. With a lick of promotional paint, the United Party, using Davy's marketing savvy, picked up enough conservative, commercial and urban votes to deliver the government a crushing defeat at the November 1928 election.

A POLITICAL PUZZLE: FIND THE 70 MILLIONS.

Trevor Lloyd, *NZ Herald*, July 27 1929. ATL: 315-2-189

United's principal platform had been concern with Coates' 'excessive' spending, but a monetary slip of the tongue probably tipped the election Ward's way. He had opened his campaign with a speech promising to borrow £7 million in a single year to bolster the economy, but eyesight or memory conspired and he read out £70 million instead. The response to this astonishing claim was so positive that United's officials subsequently blurred the issue in a masterly display of 'spin'.

With the support of Labour Party members, Ward had the numbers to complete the most remarkable comeback in New Zealand political history – fully 22 years after he first became prime minister he held the warrant again. Sadly, there was nothing remarkable about his short stewardship. Little of the £70 million materialised and a sick old man who had long ago run out of answers was no match for a depression that was tightening its grip on the world. For much of 1929 Ward's colleagues ran an administration buffeted by contracting economic activity and growing unemployment.

In the 1920s the bounce went out of New Zealand's collective step, and there was a malaise of uncertainty and insecurity in the aftermath of a devastating war and epidemic, with a yo-yo economy through most of the decade and the grand-daddy of depressions at the end of it The bright spots needed to be savoured. The 1924 All Blacks, the 'Invincibles', won every match on their tour of Britain. Culturally, stars continued to tour: violinist Jascha Heifetz in 1921 and dancer Anna Pavlova in 1926, her visit to Australasia still the cause of trans-Tasman rivalry about the origins of the confection baked in her honour.

Perhaps, in the circumstances, it was not surprising to find a rash of racial intolerance even uglier than during the 19th century. An irrational fear of Chinese and other Asians was old hat but there was also, during a time when there was a premium on conformity, a suspicious picking over of any differences among any immigrants. In part, this was because there was some enthusiasm for pseudo-philosophies like 'Social Darwinism' and 'Aryanism' which propounded the survival of the fittest and the innate superiority of Caucasian races.

New Zealand coped with the killing and maiming of the First World War – involving a quarter of the male population of military age – by generous post-war assistance to those who survived and by conferring a sort of perpetual sainthood on those who didn't. Legislation in 1921-22 decreed that the sacrifice would be

PINCHING A PLANK

Jack Gilmour, *NZ Truth*, March 21 1925. ATL: A-313-1-037

commemorated on Anzac Day, April 25, every year. And all around the country – in the cities and smallest hamlets – money was raised and war memorials were built.

It has been popularly thought that the introduction of Anzac Day was one of the building blocks of nationalism. In fact, rather than blame Britain for the battlefield slaughter there was, in the 1920s, even more emphasis than before on loyalty to the mother country. The cheerleader for this outpouring of patriotism, that went as far as compulsory flag saluting at schools from 1921, was Massey, who was a 'British Israelite', a rather disturbing cult that believed Anglo-Saxons were direct descendants of the ancient Israelites and God's chosen people.

New Zealand clung to the British apron strings so fiercely that the Balfour Declaration in 1926 and Statute of Westminster five years later were seen more as an affront than written guarantees of independence and equality. Yet despite the passion for things British, as communications technology continued to shrink the world, it was impossible to avoid the increasing economic and cultural influence of the United States.

Jazz, the Charleston and flappers were an antidote to the realities of the 1920s; the Victorian values system, which had lingered on into the 20th century, was being shrugged off as surely as the 'modern woman' discarded the physical and psychological restraints of corsetry, and revelled in the boyish look, with bobbed hair, flattened chest and dropped waist. 'Restraint' was now more a dirty word than a moral imperative.

New Zealand society beat time and flapped along with the rest of the world, tutored by the cinema, radio, the gramophone, and imported magazines. Prohibition and the 'roaring twenties' were inextricably linked in the United States, but not in New Zealand. After prohibitionists failed at the 1919 poll – the local no-licence option had gone the year before – support gradually ebbed. During the twenties, the dramatic failure and abuse of prohibition in the United States also turned opinion against the movement.

Dance marathons were briefly the rage, but music was still more likely to be enjoyed around the family piano. When the phonograph, with its limitations, was superseded there was the 'gramophone evenings' phenomenon, with concerts of imported recorded music in homes, halls and music shops throughout the country.

Radio – the first instant mass medium – arrived in 1922. Station 1YA began broadcasting in August 1926 and registered licence holders numbered over 30,000 by year's end. Stations began transmitting in Christchurch later in 1926, in Wellington the next year, and Dunedin in 1929.

Charles Kingsford Smith flew the Tasman for the first time in 1928. Thirty-five thousand watched his *Southern Cross* land at Wigram, Christchurch 14 hours 25 minutes after leaving Sydney; many thousands more listened to reports of the monoplane's progress and triumphant arrival on radio. There were sports broadcasts from the earliest days: in 1928 there was a commentary direct from New York of the heavyweight championship between Gene Tunney and Tom Heeney, the unsuccessful New Zealand challenger. Later in the year, about half a million people listened to coverage of the general election.

The cinema was sufficiently popular to encourage the building of 'picture palaces' like Auckland's 3,500 seat Civic Theatre with its Indian theme, Persian garden auditorium, and ceiling resplendent with stars and cloud effects. With censorship and prejudice at work, the authorities favoured British movies but, by 1929, when the Paramount, in Wellington, screened the first 'talkie', an overwhelming majority of the films shown were made in Hollywood. Back in 1922, Rudall Hayward, pioneer New Zealand filmmaker, was 22 years old when he shot and released his first silent feature *My Lady of the Cave*.

Electric power schemes, exploiting abundant water supplies, were now part of government works programmes. There was increasingly widespread electric lighting in city streets and homes, although the coal range, copper and mangle were slower to be replaced by labour-saving electrical alternatives.

Life in the country became more comfortable. Telephone lines ran along most country roads and electric power lines snaked into remoter areas. With milking machines reducing the drudgery in dairy farmers' lives and making larger herds more practical, there were 750,000 dairy cattle in New Zealand in 1921, twice the 1901 figure. Tractors were beginning to replace horses on farms. As the early salesmen put it, farmers didn't need to put aside several acres of wheat to feed a tractor! By the early 1920s, many sheep farmers – with over 23 million animals in their flocks – could afford motor cars, even though only the main country roads were metalled.

Efficient tramways followed city dwellers into new suburbs and bus travel was popular when the Railways Department began its Road Services branch, but nothing could slow the rapid acceleration in private car ownership. The 1925 census, the first to record motor vehicle registrations, showed 71,000 cars. Over the next five years, as the Motel T Ford was replaced by the Model A and other popular makes including the Austin 7 Salon and Chevrolet Roadster, numbers jumped to over 152,000, a hefty proportion of them of American origin.

Environmentalism was still a lonely cause but Herbert Guthrie-Smith's *The Story of a New Zealand Sheep Station*, published in 1921, and the formation of the Royal Forest and Bird Protection Society two years later were both influential in changing attitudes.

Political Roller Coaster

New Zealand, settled less than 100 years before by determined land-seekers, had such a strongly pastoral personality it was not surprising that many thousands of ex-servicemen grabbed once-in-a-lifetime chances to become farmers. During the immediate post-war boom, New Zealand could have been mistaken for a giant, frantically busy auction sale. Nearly 10,000 ex-servicemen farmers were relying on several profitable years to cover their excessive commitments and new-chum mistakes. But, as always, boom and bust were inseparable. Massey's response to the recession – an attempt to re-jig the Arbitration Court and public service salary cuts – was predictably unpopular at the 1922 election. Coates, his successor in 1925, was the beneficiary of the shrewd mix of Massey's policies in the two years before his death, but then appeared strangely impotent as the country slid into deepening depression. For three 1920s elections in a row, there were three-cornered contests as Reform's popularity fluctuated and waned. After 1922, Massey's majority depended on several independents, then Coates stormed back to an absolute majority in 1925. His subsequent indecision helped the extraordinary comeback of Sir Joseph Ward in 1928.

1. Although the original intention had been to open new soldier-settlement areas, credit restrictions were soon eased and thousands of returned soldiers bought established farms at increasingly inflated prices. *Settling the Returned Soldier*, William Blomfield, *NZ Observer*, June 9 1917. ATL: A-312-1-193
2. During the immediate post-war boom the price of everything 'ballooned'; even when there was no justification for cost increases anti-profiteering laws were too weak to make a difference. *Going Up*, Tom Ellis, *The Free Lance*, March 10 1920. ATL: A-313-3-013
3. Although farmers were not always happy with Reform's performance, the urban working class resented the special treatment Massey gave to the farming community. *"Yes, We Have No Plums Today"*, Jack Gilmour, *NZ Truth*, March 15 1924. ATL H-705-002
4. Finding work for large numbers of unemployed did not save Coates from a crushing defeat at the 1928 election. *A Helping Hand*, Trevor Lloyd, *NZ Herald*, February 18 1928. ATL: A-315-2-155

1

SETTLING THE RETURNED SOLDIER.
The Department: "Oh, he's nice and comfortable – dugout and all. Just about settle him, eh?"

2

"GOING UP."
First profiteer: "Do you think we have forgotten anything?"
Second ditto: "No."
First Profiteer: "Then 'ere goes for the H Altitude Record!"

3

"YES, WE HAVE NO PLUMS TODAY."

4

A HELPING HAND.

The Red Tide Recedes

Labour doubled its parliamentary strength at the 1922 election but it was going to take another four elections, the country's worst depression and a shift from Marxism to a variation of Douglas Credit theory to convince New Zealanders that they should elect a Labour administration. Labour, as brimming with ideas as the other parties were bereft of them, broadened its appeal after 1925, playing down controversial 'socialist' policies such as land nationalisation. Michael Joseph Savage, Harry Holland's deputy, quietly advocated pension changes and a free health service, pushed Reform into introducing a family allowance, and persuaded his colleagues that a freehold land policy was crucial to winning sufficient rural votes to occupy the treasury benches. Later in the decade, the developing depression gave Labour the opportunity to build a new image of a more benevolent and workable form of capitalism. Labour held the balance of power in 1928 and voted with United until its retrenchment policies became completely unacceptable.

1. Although Harry Holland, Labour's leader, retained his commitment to socialism, he was losing influence to more pragmatic colleagues. *From Soap Box to Silk Hat*, Jack Gilmour, *NZ Truth*, February 9 1924. ATL: A-313-1-035
2. After 1925, Labour responded to political realities and shed its radical and militant ideas well in advance of the general belief that it had done so. *Mr Facing-Both-Ways*, Jack Gilmour, *NZ Truth*, August 16 1924. ATL: A-313-1-036
3. It was popularly believed that communists dictated Labour policy: the shock waves of the Russian revolution were still reverberating; Harry Holland used angry socialist rhetoric; and the prominent party leaders had 'Red Fed' backgrounds. *The Trouble in Labour s Buzz-Wagon*, Jack Gilmour, *The Free Lance*, January 14 1925. ATL: A-313-1-040
4. Labour watered down its land nationalisation policy and then dropped the compromise 'usehold' scheme, which would have made the state sole purchaser of private land, as it became clearer it would make no progress with farmers until it accepted freehold tenure. In 1928, Labour's election platform emphasised land development. *The Wolf in Sheep s Clothing*, Trevor Lloyd, *NZ Herald*, October 24 1925. ATL: A-315-3-186

1

FROM SOAP BOX TO SILK HAT

WOULD OFFICE BE LABOR'S WE WONDER,
IF HARRY HOPPED IN AND GOT UNDER?

2

MR FACING-BOTH-WAYS.

3

THE TROUBLE IN LABOUR'S BUZZ-WAGON.

Moderate Labour to the Wild Man: "No, you don't Bolshy, not if I know it! Keep quiet or get out! It's a rocky road we are travelling and we'd soon be in the ditch if you took charge."

4

THE WOLF IN SHEEP'S CLOTHING.

A Final Hurrah

Shortly before the 1928 election, Sir Joseph Ward suddenly reappeared on the national political scene as leader of a very strange coalition of interests. The United Party claimed a tortuous genealogical connection with the old Liberal Party, but was largely controlled by right-wingers appalled by Coates' 'excessive' borrowing. It was doubly ironic that Ward should lead such a grouping at the November election and that it should defeat Coates' Reform government when Ward, by accident or design, opened his campaign with the promise to borrow a massive sum of money. In the event, the public grasped an accidental straw with the greedy enthusiasm that has influenced party manifestos ever since. Ward was prime minister again – after a gap of over two decades – but not very securely or for very long.

1. Coates had frittered away three years – and his very large parliamentary majority. He had worried his conservative colleagues without achieving compensating results; he offended Reform's traditional farming support without shoring up the business vote won in 1925. *"When the Ebb Tide Flows"*, Jack Green, *Farming First*, December 10 1928. ATL: A-311-3-014
2. Out of the blue, Ward talked about the government acquiring large land holdings and making millions of acres available for settlement. At a time when many farmers were struggling to make mortgage payments, it was a faint, distressing echo from the Liberal Party and Ward's long past glory days. *Chief Up-And-At- Em Goes on the Warpath*, Stuart Peterson, *The Free Lance*, May 15 1929. ATL: A-315-3-050
3. In another rush of blood, Ward suddenly announced there would be work for every able-bodied man within five weeks. In fact, unemployment continued to worsen. *A Jarring Note?,* Jack Gilmour, *NZ Worker*, May 29 1929. ATL: A-313-1-038
4. With the rapidly worsening world economic situation and Ward's powers of financial wizardry long since spent, United was to fare no better than Reform. *Next Week s Opening of Parliament*, Trevor Lloyd, *NZ Herald*, July 27 1929. ATL: A-315-2-164

1

"WHEN THE EBB TIDE FLOWS."

2

CHIEF UP-AND-AT-'EM GOES ON THE WARPATH.

3

The United Party Prosperity ? Band

A JARRING NOTE ? ?

CONDUCTOR JOE: "CAN'T SOMEBODY STOP THAT FELLOW? – HE'S SPOILING THE WHOLE EFFECT OF OUR MUSIC!"

4

NEXT WEEK'S OPENING OF PARLIAMENT.

Backblock Blues

The decade started promisingly for farmers on several fronts, and ended in widespread despair. About half the country's total occupied land area changed hands in the decade to 1924. But by then the optimism that had fuelled this buying and selling frenzy had gone, along with the 'war commandeer' which had held primary produce demand and prices high. Meat, wool and then dairy produce prices slumped during 1920-21, began rising again in 1922, steadied until 1925, fell, then recovered briefly in 1928 before the prolonged depression period. It was of some consolation that farming was, at the same time, making innovative and technological strides. Electrification, better rural roads and the use of fertiliser to provide permanent pasture contributed to a surge in production, particularly in dairying. Not for the last time, the response to slumping prices was feverish production of more meat, wool, butter and cheese that Britain, virtually New Zealand's sole market, had increasing difficulty in absorbing.

1. Thousands of ex-servicemen farmers, on grossly over-valued properties, needed ever-rising prices to meet mortgage payments. In a rehearsal for the greater crisis at the end of the decade, hundreds of farms were abandoned. *The Spirit of Anzac*, Jack Gilmour, *NZ Truth*, April 25 1925. ATL: A-313-1-034
2. Labour lost ground at the 1925 election, with farmers firmly behind Reform even though the troubled rural community was agitating for cheaper credit, more marketing controls and mortgage reductions. *None but the Brave*, Gordon Minhinnick, *NZ Free Lance*, April 14 1926. ATL: A-311-1-003
3. After the security of the 'war commandeer', prices tumbled and the Farmers' Union lobbied for the controlled marketing of export produce. The government set up a Meat Board in 1922 and a Dairy Board a year later. Dairy farmers were less enthusiastic than their meat producing cousins; few used the service initially and compulsory pooling of produce from 1926 was widely resented. *"Time the old idol was touched up"*, Ken Alexander, *Aussie*, June 15 1927. ATL: A-313-1-013
4. In 1927, there was jubilation in the industry when the Dairy Board was forced to modify its stance on the compulsory pooling of dairy produce. *Rejoicings in Cow-Land*, Stuart Peterson, *The Free Lance*, June 22 1927. ATL: A-315-3-056
5. With the growing numbers of motorised vehicles, the condition of roads was a major political issue in the 1920s. The 1922 Main Highways Act placed road building and maintenance under government control and Massey, very aware of the source of his bedrock support, promised major upgrading of North Island roads. *A Bad State of Affairs*, Trevor Lloyd, *NZ Herald*, ca 1922. ATL: A-315-2-106

1

"THE SPIRIT OF ANZAC"
THE SOLDIERS "CARRY ON"

2

NONE BUT THE BRAVE –
"My gracious! Here's that man again! There's no snubbing some people. I thought I settled him forever last November."

3

"TIME THE OLD IDOL WAS TOUCHED UP"

4

REJOICINGS IN COW-LAND.

5

A BAD STATE OF AFFAIRS.

South Seas Empire

Vogel and Seddon had openly expressed interest in Samoa, but Britain had its reasons for supporting United States and German claims, and Western Samoa remained in German hands until a New Zealand expeditionary force occupied the territory unopposed in August 1914. New Zealand's military administration was wrong-footed by the 1918 influenza epidemic, which decimated the Samoan population, and contributed to the destruction of neglected copra crops by the rhinoceros beetle. The situation quickly deteriorated further after Western Samoa was 'mandated' in 1920. The administration's rigid paternalism alienated the Samoans, and interference with their copra-trading monopoly antagonised the prosperous European community. A prominent mixed-blood European, O F Nelson, inspired a Samoan movement, the Mau, in 1926, sharing its leadership with Tupu Tamasese Lealofi, a high ranking chief. It was to embarrass and threaten the administration's authority during the next decade.

1. The introduction of indentured Chinese labour was to assist European plantation owners. In fact, the skewed racial views of the time decreed that Chinese-Samoan intermarriage was illegal. *A Mixed Marriage*, Tom Glover, *NZ Truth*, April 10 1920. ATL: A-313-3-032

2. New Zealand had annexed the Cook Islands in 1901 and its 'empire' extended into the southern ocean after Britain handed over nominal control of the vast Ross Dependency in Antarctica in 1923. It was to be more than 30 years before a base was established there. *Enzed s Latest Adoption*, Ken Alexander, *Aussie*, December 19 1923. ATL: A-313-1-009

3. Massey, who was not a League of Nations enthusiast, had accepted 'mandate' responsibility for Western Samoa with a noticeable lack of interest. His successor, Gordon Coates, had to deal, in 1927, with the Mau movement's initially peaceful protests and demonstrations. *"I sometimes wish that I had never offered …"*, Ken Alexander, *Aussie*, October 15 1927. ATL: A-313-1-015

4. The Mau movement, with its 'Samoa for the Samoans' slogan, wanted less Europeanisation and more local involvement in the administration. There had been numerous violence-free demonstrations before 'Black Saturday' in late December 1929 when matters got out of hand. Tamasese's death was one of a number that day. *Samoa! – Mandate pants or banned badge – which?*, William Blomfield, *NZ Observer*, March 28 1930. ATL: A-312-1-141

1

A MIXED MARRIAGE

The Massey Government "Gives Away" the Bride.

THE PLUTE PRELATE: "God bless you my children and may you increase and multiply and bring forth dividends abundantly!"

2

ENZED'S LATEST ADOPTION.

Nurse: He's a tiny child, but I doubt he will be as much trouble as the other two.

3

"I sometimes wish that I had never offered to mind this darned kid!"

4

SAMOA! – MANDATE PANTS OR BANNED BADGE – WHICH?

The Administration: "This means civilisation!"
Samoa: "And this freedom!"

Drawing the Colour Line

New Zealand's first discriminatory immigration legislation was introduced in the 1880s. At first, it was aimed at the Chinese community: the poll tax; reading 100 words of English; thumb-printing before departure to guarantee re-entry. During the First World War, when the number of Chinese had halved to about 2,500, concern shifted to the aspirations of the indentured Hindu labourers in nearby Fiji. After the war, a sudden influx of Chinese and Indian immigrants inspired the fear that they would push down wages and living standards and cause unemployment. The Immigration Restriction Act of 1920, which provided for entry applications to be granted at the discretion of the immigration minister, closed loopholes in previous legislation without overt racial overtones that would embarrass the Colonial Office. Chinese were allowed about 100 entry permits for several years until economic conditions worsened again. The iniquitous poll tax was last levied in 1934 and finally abolished a decade later.

1. There was apprehension when New Zealand was asked, at the 1917 Imperial Conference, to allow wives and children of already settled Indians to enter the country. *The Coming Artist*, William Blomfield, *NZ Observer*, 1919. ATL: A-312-1-192
2. Returned servicemen were strident objectors to Chinese and Indian immigration – employment fears overlaying racist feelings. The RSA led an often vicious protest movement. *No Man s Land – New Zealand Home Front, 1922*, Tom Ellis, *The Free Lance*, March 15 1922. ATL: A-313-3-031
3. Despite evidence to the contrary, there was a strongly developed fear that Asian immigrants – not to mention Bolsheviks – would swamp New Zealanders of 'British' stock in a wave of debauchery, drug-taking and violence. *And Still They Come!*, Jack Gilmour, *NZ Truth*, February 21 1925. ATL: A-313-3-045
4. News, in 1927, that some foreigners had been killed in riots in China suggested, to some, that behind their inscrutable exteriors Chinese were a potential danger to New Zealand society. It was conveniently forgotten that an elderly Chinese man had been murdered in Wellington in 1905 by a European demented by his anti-Asiatic crusade. *John Chinaman at Home – and Abroad*, Stuart Peterson, *The Free Lance*, April 6 1927. ATL: A-315-3-055

1

THE COMING ARTIST.

2

NO MAN'S LAND – NEW ZEALAND HOME FRONT, 1922.

3

AND STILL THEY COME!

4

JOHN CHINAMAN AT HOME – AND ABROAD.

The Shylock Syndrome

There was a strange, almost schizophrenic attitude towards the Jewish community in New Zealand. Jewish traders had been in the country, and well accepted, from the earliest days of European settlement, and there had been no barriers to individuals achieving high public office or stunning commercial success, although there were also the deeply engrained stereotypes that had travelled intact from the old world to the new. Sir Julius Vogel, the country's most influential politician during the 1870s, preferred to work behind the scenes rather than be premier, in part because he was well aware of latent anti-semitism. Possibly prejudices were less overt in the law; certainly Sir Michael Myers was a widely admired chief justice and held the country's highest constitutional position on several occasions in the interregnum periods between governors-general. Names like Davis, Hallenstein, Levin and Nathan symbolised commercial success; these families were also leading members of a worldly, sophisticated and cultured haute bourgeoisie, a new urban phenomenon in a still comparatively raw colonial society.

1. A cartoonist's interpretation of the news that the Prince of Wales, on a state visit, did not expect locals to be formally dressed at official functions. In fact, Jewish New Zealanders were more likely to be major importers, large retailers or significant manufacturers. *Commotion in the Second-Hand Goods Trade*, Tom Ellis, *The Free Lance*, April 7 1920. ATL: A-313-3-030
2. Prominent Jewish families of the time were amongst the most generous of public benefactors, but one lingering perception was that personal wealth at any cost was an all-consuming goal. *"Vot s your idea of Heaven, Izzy?"*, Ken Alexander, *Aussie*, June 15 1925. ATL: A-313-1-011
3. One of the clichés that cartoons like this gave credence to was that Jews put possessions before people, exhibiting a materially-based meanness of spirit. *"Vas you the fellow ..."*, Gordon Minhinnick, *The Artists Annual*, 1929. ATL: A-311-1-007
4. To some, 'Jewishness' symbolised less desirable aspects of modern capitalism and a financial system that involved the secretive, devious manipulation of money for the benefit of 'insiders'. *Finance*, George Finey, *The Artists Annual*, 1929. ATL: A-311-1-008

1

COMMOTION IN THE SECOND-HAND GOODS TRADE.

Perlemutter No. 2: "Ach, Abe, ve are ruined! Vat shall we do?"
Polash the Second: "Holy Jerusalem! Our fancy goods will sink us if bell-toppers and frock-coats are not the rig for meeting the Prince."

2

"Vot's your idea of Heaven, Izzy?"
"Vy, celluloid buildings, an' Jewish fire brigades."

3

"Vas you the fellow who saved my little Ikey from drowning ven he vas fishing?"
"That's me, mister."
"Vel – vere's de sinker off his line?"

4

FINANCE.

Moving Right On

New Zealand might have been down in the depression dumps twice in the 1920s, but the tempo of life turned up several notches – with frenetic flappers on the dance floor, an explosion of motor cars, trucks and buses on roads designed for the horse and cart era, the first flight across the Tasman, and instant contact with the world at the turn of a radio knob. New Zealand's enthusiasm for motoring was unbounded. By the end of the 1920s, the number of cars had doubled in five years to about 152,000 and truck numbers had trebled to over 13,500. There was now one car to every 9.6 New Zealanders compared to 1:14.8 in Australia and 1:47 in Britain. As New Zealand's end-of-the-world isolation lessened, the country's small tourist industry, based at Rotorua, the 'Thermal Wonderland', since the early 1880s, was about to change.

1. South Island entrepreneur, Rudolph Wigley wanted some of the tourist action. His Mount Cook Motor Co ran service cars from Timaru to Queenstown as early as 1906 and to Mt. Cook from 1918, the year the last horse-drawn coach service ended in the South Island. Wigley pointed out that American tourists were spending £140 million in Europe and New Zealand's total tourist revenue in 1922 was only £800,000. *Haere Mai, Uncle Sam!*, Skipper, *The Free Lance*, December 5 1923. ATL: A-315-3-057
2. There was even interest in packing more into a day. Sir Thomas Sidey, a minister in the 1928-31 United administrations is remembered, if at all, for his passionate advocacy of daylight saving. New Zealand clocks were advanced one hour from November 6 1927 to March 4 1928 as a summer time-stretching device. After further experimentation, daylight saving became a calendar fixture from 1946, to the continuing bane of dairy farmers in particular. *Proposed Monumental Group*, Ken Alexander, *NZ Artists Annual*, Christmas 1927. ATL: A-313-1-012
3. With more cars travelling, the country roads were sometimes in better condition than those in town. In Taranaki, which had toll gates to raise money for local roads, there was one car to 5.5 people, only marginally higher than the United States' ratio. Ford's pioneering Model T era ended in 1927 and the new Model A was available in New Zealand the next year for £245, with one hour's free driving tuition thrown in. *A Summer Holiday Impression!*, Trevor Lloyd, *Auckland Weekly News*, December 23 1920. ATL: J-065-046

1

HAERE MAI, UNCLE SAM!

Miss Maoriland: "Now, if I can make him turn this way, he mightn t be so keen about spending his money on that old frump Europe!"

2

PROPOSED MONUMENTAL GROUP IN HONOUR OF MR T. K. SIDEY.

A SUMMER HOLIDAY IMPRESSION!

5: 1930-1939
DARK DAYS AND A NEW DAWN

As the new decade began, a desperately ill Joseph Ward clung to life and the prime ministership. His colleagues were in no particular hurry for him to resign, in part because there was no standout successor, but the inevitable finally happened at a bedside conference in May 1930 seven weeks before his death when Ward was replaced by his deputy George Forbes. Forbes masked his indifferent ability with a stubborn rigidity of purpose, but it was an impossible situation: the new prime minister found himself facing one of the greatest economic crises of modern times as the head of a government of particularly mediocre talent. Also minister of finance, Forbes introduced standard deflationary measures that swelled unemployment without lessening a worrying deficit.

Labour, which had supported United at the 1928 election on the lesser of two evils principle, was loudly critical of the niggardly and temporary relief schemes that tinkered with the rapidly rising number of unemployed, and withdrew its backing in early 1931 when Forbes retrenched further, the one course of action in his limited political repertoire.

Reform could work with United, or force an election nobody wanted. Gordon Coates, who had a low opinion of Forbes and his colleagues, provided grudging support before finally agreeing to a coalition government. Known as 'Honest George', possibly because he lacked the imagination to varnish the truth even a little, Forbes remained prime minister while Coates and his Reform colleagues took charge of the key portfolios.

The coalition won the December 1931 election, although Labour's vote continued to increase steadily. Overall, the electorate still preferred unsatisfactory predictability to promising uncertainty.

Far more decisive than when he had been prime minister, Coates, minister of public works and with responsibility for employment, set up relief camps in the countryside, weakened the Arbitration Court's role in wage setting and increased the unemployment tax. However, frustration boiled over and the 1932 riots in Dunedin, Auckland and Wellington rattled the government into modifying some of the more draconian aspects of its policies. Unemployment soared to about 80,000 by September 1933, but it was not until 1934, after an inexcusable delay, that the government finally announced an unemployment benefit.

The combination of seemingly intractable problems and a head-in-the-sand government led many New Zealanders to seek solutions in unlikely places. There was a full spectrum of choice: the Communist Party, the Douglas Social Credit movement and even the New Zealand Legion which, in 1933, wanted to replace party government with the sort of inspirational leadership then showcasing in Germany and Italy.

Through the twenties and into the 1930s, successive prime ministers and governments took only a perfunctory interest in international affairs, happy to sub-contract foreign policy to Britain. Even though New Zealand was a signed up member, the League of Nations was viewed with suspicion, if at all. However, it was a rather different matter when New Zealand's interests were directly affected, as they were when export receipts nose-dived 44 percent between 1929 and 1933.

At the Imperial Economic Conference in Ottawa in July 1932, Coates was prominent in persuading Britain to give preferential trade treatment to a range of agricultural products from the dominions. Buoyed by this, he came back determined to boost farm incomes rather than screw them down further. Aided by a 'brains trust' of young economists, he turned current thinking on its head, devaluing the New Zealand pound, setting up the Reserve Bank to take control of currency and money supply from the trading banks, and the Mortgage Corporation to help farmers refinance their loans. Although these policies contributed significantly to economic recovery, they infuriated conventional conservative thinking, each an assault on the sanctity of the private enterprise system.

In fact, private enterprise was about to be under far greater threat from the Labour Party.

When Harry Holland, an uncompromising socialist, died in 1933, Michael Joseph Savage became Labour's leader. Someone less like the bestial, ape-like Bolshevik agitators of 1920s cartoons would be difficult to imagine. Savage's gentle, genteel approach and an attractive parcel of policies dependent on the availability of credit administered by a central banking authority – notably the guaranteed price for farm produce and a free national health service – appealed particularly to those groups which had felt most impotent during the depression years.

At the 1935 election, delayed by the economic crisis for a year, it was clear that the public was no longer apprehensive about giving Labour a chance to govern. Dairy farmers, shopkeepers and clerks combined with trade unionists to sweep Labour into power with a clear mandate to get on with their seemingly radical restructuring of the economy.

The winning margin was no greater than Coates' in 1925, but there was little doubt in anyone's mind, as the press warned before and lamented afterwards, that this was the greatest shift in power since 1890.

Armed with the heavy guns of state planning and control, Labour lost little time in attacking the economic

What the ---? Why the ---? How the ---!!

Ken Alexander, *The Free Lance*, October 7 1936. ATL: A-313-1-052

forces that had caused so much depression suffering. But while the National Party opposition – reinvented from the remains of the United, Reform and Democrat parties – and a determinedly conservative press conjured up visions of the great red hand of socialism sweeping away farms and homes, Labour's left wing was frustrated by the party leadership's cautious, middle-of-the-road orthodoxy. Certainly, Labour's leaders were now less committed to socialist theory than to the practical possibility of achieving social justice for New Zealanders, of securing a universal minimum standard of living.

As Labour began to make up for a great deal of lost time in 1936, an escalating flight of capital seriously depleted New Zealand's sterling reserves in London. Import licensing and exchange controls were used in an attempt to plug the outward flow, but the government was not diverted from its goal of giving people more purchasing power to stimulate a sluggish economy that would, in turn, boost employment and trigger further demand. State control of the newly-established Reserve Bank was at the heart of this economic recovery.

An ambitious state housing programme, guaranteed prices for dairy produce, the nationalisation of commercial radio, and compulsory union membership linked to a 40-hour working week were some of the sweeping changes.

Savage also forged a long-lasting political alliance with the Ratana movement; for neglected Maori it meant education, health, employment, and land settlement initiatives. For the first time Maori was receiving all the benefits available to pakeha.

Internationally, Labour's approach was markedly different as well. Savage took an altogether more detached and objective view of New Zealand's foreign policy interests than his predecessors, criticising Britain's weak response to Japan and questioning the effectiveness of the Singapore naval base at the 1937 Imperial Conference.

In 1938, Savage introduced Labour's social security programme, the most comprehensive 'cradle to the grave' legislation in the world. It provided a universal, free health system, a means-tested old-age pension at age 60 and universal superannuation at 65. The subsequent election was another triumph for Labour and its leader.

By now Savage was gravely ill; he had delayed an essential operation until the social security legislation became law and the election was won. In late August 1939, a week after he came out of hospital, finally having had the operation, New Zealand was at war with Germany. Despite their long devotion to pacifism, Labour's leaders were convinced that fascism had to be halted by force. Ironically, it took New Zealand's declaration of war for the aloof, conservative and unsympathetic British government to offer the bulk produce purchase agreements Labour had desperately needed to fund its reform programme.

ONE PLACE WHERE THE STRANGLEHOLD IS PERMITTED.

A.S. Paterson, *Dominion*, ca 1938. ATL: A-313-1-023

It was a difficult decade, but by its end a great many New Zealanders were living more comfortably than at the beginning. It was a worrying decade too: in 1930 there was widespread anxiety about when the depression would end and by 1939 fear about the number of lives another world war would engulf.

During the depression, most of those in work lived a more spartan life than they had grown accustomed to as public service and other salaries were cut. For those out of work, and with no immediate hope of any, it was much worse; families lived in shacks, in town and in the country. Thousands, particularly children, were always hungry.

Fashion, for those who could afford to follow it, had dropped the boyish look for much more feminine styles and elaborate materials. For other New Zealanders there was more interest in converting sacks into rain capes and boys' trousers, in unpicking the remains of old jerseys to knit new ones, and in stuffing cardboard into the bottom of worn through shoes.

Farmers who had been among the first to buy cars a decade or more before were now putting their vehicles up on blocks and rarely leaving their properties. Some farmers paid their doctor's bill in meat and vegetables there was no longer a profitable market for. Soon many were walking off their farms, no longer able to pay their mortgages.

If the depression wasn't enough, Napier was literally shaken to pieces in February 1931 in an earthquake that killed 255 in the city and neighbouring Hastings. The one good thing about New Zealand's worst civil disaster was that out of the rubble grew one of the world's most impressive assembly of Art Deco buildings, using the popular, opulent architectural style that – with its bold and sweeping curves, zigzag and stepped forms, chevron patterns and sunburst motifs – was an exuberant reaction to the depression.

The Liberals had built some worker housing in the 1890s, but Labour's new Department of Housing was promising – and delivering – on a very different scale. For the next decade and beyond an average of 2,500 state houses were built every year; sturdy, squarish, facing the sun (a revolutionary idea at the time), with ample cupboards and built-in wardrobes, and attached laundries – dream homes for many who had never dared to envisage such a dream.

Austerity eased as the decade lengthened. In many homes, carpets were covering wooden floors or linoleum for the first time. Living room suites were replacing single arm chairs; 'time payment' was easing the burden of paying for the radios, electric stoves, water heaters and refrigerators that were adding to domestic comfort and convenience.

Despite the preferential trade agreements that tied Britain and New Zealand even more tightly together, the growing influence of the United States and the American way of doing things was inexorable. With the widening range of competing consumer products, marketing and its advertising sidekick, both American inventions, were much more in evidence.

The 'branding' of packaged goods had 19th century beginnings, with the mass production of many household items. From the late 1920s, the range of consumer brands in New Zealand increased rapidly and, at the same time, the marketing of consumer durables – from vacuum cleaners to refrigerators – was fanning out from the United States. There had been advertising agencies of a sort from the 1890s, but it was not until the 1930s, with the wider distribution of daily newspapers and the beginning of commercial radio, that recognisably modern agencies emerged. J Walter Thompson, the giant US advertising agency, beat its international rivals to New Zealand by decades to 'service' General Motors, which had opened a car assembly plant. Other sophisticated international marketers like Colgate-Palmolive and Unilever were now manufacturing their products in New Zealand as well.

The closely twinned eras of marketing and mass media were just dawning, but they were already beginning to change perceptions about people in the news. There had been heroes before, but Jean Batten, when she made the first ever direct flight from England to New Zealand in 1936, and Jack Lovelock, winning the 1,500 metres at the Berlin Olympics the same year, were now 'personalities'.

In the 1920s, the number of American cars in New Zealand was much higher than some figures suggest. Ford, the archetypal American car, came from Windsor, just across the Detroit River from the United States car capital, and this bit of geographical dexterity was even more useful after the 1932 agreement that secured preferential trade preference for the dominions. Even so, the percentage of British-sourced cars increased sharply during the 1930s and were dominant until the 1960s.

Whatever the make of car, and despite the depression years, there were many more of them on New Zealand roads by the end of the 1930s, with an attendant increase in fatalities and attempts to reduce them. By the end of the 1920s, road deaths were nearly three times higher than at the beginning of the decade and they climbed again in the 1930s, with an understandable dip during the most difficult years, to reach 246 in 1939. By 1925 licences were compulsory for all drivers, and during the next decade speed limits were introduced for the first time, the first edition of the Road Code was published and warrants of fitness were required for all vehicles not already certificated.

By 1939, commercial aeroplanes flew between New Zealand's principal cities and, a year later, Auckland and Sydney were linked by regular flying-boat services. But for most people, travel and passenger trains were synonymous in the 1930s. Sir Joseph Ward's funeral cortége processed by train through the South Island; Michael Savage's train journey from Auckland to Wellington, after he became prime minister in 1935, was punctuated by ecstatic welcomes at railways stations along the main trunk line.

Despite, or possibly because of, the difficulties and deprivation, New Zealand remained a god-fearing country. In the mid-1930s, about 40 percent of New Zealanders claimed to be Anglicans and nearly 25 percent Presbyterians, with Roman Catholics steady, as they had been for some time and would continue to be, at about 15 percent of the population. Active involvement was probably 10-15 percent of nominal memberships. Followers of the Ratana faith, the largest Maori church, grew significantly during the 1920a and declined slowly after that.

It was a sign of New Zealand's growing cultural confidence that local book publishing began in the early 1930s, led by A H and A W Reed, formerly Dunedin booksellers. One of their first books was James Cowan's *Tales of the Maori Bush*. Academic books, like J C Beaglehole's *Exploration of the Pacific* (1935) and Peter Buck's *Vikings of the Sunrise* (1938), still benefited from the added clout of major international publishing houses.

A new breed of fiction writers was at work. They questioned established ideas and conventions; their characters were pakeha and England was 'home', but there was also a growing sense of New Zealand nationalism. John Mulgan's novel, *Man Alone*, published in London in 1939, has been seen as a watershed in the country's fiction.

There was a small, appreciative audience for the work of a growing number of poets, including A R D Fairburn, Allen Curnow, Charles Brasch and Denis Glover, the latter's Caxton Press often the publisher. *Conversations With My Uncle*, the first book by Frank Sargeson, to become the most influential writer of his generation, was published in 1936.

The *New Zealand Listener*, journal of the Broadcasting Service, was launched in 1939, beginning its long tenure as the country's leading cultural magazine.

New Zealand theatre audiences continued to enjoy imported plays and actors, prominent ones including Sybil Thorndike, Lewis Casson and Fay Compton. Musical imports included a 17-year-old Yehudi Menuhin in 1935, American tenor Richard Crooks the next year and conductor Malcolm Sargent in 1939. For stay-at-homes and those addicted to the new medium of radio, the era of serials had begun, with most, like *Dad and Dave from Snake Gully, Dr Paul, Portia Faces Life*, and *Life with Dexter*, coming from Australia. In 1936 the broadcasting of Parliament began, but 'Aunt Daisy' made a greater impact; Daisy Basham's rapid-fire delivery and her 'A Bicycle Built for Two' theme were to be a weekday morning institution for the next quarter century.

Racing probably ranked next to rugby in the sporting pantheon, although there were more clearly defined social distinctions, with the owners and club stewards in the members' stand and the 'punters' crowded along the rails. The depression hit attendances, but the racing community's spirits were briefly buoyed by the performances of Phar Lap, the country's greatest racehorse, in Australia and North America during 1930-32. However, barely a fortnight after winning an important race in Mexico, Phar Lap died suddenly in the United States in April 1932. The 1930s was that sort of decade.

Cruel Cuts

When Labour withdrew its voting support from United in early 1931 – after George Forbes decreed no payments without work and 10 percent wage cuts – the eventual 'fusion' of United and Reform was inevitable. Effectively government leader but not prime minister, Coates was more decisive than before, but measures he introduced were harsh and seemingly callous. The city riots that followed in 1932 were flashpoints of frustration rather than planned acts of political violence in response to specific legislation. Coates was jolted into making some concessions and, by the time unemployment peaked in late 1933, relief camps were being run with a more satisfactory mix of efficiency and humanity and the building industry had been given a financial shot-in-the-arm. As important for the country's recovery, Coates made sure, via a bitterly opposed devaluation and other measures, that farmers' incomes began to inch up again. By the 1935 election a rapid world recovery was already giving a fillip to export prices.

1. The decision of United and Reform to 'pull together' later in 1931 was based more on mutual impotence than shared optimism. Forbes and Coates, leaders of the two almost identically conservative parties, divided up cabinet posts before and after the 1931 election which the National coalition won handsomely. *Pull Together,* Jack Gilmour, *The Free Lance*, December 31 1930. ATL: J-044-006
2. He was hardly 'new blood', but Coates returned from an economic conference in 1932 determined to attack the depression with more innovative, less defensive, policies. *Give Young New Zealand a Chance!,* Stuart Peterson, *The Free Lance*, December 7 1932. ATL: A-315-3-064
3. Export prices began to recover in 1933 and farm incomes were further boosted by the increases in production farmers were now getting from the grasslands revolution. *Signs of a Thaw*, Trevor Lloyd, *NZ Herald*, September 27 1933. ATL: B-115-024
4. The depression hardly touched some New Zealanders; the worst affected were the unemployed, unskilled, over-mortgaged small farmers, most Maori, and women. The 1930 Unemployment Act obliged women in the paid workforce to pay an unemployment levy while excluding them from relief payments when unemployed. *Women in the Depression*, Kennaway, *Tomorrow*, July 24 1935. ATL: J-065-051
5. Labour continued to gain seats in 1931 and, as the only party untarnished by the subsequent harsh and ineffectual retrenchments, steadily garnered more support over the next four years. The fate of both United and Reform had been sealed long before the depression lifted. *A Friend s Passing*, Jack Gilmour, *NZ Truth*, October 2 1935. ATL: A-313-1-025

1

PULL TOGETHER – THE RESOLUTION FOR 1931.

2

GIVE YOUNG NEW ZEALAND A CHANCE!

The schoolboy: "Say, mister, you're tired and these chaps are dug in. Please let me have a go at them."

3

SIGNS OF A THAW.

4

5 A FRIEND'S PASSING

The Forbes & Coates Show

After Sir Joseph Ward died in June 1930, George Forbes – only prime minister because his cabinet colleagues were even less likely contenders – met the worsening depression with retrenchments, the severity of one dictating the harshness of the other. The unlikely alliance with Labour was over early in 1931, and Forbes stumbled on with unofficial Reform support for several more months before Coates agreed coalition terms. At first, with Reform's Downie Stewart a thoroughly orthodox minister of finance, Forbes was sufficiently encouraged to campaign vigorously and successfully for 'national solidarity' at the 1931 election. In time, though, Coates' growing disquiet with the administration's wallowing indecision led to the raising of New Zealand's exchange rate to assist the farming community. When Stewart resigned, and Coates became finance minister, Forbes was largely marginalised, in part coping with the situation by taking several extensive overseas trips. In the months before the 1935 election, Coates cautiously eased the unemployment tax and restored pensions and wages a measured step or two behind rising export prices.

1. As the depression deepened, with no end in sight, Forbes pressed Coates to join in a coalition and share responsibility for the draconian cuts and retrenchments that orthodox thinking deemed necessary. A reluctant Coates, who had little enthusiasm for being associated with United's bungling, finally agreed to a National coalition. *Leaving the Coalition Tent*, Stuart Peterson, *The Free Lance*, December 9 1931. ATL: A-315-3-063
2. The National coalition had a comfortable victory at the 1931 election, taking 51 seats to Labour's 24. Nevertheless, Labour continued to make steady progress, winning five more seats than in 1928. *And the Villain Still Pursued Them*, William Blomfield, *NZ Observer*, December 10 1931. ATL: A-312-1-150
3. Whatever the problem – even rabbits, white butterflies and ragwort – Forbes had a very small armoury of tried and often quite inappropriate responses. *The Way Out*, Trevor Lloyd, *NZ Herald*, April 11 1934. ATL: B-115-002
4. Voters swept Labour to power in 1935, remembering, with considerable bitterness, the harshness of many of the coalition's policies. The National Political Federation was decimated at the election and Labour had little effective opposition within or outside parliament during its early years in power. *The Rising Tide of Labour*, Fox, *Standard*, February 4 1937. ATL: A-312-2-058

1

LEAVING THE COALITION TENT FOR A PERMANENT HOME.

2

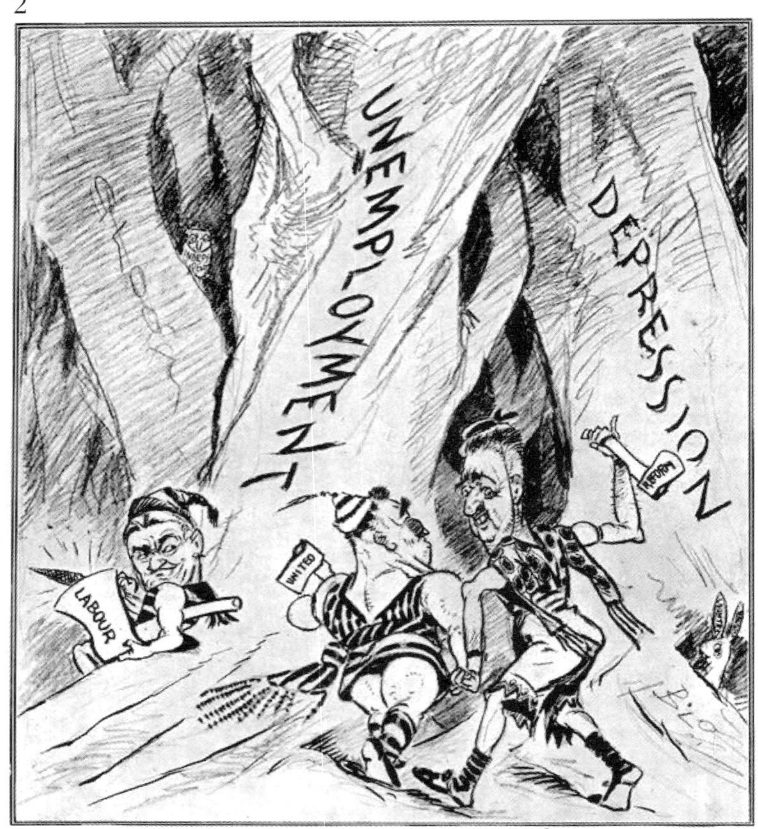

AND THE VILLAIN STILL PURSUED THEM.

The Coalition babes in the Wood (in unison): "I think we've thrown that wicked man off the scent at last."

3

THE WAY OUT.

4

A Gentle Savage

A number of New Zealand prime ministers have been respected, but none was loved like Michael Joseph Savage, the genial, benevolent little cellarman from Australia who became Labour's leader after Harry Holland's death in 1933. 'Micky' Savage entered parliament in 1919 after years of service in the moderate wing of the Auckland trade union movement. From the beginning he worked in his quiet, unobtrusive way to widen Labour's appeal beyond the union movement, advocating pension changes and a free health service, and persuading his colleagues that a freehold land policy was crucial to winning sufficient rural votes to occupy the treasury benches. Labour's smiling, owlish, favourite-uncle sort of leader could not have been more different from the image of the brutal, barricade-storming socialist. His patent honesty, idealism and talent for comforting, inspiring but vague generalisations, reassured voters previously apprehensive of Labour.

1. Delayed for a year, the election finally held in November 1935 was a momentous victory for Labour and their 63-year-old leader, his quiet charisma and moderate views contributing significantly to the result. *"Going, Going G ....",* Gordon Minhinnick, *NZ Herald*, October 25 1935. ATL: A-311-1-010
2. In place of equivocation and uncertainty, Labour offered a simple, easily understood solution to the country's troubles at the 1935 election. The National Political Federation, an uneasy alliance of Reform and United politicians, won only 19 seats. *The Story of the Pyramid*, Ken Alexander, *Point Blank*, December 16 1935. ATL: A-313-1-042
3. While Savage's well-tuned political instincts warned against an avalanche of new legislation, the first Labour government's programme during 1936 made most administrations, before and since, look like timid procrastinators. *The Mushroom Season*, Trevor Lloyd, 1936. ATL: C-109-027
4. Savage's consensus approach held caucus factions and strong personalities together for the stunning 1938 victory, with nearly 53 percent of the electorate voting for Labour – almost 10 percent more than in 1935. The newly-minted National Party, a re-invention of the United, Reform and fledgling Democrat parties, and its leader Adam Hamilton, were soundly trounced. *'Now Then'*, Gordon Minhinnick, *NZ Herald*, 1938. ATL: A-311-1-015

1

"GOING, GOING, G..."

2

THE STORY OF THE PYRAMID.

3

THE MUSHROOM SEASON.

4

'NOW THEN.'

Up, Up and Away

One of Savage's favourite expressions was 'Onward and Upward', and it neatly summed up Labour's purpose and performance. The new government might have shifted from the destruction of capitalism to its peaceful modification but it got on with the job immediately and with revolutionary zeal. Labour's principal promise was to insulate New Zealand's economy from international pressures. Walter Nash, the finance minister, believed the Reserve Bank takeover was the key to the state control and planning that would stabilise the economy. Labour attacked unemployment by stimulating the local market with higher wages and by freeing farmers of liabilities and uncertainty, with cheap Reserve Bank credit the source of funds. There was as much, if not more, apprehension about Labour's social policies which were wrapped up in the 1938 Social Security Act. This, the beginning of 'cradle-to-grave security', provided a universal, free health service, a means-tested old-age pension at age 60 and universal superannuation from 65, funded from a single universal tax subsidised by government.

1. In 1936 Nash was responsible for the most important legislation, with Savage reassuring the country the revolution had not arrived. *Into the Stratosphere*, Ken Alexander, *The Free Lance*, April 29 1936. ATL: A-315-3-066
2. Labour was clear-sighted about how vital the recovery of farming and increases in the volume and prices of export produce were to the overall health of the New Zealand economy. *Always Hungry*, Jack Gilmour, *NZ Truth*, September 8 1937. ATL: A-313-1-027
3. Higher tax receipts were only one component, along with internal loans and rising export prices, in Nash's strategy to cover the massive increases in government spending. A social security contribution – a special tax of 5 percent – was introduced on individual and company incomes in 1939. *The Gourmand*, Alec Garmonsway, *NZ Observer*, September 22 1938. ATL: A-313-9-004
4. In fact, the NZ branch of the British Medical Association was a major obstacle to the free health scheme, claiming it destroyed the personal relationship between doctor and patient and that only the poorest should receive a completely free service. In 1939, with the scheme now operating, the BMA refused to co-operate, citing payment and other concerns. The medical profession's image suffered until, in 1941, most doctors agreed to a universal, fee-for-service system. *There s No Telling*, Gordon Minhinnick, *NZ Herald*, July 1 1938. ATL: A-311-1-014

1

Into the Stratosphere.

2

ALWAYS HUNGRY

3

THE GOURMAND.

4

THERE'S NO TELLING.

Guarantees for Country Cousins

Critical to Labour's plan to revive agriculture was the 'guaranteed price' or compulsory purchase of farm produce. In part because the dairy industry was already significantly centralised, only dairy exports came under the purchase and marketing provisions of the Primary Producers Marketing Department. (Labour did not finally abandon the possibility of adding meat and wool until after the war.) The dairy farmer's reasonable standard of living was guaranteed by a set annual price, with purchases financed by the Reserve Bank. The government intended to recoup its outlay from reciprocal trade agreements with Britain and other countries. Initially, Britain refused to consider bilateral, bulk-trading deals, which were unfashionable at the time. Fortuitously, Labour's economic gamble was reprieved by the war and by Britain's blanket purchase of meat and dairy exports. The guaranteed price scheme received a mixed reception from farmers, although compulsory purchase undoubtedly provided stability and security for small struggling ones.

1. At a time when New Zealand farming was reeling, 'Buy British Goods' seemed like an empty slogan when Britain was preferring Danish butter to New Zealand's – and at threepence a pound more. At the Imperial Economic Conference in Ottawa in 1932, Coates helped convince Britain to give preferential agricultural product treatment to New Zealand and other dominions. *Is This John Bull s Style of Imperial Preference?,* Jack Gilmour, *The Free Lance*, October 22 1930. ATL: A-313-1-041
2. Coates' attempt to boost farm incomes by a devaluation was another not very successful 'band-aid' solution. In short order, prices for frozen meat, butter and cheese and crossbred wool all fell, in some cases to about the amount of the increased exchange rate. *Doubtful Blessing of High Exchange*, Stuart Peterson, *The Free Lance*, February 22 1933. ATL: A-315-3-065
3. Set annual prices were primarily based on the average for the previous decade which, in tandem with costs, had been low during the depression years. Now, with Labour's expansionary policies, costs were rising sharply. *He got the Honey, but …,* Ken Alexander, *Point Blank*, January 1937. ATL: A-313-1-043
4. This was wishful thinking on the cartoonist's part. While there were some concerns about the guaranteed price scheme, Labour significantly increased its total vote at the November 1938 election. *Killing the Goose*, Alec Garmonsway, *NZ Observer*, October 27 1938. ATL: A-313-9-006

1

IS THIS JOHN BULL'S STYLE OF IMPERIAL PREFERENCE?

2

DOUBTFUL BLESSING OF HIGH EXCHANGE.
The farmer (to Coalition Chiefs): Hi, there; you didn't tell me this pup would bite!

3

He got the Honey, but…!

4

KILLING THE GOOSE.

Heads in the Sand

Until Labour came to power, New Zealand echoed Britain's League of Nations 'appeasing' sentiments, and defence policy largely rested on assumptions about the high-seas supremacy of the British Navy. Labour was deliberately misled by Britain about the Royal Navy's war-time ability to send a fleet to Singapore before the fall of the naval base on which New Zealand had spent heavily for a decade. Already contemplating the inevitability of war, Labour had multiple concerns: New Zealand's inadequate defences; Japan's blatant militarism that had turned the Far East into the Near North; and the Singapore naval base as an increasingly uncertain first line of defence. Consequently, it was surprising that, when New Zealand went to war on September 3 1939, the government was prepared once again to send its volunteer and conscript army to fight in the Middle East and Europe.

1. In 1931, depression financial restraints forced retirements from the army's permanent force – leaving 86 officers and 263 other ranks. The territorial force became voluntary, numbers dropping from 16,990 to 3,655. Later in the decade, Labour's pacifist leaders backed away from compulsory military training, but early in 1939 Savage called for 50,000 home-defence volunteers. *The Funeral*, Trevor Lloyd, *NZ Herald*, July 22 1930. ATL: A-315-2-191
2. Despite their long devotion to pacifism, Labour's leaders were, by 1936, convinced that fascism had to be halted by force. The general public was more complacent, and an attempt to form a branch of the NZ Defence League in Wellington netted only 30 interested persons. *The Ostrich*, William Blomfield, *NZ Observer*, October 29 1936. ATL: A-312-1-190
3. When Savage and Nash attended the coronation of King George V1 in 1937 there was a cool reception from a sniffy British government alarmed at the rundown in New Zealand's sterling reserves in London, suspicious of 'welfare state' developments, and miffed at opposing stances at the League of Nations. Consequently, Nash's attempts to negotiate bulk trading agreements were rebuffed. *Food for Thought*, Gordon Minhinnick, *NZ Herald*, June 22 1937. ATL: A-311-1-012
4. At the 1937 Imperial Conference that followed the coronation, Savage was unimpressed by Britain's claims about the effectiveness of the Singapore naval base, should Japan invade the Pacific, and said so bluntly. It officially opened on February 14 1938. *Basking in the Shade*, Jack Gilmour, *NZ Truth*, February 16 1938. ATL: A-313-1-028

1

THE FUNERAL.

2

THE OSTRICH.

3

FOOD FOR THOUGHT.

4

BASKING IN THE SHADE

The Medium and the Message

Labour won the 1935 election despite a strongly antagonistic press that predicted a coalition win until the last days of the campaign. The coalition was well aware of the potential potency of radio, now past its infant, crawling stage, and had been implicated in the jamming of 1ZB, the Auckland radio station, during a pre-election broadcast by the popular Rev. Colin Scrimgeour who was expected to advise his listeners to vote against the government. It was hardly surprising that the new Labour government had plans for the first instant mass medium – there were 50,000 licensed radio receivers in 1930 and over 300,000 by 1939. Control of broadcasting shifted from government-appointed board to state department; Savage's friend 'Uncle Scrim' was a controversial appointment as controller of commercial broadcasting; the broadcasting of parliament began; Labour allocated political time in line with parliamentary strength – and to its advantage for the 1938 election when party propaganda was presented as news from the prime minister's department.

1. *Tomorrow*, a small but influential left-wing periodical, edited by artist and cartoonist Kennaway Henderson, was trenchant in its opinion that the public were pawns, and the press the propaganda arm of international capitalism. *Pawns in the Game*, Kennaway, *Tomorrow*, November 25 1936. ATL: J-065-062
2. In 1937, James Shelley, education professor turned director of the national broadcasting service, announced plans to build an impressive broadcasting headquarters in Wellington including a conservatorium of music and drama. Foundations were dug before the war brought an abrupt end to the project. Broadcasting House, finally opened in 1963, was a much more modest building. *Castles in the Air*, William Blomfield, *NZ Observer*, February 4 1937. ATL: A-312-1-191
3. It was the view of Labour supporters that the mainly conservative press was in the hands of 'vested interests'. Certainly National Party advertising and newspaper editorials were barely distinguishable. *Vested Interests ….*, Fox, *Standard*, September 16 1937. ATL: A-313-2-013
4. Savage saw radio as having cultural as well as information roles. Whether New Zealanders, or the rest of the world, would welcome the colourful language of Bob Semple, ex-Australian miner and 'Red Fed' orator, was a moot point. *Telling the World*, Gordon Minhinnick, *NZ Herald*, January 27 1937. ATL: A-311-1-011

1

PAWNS IN THE GAME.

2

CASTLES IN THE AIR

3

Vested interests: "We must see that nothing gets into our press about this."

4

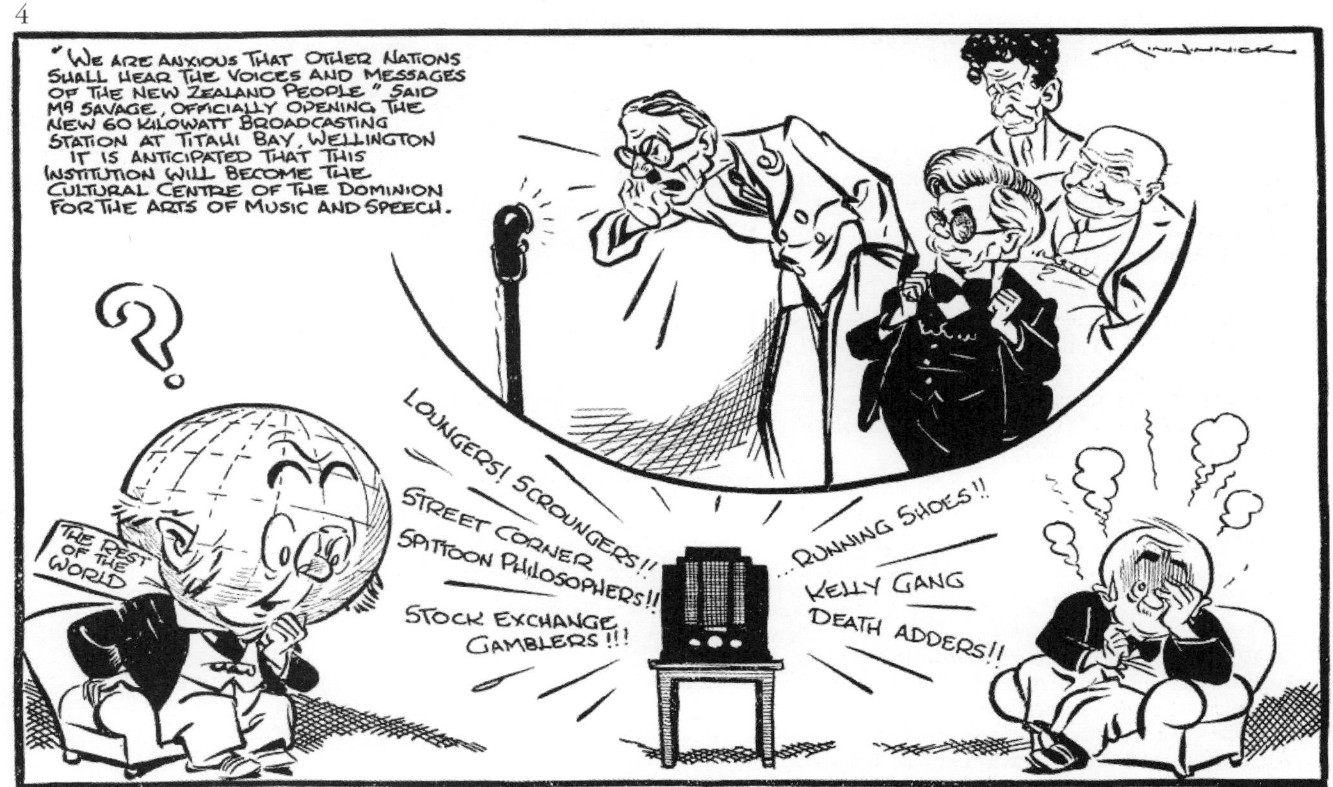

TELLING THE WORLD.

Life (More or Less) as Usual

It was known as the 'great' depression because its stranglehold over much of the world was worse than encountered before, but in New Zealand there was something of a gap between subsequent mythology and reality at the time. Undoubtedly, the depression years – particularly 1930-33 – were felt right across New Zealand society. But the pain and hardship was felt very unevenly. Wages fell, whether by government edict or employer tightening, but consumer prices dropped even further. Unemployment was higher than before, but considerably less than elsewhere. For those unemployed, or already struggling, life was grim as evidence of malnutrition, inadequate clothing and housing and desperate abortions shows. For those still in work, or with an income, life carried on much as before, but with a sense of just staying afloat. There were still rugby tours and race meetings; movies screened and the pubs were open; but it was as if the nation's metabolism had slowed. Even those who could afford to spend went into squirrelling mode. Less food was eaten, beer consumption dropped by 30 percent between 1929-33, on-course betting and cigarette smoking halved. For a few years the future looked bleak, uncertain, but then the sun broke through ....

1. All Black tests can put a spring in the step, the 'feel-good factor' useful in an election year or in a deepening depression – as long as the All Blacks are winning. In this 1930 series, New Zealand lost the first test, then won the next three. *Britain Victorious in First Rugby Test*, Trevor Lloyd, *NZ Herald*, June 23 1930. ATL: A-315-2-013
2. Bookmakers were a colourful part of the racing scene until banned in 1910. While no longer 'on-course', they were still in business, operating out of public bars and over the telephone – and paying no tax. A 1935 suggestion that off-course betting be reviewed was rejected by Savage. *Business as Usual*, Gordon Minhinnick, *NZ Herald*, July 15 1935. ATL: A-311-1-054
3. Vehicle sales halved between 1930-31 and halved again by 1933. Yet during the decade car registrations went up 39 percent, New Zealand now recording the second highest density in the world. *A Short History of the Depression*, Gordon Minhinnick, *NZ Herald*, July 26 1932. ATL: A-311-1-009
4. In 1938 Peter Fraser announced that women would now be allowed to join the police force. The first 10 women police graduated in 1942. *Help!,* Jack Gilmour, *NZ Truth*, May 11 1938. ATL: A-313-1-030
5. In 1939, after false starts, international air travel began when Imperial Airways flying boats began a regular, scheduled service to Australia. The next year the government combined with British and Australian interests to form Tasman Empire Airways (TEAL). *Bogged,* Jack Gilmour, *NZ Truth*, February 23 1938. ATL: A-313-1-029

1

BRITAIN VICTORIOUS IN THE FIRST RUGBY TEST.

2

BUSINESS AS USUAL.

3

A SHORT HISTORY OF THE DEPRESSION.

4

HELP!

5

BOGGED

6: 1940-1949

WAR AND FRETFUL PEACE

Savage had been too ill to read New Zealand's declaration of war in Parliament on September 3 1939; his deputy Peter Fraser did this and took charge of both the country's war preparations and ugly skirmishes within the Labour caucus. John A Lee, who did not agree with the government's cautious economic approach, and was frustrated by an under-secretaryship that satisfied neither his abilities nor his ego, was expelled from the party for a barely disguised attack on the dying prime minister's mental health.

By the time Fraser had succeeded Savage at the beginning of April 1940, he had travelled to London and forged a cordial personal relationship with Winston Churchill and achieved an immediate rapport, that developed into close friendship, with Bernard Freyberg who subsequently commanded the 2nd New Zealand Expeditionary Force.

Given New Zealand's inadequate defences, scepticism about the Singapore naval base, and the obviously expansionist intent of the Japanese, it was surprising that the Labour government once again sent its army to fight in the Middle East and Europe. By early October 1939, nearly 15,000 young New Zealand men had enlisted voluntarily. Three months later the First Echelon of the 2nd NZEF, over 6,500 officers and men, sailed to Egypt; the Second Echelon, totaling nearly 6,850 followed in May, its final destination Scotland.

At home, Fraser lost no time in 'mobilising' the nation. A raft of measures – censorship and emergency regulations that gave the government unprecedented control over people and property – were pushed through parliament. When Fraser, jailed for sedition during the First World War, introduced the legislation authorising conscription, there was surprisingly little opposition. Over the next five years 306,000 men between the ages of 18 and 46 were called up for service in the armed forces.

However, Peter Fraser was determined New Zealand troops would not be again on the receiving end of some of the War Office bungling that strained relations during the First World War. He and General Freyberg agreed that the New Zealand Division was the expeditionary force of a sovereign state and not part of the British army. Unfortunately, there remained a gap between theory and practice. New Zealand suffered heavy casualties in Greece and Crete, poorly planned campaigns Fraser and Freyberg had agreed to without adequately consulting each other.

Following the attack on Pearl Harbour by the Japanese, one of the most difficult decisions Fraser had to make was whether to recall the country's troops from the Middle East – as the Australians did. Responding to Churchillian pressure, Fraser persuaded a doubtful parliament and public that the great bulk of the country's troops should remain in the Northern Hemisphere. A defenceless New Zealand hung on tensely, with a token naval and air force presence and a Home Guard that often drilled with wooden guns, until waves of US marines and GIs arrived – an advance guard of the continuing, insistent American assault on New Zealand's young, transplanted culture.

Understandably, Fraser was anxious to share responsibility for unpopular war-time restrictions with the National Party in a coalition administration. Sid Holland, who replaced Adam Hamilton as National Party leader in late 1940, refused to be drawn into the inner war cabinet, which included Hamilton and Coates. Holland did, though, agree to the postponement of the election due in 1941 and, in June 1942, he eventually accepted Fraser's offer of a seat in the war cabinet and in a specially constituted war administration along with five National colleagues. Although he was given responsibility for all war expenditure, Holland saw more political capital in being the government's chief critic and, after just three months, used the court's lenient treatment of striking Huntly coal miners as the excuse to end National's grudging co-operation. The Federation of Labour was more amenable, the mutually acceptable accommodation between Fraser and F P Walsh, the powerful FOL leader, ensuring the smooth running of the government's economic stabilisation policies. The introduction of compulsory unionism in 1936 had greatly strengthened Walsh's position, and he was now happy, in return, to guarantee the government an acquiescent union movement.

During 1943 the war tide turned. The 2nd NZEF, now the 2nd New Zealand Division, was part of a victorious allied 8th Army that defeated the Axis forces in North Africa before turning its attention to Italy. In the air, one in every 12 Battle of Britain pilots had been a New Zealander. No 75 (NZ) Squadron clocked up thousands of bombing sorties over Europe; No 15 Squadron flew Mosquito fighters in the Pacific theatre. The most famous naval engagement involving New Zealand naval personnel was the defeat of the German battleship *Admiral Graf Spee* by the *Achilles* and two other cruisers.

Labour won the next election, finally held in September 1943, but its reduced majority reflected the tightening grip of heavy taxation, rationing and economic stabilisation.

Foreseeing the United States' importance in the post-war world, Fraser had by now dispatched Walter Nash, his deputy, to Washington to ensure New Zealand had some say in both the Pacific war and in decisions already beginning to shape the future. Trans-Tasman relations were improved when the two Labour administrations signed the Canberra Pact in early 1944.

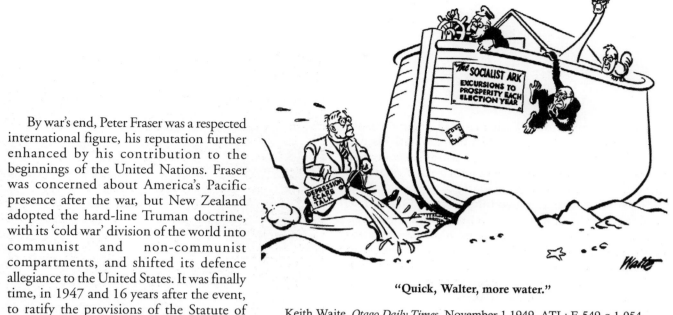

"Quick, Walter, more water."

Keith Waite, *Otago Daily Times*, November 1 1949. ATL: E-549-q-1-054

By war's end, Peter Fraser was a respected international figure, his reputation further enhanced by his contribution to the beginnings of the United Nations. Fraser was concerned about America's Pacific presence after the war, but New Zealand adopted the hard-line Truman doctrine, with its 'cold war' division of the world into communist and non-communist compartments, and shifted its defence allegiance to the United States. It was finally time, in 1947 and 16 years after the event, to ratify the provisions of the Statute of Westminster which spelt out New Zealand's legal and political independence from Britain.

At home, though, Fraser was bogged down by the sort of expediency that catches up with weary governments that have been in power for years. Labour's desperately tired leaders faced the 1946 election after a tumultuous decade of fundamental changes in the control and management of the economy, establishment of the welfare state, and a war that absorbed nearly one-third of the male workforce into the armed services. There was a sputter of crusading spirit left – the family benefit made universal, mothers receiving the generous sum of 10 shillings for all children under 16 years of age – but Labour was now more concerned with safeguarding what it had achieved than taking fresh tilts at the capitalist system.

The 1946 election was a close run thing, the four Maori seats the difference. Holland had worked hard at building National's voter base and positioning it as the party of innovation and as the zealous supporter of private enterprise, committed to breaking down the continuing pattern of controls and restrictions.

Labour had now run out of steam, the public was tired of shortages and controls, and militant trade unionists were flexing their muscles. As well, Labour's core support was shaken by Fraser's increasing dependence on union hard man Walsh and his determination, based on his gloomy assessment of the likelihood of peace in a world of belligerent superpowers, to introduce peacetime conscription. He tried, but failed, to deflect widespread criticism by calling it 'compulsory military training'.

Nobody was surprised when National won the November 1949 election in resounding fashion.

By its rather staid standards, New Zealand let its hair down at the beginning of the decade to celebrate a century of European settlement. Not even the declaration of war less than two months before could dent enthusiasm for the New Zealand Centennial Exhibition which opened on November 8 1939 and ran through to the beginning of May 1940. Over 2.5 million people visited the exhibition at a time when the country's population was about 1.5 million. Covering 55 acres of land near Wellington airport, the exhibition was an unabashed appeal to nationalism and the government's role in New Zealand life, with scant regard to Maori sensitivities. The 'Dominion Court' included a massive diorama with cities, ports, rail and roads all in place; the 100,000 square feet 'Government Court' featured the Health Department's walking and talking robot 'Dr Wellandstrong'. An impressive use of electricity and neon – involving over 37,000 lights – showcased the latest source of power. But what drew the fun-starved crowds back for repeat visits was 'Playland' with its dodgems, Crazy House and roller coaster.

In 1940s New Zealand, the 'average' and the 'norm' were more comfortably accommodated than the markedly different. The fact that the gap between the highest and lowest incomes in the country was the smallest in the world was considered an achievement rather than an aberration. In wartime particularly, pacifists were sufficiently different from the norm to be a considerable embarrassment. Over 800 conscientious objectors, many of them pacifists, were sent to detention camps, and several of their leaders went to prison.

Women played a significant role in New Zealand's war effort. Nearly 650 nurses served in the Middle East, Italy and the Pacific; from 1942 'voluntary aids' were sent overseas to release male medical orderlies for active service. At home, also from 1942, women aged between 18-30 were drafted into 'essential' work as railway porters, tram conductors and in other previously men-only occupations, and swelled their numbers in industry by nearly 50,000 in three years. Others joined the Women's Land Service

"PEACE ON EARTH, GOODWILL TO MEN."

Neil Lonsdale, *NZ Observer*, December 25 1940.
ATL: A-316-4-003

and worked on farms. With many of their menfolk volunteering for 26 (Maori) Battalion, Maori women formed the Maori War Effort Organisation, encouraging their sisters and daughters to move from isolated rural areas to work in essential industries.

There was a restrained mood after the war. There might be little poverty, but with restrictions remaining there was little scope for frivolity. Some young women, swept away by the seeming sophistication and affluence of 'rest and recreation' GIs, became American war-brides; the rest settled down to secure, if more prosaic, lives as suburban housewives and 'baby boom' mothers.

Over the decade from war's end, 10,000 ex-servicemen were assisted onto farms, but in a carefully controlled way that avoided the wholesale land speculation following the First World War.The war had been a great leveller: more Maori now lived in what had been largely pakeha cities; city professionals and farm workers had soldiered in the same units. Nevertheless, town and country differences remained, the farmer more community-minded than the average city dweller, anonymous in his suburban street. And the sheep farmer still had some claim to the 'aristocrat' tag, particularly when export prices were on the rise.

Life might never be the same again, but it was not all that different either. American servicemen might have created a fleeting market for a decent cup of coffee, but the idea of 'eating out' had not developed further than a milk bar snack after the almost mandatory Friday night shopping expedition. Stocking the cupboards with home cooking was encouraged by *The New Zealand Women's Weekly*, which had been extolling womanly virtues since 1932. Much of Aunt Daisy's 1954 cookbook, for example, was devoted to 'tin-fillers', including eight types of sponge cake.

With city populations growing, in part because of a steady stream of 'Ten Pound Pom' immigrants in the postwar years, the sanctity of the quarter-acre section pushed suburbia out to occupy areas as large as overseas cities with 10-times more people. Some of the more overt American influences were yet to come, yet the expansiveness of town planning and comparative social mobility owed more to North America than Europe.

Labour's leaders were a dour, earnest lot and frivolity was not something they encouraged. They were passionate about achieving 'equality', but life was a serious business, to be lived seriously even when there wasn't a depression to contend with or a war to struggle through. Aside from an occasional visit to the theatre, Peter Fraser's idea of fun was to sit around the fire with his wife, reading book passages to each other. During Labour's 14 years in power, shops kept strictly regimented hours during the week, only dairies opened at weekends, restaurants were as rare as the endangered bird species New Zealanders were beginning to hear about, and hotels were better known for their public bars and the 'six o'clock' swill than for fine dining. The surburban weekend was as strictly orchestrated as the rest of life: the lawns and vegetable garden, cleaning and polishing inside, painting and repairing outside, and the ritual cleaning of the car most families now owned. The routine was most likely to be interrupted by a Saturday afternoon rugby match, a Saturday evening at 'the pictures' or Sunday afternoon 'drive' to nowhere in particular or to visit elderly relatives.

The general greyness extended to fashions that were like the uniforms of a civilian army. Hats continued to be compulsory out-and-about wear for both men and women, and milliners and hat shops were kept busy until, for reasons as inexplicable as the compulsion to wear them, they were suddenly out of favour.

The motoring boom stalled. Petrol rationing, introduced in early October 1939, narrowed travel horizons to about 150 miles worth of petrol a month, and encouraged ingenious experiments with coal gas and kerosene. When the government requisitioned pre-war used cars and then most new vehicles, there were 20 eager prospective buyers for every new import, even when prices soared 50 percent. At the end of the decade 70 percent of the 230,000 registered cars in the country were over 10 years old.

Labour's leaders had less first-hand experience of children than most politicians before or since, but they had a deep and practical concern about their health and education.

By the late 1940s all children received a medical examination on starting school and then at intervals during their primary years. Those not 'thriving' were sent to health camps. Existing camps were taken over by the government in 1938 and permanent ones opened in the 1940s and later. Following the polio epidemic in 1947, which closed North Island schools for over four months, preventative programmes were introduced for tuberculosis and the Salk polio vaccine was available from the mid-1950s. Also in 1947, the government funded regular visits to dentists and dental clinics for all children until they were 16.

Labour, and the educationists it appointed, responded positively to international research identifying childhood as a distinct stage in human development. The number of kindergartens doubled during the first half of the decade and the less formal Playcentre pre-school movement, begun in Wellington by the wives of prominent educationists in 1940, spread around the country. With government assistance to both organisations, pre-school education expanded rapidly.

During the early years of his lengthy tenure, C E Beeby, the innovative educational psychologist who headed the Department of Education from 1940, there were significant changes to primary and secondary school curricula, a new physical education regime, expansion of school libraries, special programmes for the disabled, and the raising of the leaving age to 15 – all with the aim of providing equality of educational opportunity.

The visual arts blossomed in the 1940s. By now Evelyn Page and Toss Woollaston had developed distinctive, if not always approved of, styles: significant new names included Rita Angus, Eric Lee-Johnson and W A Sutton. However, even art aficionados still struggled with 'modern art'; in 1949 the advisory committee at Christchurch's McDougall Art Gallery rejected Frances Hodgkins' 'Pleasure Gardens', which had been purchased by public subscription.

The depression, 'talkies' and the war ended regular tours of New Zealand by British and American professional theatre companies. This was, if anything, a stimulus to greater local activity: Wellington's Unity theatre was a distinguished addition, in 1942, to the growing number of amateur dramatic societies; Ngaio Marsh's Shakespearean productions for the Canterbury University Drama Society from 1944; and the first production of *The Axe*, a pioneering verse play by Allen Curnow, in 1948.

Film was an increasingly popular entertainment and information medium. In early 1940, the sound version of Rudall Hayward's *Rewi's Last Stand*, considerably different from the silent one, was screened for the first time. The government established the National Film Unit in 1941 and, in the pre-television era, its *Weekly Review* newsreel provided local and overseas war information.

The 1946 creation of the National Orchestra of the NZ Broadcasting Service was another sign of a maturing culture, as was, during the 1940s, the growing oeuvre of Douglas Lilburn, who was to become one of the country's most prolific and influential composers.

The war was a source of stimulus to writers, like Dan Davin and Eric McCormick, who joined the armed forces, an opportunity to view their country from a fresh perspective. In New Zealand, *Landfall*, a quarterly founded by Charles Brasch in 1947, gave a new edge and purpose to literary criticism. A 1945 anthology of New Zealand poetry, edited by Allen Curnow, was attacked by young poets like James K Baxter and Louis Johnson; nationalist themes – including isolation and alienation – should give way, they argued, to more universal and international ones.

Rugby was a war casualty for a decade, with only seven tests played between 1938 and 1947, all against Australia, and five of them across the Tasman. The New Zealand Army Kiwis played dashing rugby during post-war celebrations in Britain, but that wasn't much consolation to local fans. The 1949 All Black tour of South Africa was no cause for celebration either off the field or on it: despite vigorous protests, New Zealand acquiesced to the demand that no Maori tour; and all four tests were lost in stolid, ugly, forward-dominated contests.

Environmentally, there were several developments during the 1940s that were to be of long-term significance. The Abel Tasman National Park was established in 1942; possums were no longer a protected species after 1946 (there had been open season on mustelids since 1936); the takahe was rescued from assumed extinction in Fiordland in 1948; and the Forest Act, with its indigenous forest controls, was passed in 1949.

Where Britain Goes, We Go

In declaring war, Savage said, of Britain: "Where she goes, we go; where she stands we stand". And that meant the government was prepared once again to send its young men to fight in the Middle East and Europe. In retrospect, it was a surprising response given the British government's view of the upstart Labour administration, and a clutch of local concerns ranging from pointless First World War deaths to Japan's obvious territorial ambitions and the country's almost total lack of defence preparedness. The two army divisions that served overseas were New Zealand's major military contribution to the allied war effort. General Freyberg, the country's most famous soldier, commanded the Second Division, from the ill-judged foray into Greece and the desperate defence of Crete, and then through the Middle East campaigns as part of the Eighth Army. In December 1942, a secret session of parliament decided the Second Division should stay in the Middle East despite Japan's rapid advance southwards. Later, Freyberg led the regrouped division during the Italian campaign. The Third Division, under General Barrowclough, played a peripheral role in the Pacific theatre during 1943.

1. Because of the seriously deteriorating war situation, in October 1941 it was agreed to delay the election until 1943. Labour retained the treasury benches with a reduced majority. *Interval for Voting*, Gordon Minhinnick, *NZ Herald*, June 20 1941. ATL: A-311-1-018
2. Nevile Lodge went to war as a corporal in the Second NZEF. Captured at El Alamein, he sold his first cartoons while a prisoner of war in a prison camp in Italy. *"It s funny ....."*, Nevile Lodge, ca 1943. ATL: DX-024-002
3. The saga of the Second NZEF – in and out of the front line – in the Middle East, Greece, Crete and Italy. *This is My Story, This is My Song*, Neville Colvin, *NZEF Times*, May 14 1945. ATL: B-154-221

1

INTERVAL FOR VOTING.

2

3

THIS IS MY STORY, THIS IS MY SONG
RTO
ADOLF HERE I COME-
EGGS-A-COOK
VERY NICE, VERY SWEET
VERY CLEAN, VERY HYGIENE
GETTING BROWNED OFF
THE MAADI BUST
CAIRO
BED & BREAKFAST
FDC
GEOLOGY COURSE
SHUFTI-SHAFTO'S
BUG-HOUSE
BAB-EL-LOUK
EL MREIR DEPRESSION
WEED KILLER
STUKA VALLEY
NECESSITY
THE TINY TANK
MINISTRY OF INFORMATION
GEZIRA
COOKED TOURS
SUNNY ITALY
NAPLES
MOSTKITOS AND MOSTWASKIS
THE PIPPLE OF NEW ZILLOND THANK YOU —
ROMAN ARCHITECTURE
ITALIAN STREET SCENE
ITALIAN COUNTRYSIDE
HIGH OCTANE
SHOOT DAT TIGER
THE MAORI MOUNTED RIFLE BATTALION
VICTORY
IT'S HAD IT
I HEARD - AND HE RECKONS
SPERIAMO
— YOUR GUESS IS AS GOOD AS MINE
— NEVILLE COLVIN —

War Work

Labour fought the war, abroad and at home, as vigorously as it had laid the foundations of the welfare state from 1936-39. Despite increasing manpower problems – with so many New Zealanders in the armed forces – farm production was boosted to feed Britain and US armed forces in the Pacific. The government felt the prodigious wartime effort could be achieved only by the introduction and unblushing enforcement of emergency regulations that severely limited freedom of speech and personal liberty – there was much stricter press censorship in New Zealand than in Britain and little tolerance of aliens, conscientious objectors, and others morally or ideologically opposed to the war. Clearly, Labour was most committed to safeguarding standard-of-living gains and used its emergency powers to enforce price stabilisation and wage controls. Labour was also determined to pay war costs as they were incurred. Every effort was made to increase dairy and meat production to maximise export income; heavy taxation and internal loans absorbed surplus money supply.

1. In addition to the export push, there was – given the difficulty and cost of imports – a strong emphasis on eating, smoking and 'buying New Zealand'. During the war the volume of manufacturing output jumped 30 percent. Local cigarette production doubled. *The Patriot*, Gordon Minhinnick, *NZ Herald*, April 3 1941. ATL: A-311-1-017
2. The BMA's continuing obstruction of Labour's universal health scheme was seen increasingly as economic self-interest – and all the more deplorable in war-time. Most doctors gave way in 1941. *St Sebastian – 1941*, H W Bennett, *NZ Observer*, September 24 1941. ATL: J-065-056
3. Three ships mined or sunk by German raiders close to New Zealand underlined how defenceless the country was. The Home Guard, a sort of ill-equipped 'Dad's Army', topped 120,000 in numbers but was only slightly better than nothing until the first US troops arrived in mid-1942. *Getting Nearer Home*, J C Hill, *Auckland Star*, June 1940. ATL: A-314-3-003
4. The five-day, 40-hour week was a major Labour achievement but under emergency war regulations many worked longer hours (watersiders up to 84 a week) without overtime payments. *"What did you do ....?"*, Fox, *Standard*, June 12 1941. ATL: A-313-2-039
5. Rationing began with petrol in 1939, followed by tea and sugar, and then, after the 1943 election, a number of basic commodities including butter, meat and cheese. *Buttercuts and Dazes*, Gordon Minhinnick, *NZ Herald*, October 7 1943. ATL: A-311-1-020

1

THE PATRIOT.

2

ST SEBASTIAN – 1941
(The B.M.A. suffering the 'slings and arrows of outrageous fortune' at the hands of New Zealand's Labour Government – After Botticelli's famous painting of the early Christian martyr, who was left for dead by the Roman Emperor Diocletian's archers).

3 GETTING NEARER HOME.

4

5

BUTTERCUTS AND DAZES.

The Master Politician

Although Peter Fraser played a part in shaping Labour's election-winning 1935 policies and tactics and was an effective health and education minister, he succeeded Savage in 1940 mainly because of his political judgment and skill. The stereotypically dour and industrious Highland Scot, Fraser came to New Zealand as a young militant socialist and was jailed for his anti-conscription beliefs. He was much tougher and shrewder than Savage and an able, energetic war-time leader. He appeared untroubled by the harshly restrictive measures the war and then the post-war situation justified. An increasingly conservative 'cold war' convert, his promotion of peace-time conscription offended many loyal supporters and his unwillingness to ease restrictions increasingly antagonised the rest of the country. Together, they made National's 1949 victory all the more inevitable.

1. A prominent parliamentarian by 1927, Fraser admitted that while a great majority of unemployed were genuine cases, there were some "wasters in the Labour class". *The Waster – Peter Removes the Halo*, Stuart Peterson, *The Free Lance*, February 16 1927. ATL: A-315-3-054
2. Labour's leaders had strong personal philosophical objections to conscription, and it was not until July 1940 that the government agreed to conscription by ballot. *Nightmare*, Maxwell, *Otago Daily Times*, May 25 1940 ATL: J-065-067
3. While Fraser visited London and Washington several times during the war and impressed with his clear-sighted views on international affairs, his reputation at home was unravelling. *The Great Barnum*, H W Bennett, *NZ Observer*, September 13 1944. ATL: J-065-066
4. Weary after over a decade in power, Labour scraped home at the 1946 election, its Maori MPs making the difference. With the public unhappy with continuing restrictions, and some unions more militant, National was sniffing a change in the electoral breeze. *"What! You can t see ANY of them?"*, Neville Colvin, *Evening Post*, November 21 1947. ATL: A-317-078
5. While Labour was under increasing pressure at home, Fraser was widely respected internationally, chairing the trusteeship committee at the conference that created the United Nations. *Call of the Wild*, Gordon Minhinnick, *NZ Herald*, February 22 1946. ATL: A-311-1-022

1

THE WASTER – PETER REMOVES THE HALO.

2

NIGHTMARE!

3

THE GREAT BARNUM.

4

"What! You can't see ANY of them?"

5

CALL OF THE WILD

Chalk & Cheese

Aside from Fraser, the most prominent members of Labour's cabinet – one of the most capable and industrious in New Zealand's history – were Walter Nash and Bob Semple, two men who could hardly have been more different. Nash, a 'Christian socialist' from the English Midlands, and in many ways Labour's ablest minister, joined Labour from a commercial rather than a trade union background. As party secretary, then MP, he was a major force, organising, writing the 1935 manifesto, and helping frame the social security and guaranteed price schemes. During the war he regularly represented New Zealand at war councils in Washington and London. Bob Semple, one of Labour's most colourfully outspoken ministers, had preached socialism with evangelical fervour, and was widely known as 'Bob the Ranter'. An Australian-born miner and 'Red Fed' orator, Semple was imprisoned in 1916 for opposing war-time conscription. In June 1940, he drew the marble for the first conscription ballot under the just enacted national service emergency regulations.

1. Walter Nash, Labour's minister of finance, funded the government's ambitious schemes – his approach more orthodox than the party's credit reformers wanted – and administered war-time price and wage stabilisation. Nash's determination to 'tax to the economic limit for war purposes' and encourage import substitution was spectacularly successful in avoiding post-war debts. *Our Political Paragon*, J C Hill, *Auckland Star* ca 1940. ATL: A-314-3-004
2. Coates had devalued the NZ pound in 1933; Nash returned the exchange rate to parity with sterling in August 1948 to ease inflationary pressures. Sterling balances were at very high levels. *"Sixth Floor Going Down Ground Floor!"*, Gordon Minhinnick, *NZ Herald*, August 21 1948. ATL: A-311-1-027
3. Semple viewed the world in simple, black-and-white terms and the public works portfolio, in a period when it got back to the business of the nation's physical development, suited his personality perfectly. *His Mark*, Gordon Minhinnick, *NZ Herald*, July 21 1948. ATL: A-311-1-026
4. There was an enduring image of Semple at the controls of a giant tractor crushing an old wheelbarrow and shovel. In his fiefdom, wages and jobs expanded, machinery grappled with the tougher work and schemes proliferated. *Ole Man River*, Gordon Minhinnick, *NZ Herald*, July 3 1948. ATL: A-311-1-023

1

OUR POLITICAL PARAGON

2

"SIXTH FLOOR GOING DOWN GROUND FLOOR!"

3

HIS MARK

4

OLE MAN RIVER

Out of Puff

After a no-holds-barred campaign in 1946, Labour struggled back to the treasury benches. In power since 1935, including six uncertain, spartan, war-time years, the government had steadily lost its temporary dairy farmer support, yet it did little to ease unpopular war-time restrictions. Stabilisation policies were retained for fear of a post-war slump, and food rationing was continued to maximise exports to Britain. Although Britain's recovery was vital to the local economy, the government showed little sympathy for the understandable frustrations of New Zealanders who expected a return to greater private affluence. The government did not placate its own caucus despite a substantial child allowance increase, and nationalisation of coal mines and the Bank of New Zealand. Labour's 1949 loss was all the more inevitable when party solidarity was shattered by Fraser's 'cold war' obsession with peace-time conscription – New Zealand's contribution to vigilance against the supposedly creeping tentacles of international communism.

1. There was a steady rise in the number of strikes and Fraser, who was MP for Wellington Central until 1946, was well aware that the government's 'weakness' in handling them would have electoral consequences. *Let Battle Commence*, Gordon Minhinnick, *NZ Herald*, July 9 1946. ATL: A-311-1-024
2. The electorate was tired of rationing, shortages and state control, but Labour did not loosen its grip. It very nearly lost the 1946 election, 'life-saved' by the margin of the four Maori seats. *Opening the Life-Saving Season*, Neville Colvin, *Sports Post*, November 9 1946. ATL: B-154-069
3. By 1949 the government's relations with more militant unions, particularly the watersiders, had deteriorated badly. *"The Government Takes a Most Serious View ....",* Gordon Minhinnick, *NZ Herald*, March 10 1949. ATL: A-311-1-028
4. Some thought the national health service had gone too far; social services accounted for 3.3 percent of national income in 1928 but 16 percent in 1949. *Free Medicine*, Gordon Minhinnick, *NZ Herald*, May 13 1948. ATL: A-311-1-025
5. National wanted to play a more open, less restrictive 'game' Labour wanted to maintain the 'tight five' control that had produced economic stability. *Test Match Tactics*, Neville Colvin, *Evening Post*, May 13 1949. ATL: E-549-q-01-024

1

LET BATTLE COMMENCE!

2

3

"The Government takes a most serious view…"

4

FREE MEDICINE.

5

TEST MATCH TACTICS.

Right for a Change

In the late 1930s there had been scant opposition to Labour's legislative programme. Although Adam Hamilton led a better organised National into the 1938 election, the party made little progress until Sid Holland toppled him in late 1940. National had not approved of Hamilton and Coates joining the war cabinet mid-year and Holland rebuffed several invitations to join it, though he did agree to the postponement of the 1941 election until 1943. He also took some of his front-benchers into the 1942 war administration, with its seven Labour and six National representatives, but he marched them out again after only three months. Hamilton and Coates returned to the war cabinet as individuals, but there were no further attempts to bridge party differences. Under Holland's tough-talking leadership, National tagged Labour the 'shortage government', attacked centralised state control and steadily won support.

1. Adam Hamilton, with a drooping gait and a personality to match, had the unenviable task of trying to unite the surviving remnants of the largely discredited United, Reform and Democrat parties. His comment that the party held fast to "whatever was good in the past" did not inspire universal confidence. *Vulcan s Waterloo*, Fox, *Standard*, February 18 1937. ATL: A-313-2-003

2. In 1943 and 1946, National, swallowing the concept of social security without any signs of philosophical indigestion, reduced Labour's majority. *"On Me, It Looks Better"*, Fox, *Standard*, March 8 1945. ATL: A-313-2-059

3. It was a pattern that was to become familiar; National accepted Labour's major policies, quibbling only at 'socialistic' implementation. *Getting Him Ready for the Big Race*, Fox, *Standard*, July 11 1946. ATL: A-313-2-048

4. It rankled National that only the four Maori seats had been the difference between winning and losing the 1946 election. *"If only he had a drop of Maori blood ....",* Neville Colvin, *Evening Post*, July 3 1947. ATL: J-065-054

5. After the 1946 election, and despite Labour's economic successes, National struck a very basic chord with the public as the private enterprise champion which would put an end to unnecessary controls and restrictions. *NZ is Wrecked*, John McNamara, *Southern Cross*, 1947. ATL: A-369-079

1

2

3

GETTING HIM READY FOR THE BIG RACE

4

"If only he had a drop of Maori blood in him – he'd be a crackerjack!"

5

Screwed Down and Up-Tight

At the beginning of the decade it looked as if a new, exciting era was opening up, New Zealand's isolation ended by trans-Tasman flying boats that landed in Auckland and Sydney harbours like giant, ponderous ducks. But while a great many young New Zealanders travelled, to war rather than on holiday, life in New Zealand took on an austerity still well-remembered from the depression years. When the war was over the country hankered for a return to normality and the uninterrupted certainty of everyday life. It was about 'nesting', and the dream of happy nuclear families in mushrooming suburbia was the romantic ideal. However, the elderly, straight-laced politicians in control continued a number of war-time measures like rationing.

1. Although Australia was, potentially, now so much closer, for most people there was no rush to international air travel after the war. Some New Zealanders had seen the first jet aircraft that visited in 1946 but it was to be a long time before they were heard regularly in the skies over New Zealand. *Another Milestone Gone*, Neil Lonsdale, *NZ Observer*, May1 1940. ATL: A-316-4-002
2. The state continued to regulate drinking habits with a heavy hand. Six o'clock closing had begun in 1917 and, to the astonishment of many, was retained by a large majority at a 1949 referendum. *State Control*, Neville Colvin, *Evening Post*, September 4 1946. ATL: J-065-053
3. War news on the radio was now about rugby. In 1949 the All Blacks toured South Africa for the second time, the first visit 21 years previously. In a dour, bruising 25-match tour the All Blacks lost all four test matches. *Bedtime Story*, Gordon Minhinnick, *NZ Herald*, September 6 1949. ATL: A-311-1-029
4. Even though petrol rationing remained through the decade, the annual family holiday was an important part of returning normality. Throughout the country there were motor camps, usually run by local authorities, with camping and caravan sites affordable for most New Zealanders. *"Hoi – why can t you use the gate like everyone else?"*, Neville Colvin, *Sports Post*, April 8 1950. ATL: B-154-104

1

ANOTHER MILESTONE GONE

2

State Control.

3

BEDTIME STORY

4

7: 1950-1959
1951 AND ALL THAT

The 1950s – and the following decade – were final vindication for the back-breaking, are-things-going-to get-better decades of toil that had transformed New Zealand from primeval forest to productive farm land. There was now unprecedented and widely-based prosperity.

National, the product of the unpromising remnants of the Reform and United parties, was in charge, and successfully so. Although Adam Hamilton had helped to unite the warring factions, it had been Sidney George Holland, party leader from 1940, who put muscle into National's performance. The party's gains at the 1943 and 1946 elections were helped by a combination of its private enterprise credo with Labour's concept of social security.

Labour's commitment to state control looked even more unpalatable after the war and, with National backing its call for more competition and free enterprise with an efficient party organisation, there was an increasing inevitability about a change of government.

National won the 1949 election with a comfortable 12-seat majority. Holland's role was now more to undo than to do. To general relief, he progressively ended wartime rationing of butter and petrol; freed up import licensing to some extent; removed price controls on urban land; allowed tenants to buy their state houses; and gave majority control of agricultural boards to the producers.

Two of Holland's principal election planks had been abolition of parliament's upper house, the Legislative Council and, more controversially, of compulsory unionism. The first was something of a personal crusade; the second had all his caucus firmly behind it.

The ineffectual Legislative Council, its membership heavily weighted with pensioned off Labour MPs and sympathisers, was an obvious target for the first-term National administration. In 1950 Holland appointed to the Council sufficient National supporters, dubbed the 'suicide squad', to carry a vote for its dissolution. This duly happened in August 1950.

Once controls were lifted, after the long period of enforced economic stability, living costs began to rise sharply and militant unions, with little faith in any politicians and none in Fintan Patrick Walsh's Federation of Labour, increased the tempo of their disruptions and stoppages. There was a growing feeling that some unionists were holding the country to ransom; all vital exports passed through the ports and, before much mechanisation, the hands of waterside workers. Certainly, the strategically important and most militant unions – watersiders, seamen, freezing workers and miners – were best placed to push for monetary and other concessions.

Coupling a shrewd awareness of public feeling with personal relish for the task, Holland set about smashing the militant unions. He was helped by divisiveness in the union movement over the resulting 1951 wharf stoppage which involved clashes of personalities as well as principles.

At the beginning of 1951 a wage demand confrontation between shipowners and watersiders gave Holland the opportunity to impose emergency regulations. The Watersiders' Union was de-registered and its funds seized; the armed forces worked the wharves; freezing workers and miners struck in sympathy. The strike lasted 151 bitter days until July 11 – nearly five months of industrial strife, hardship for strikers and their families, considerable economic loss, and a loathing of right-wing governments that would fade only slowly. For Holland it was almost complete victory; compulsory unionism might have survived but the most militant and strategically important unions were broken.

The 1951 confrontation, and easily inflamed public fears about communism, provided National with the opportunity to call the first snap election of the century. Snared by a divided union movement and its own conservatism, Labour was accused of 'fence-sitting' during the waterfront crisis, and of communist sympathies during the rough election campaign that resulted in National's majority increasing to 20 seats. It did not seem to matter that National had belied its free-enterprise claims with repressive legislation infringing personal liberties.

National did much to smother opposition with a diligent pursuit of political consensus; Labour was hamstrung by its shared commitment to safeguarding the new levels of prosperity and to sheltering under the United States' defensive umbrella, with its accompanying involvement in the Korean War and signing of ANZUS and SEATO pacts. The 1951 signing of the ANZUS treaty with the United States and Australia was an important foreign policy development, Holland seeing no contradictions as he endlessly repeated his trade-related mantra that he was "a Britisher through and through".

High export returns during the early 1950s launched a sustained period of economic growth. A farmers' cabinet, with Keith Holyoake an able and energetic minister of agriculture, gave top priority to the rural sector; there were also solid achievements with forestry, road-building, power generation and housing. Not surprisingly, the 1954 election was won comfortably. Holland who, unusually, had been minister of finance as well as prime minister since winning the treasury benches, now relaxed his tight political and policy grip a little. He was no intellectual, but wise enough to delegate authority to talented cabinet colleagues, and this included passing the finance portfolio to Jack Watts.

Holland's health declined during 1956 but, ill though

he was, he would not hand over to Keith Holyoake until less than three months to the 1957 election. It was insufficient time for Holyoake, the loyal deputy for nearly eight years, to settle comfortably into the prime ministership.

Despite challenges, Labour's Walter Nash had been leader of the opposition since Peter Fraser died in December 1950. Now, in 1957, the imminent introduction of Pay As You Earn (PAYE) income tax provided both political parties with the opportunity to tempt voters with tax concessions. Labour's £100 tax rebate, coupled with the promise of 3 percent loans for housing and the abolition of compulsory military training, resulted in the narrowest of victories. At 75, Walter Nash became New Zealand's oldest incoming prime minister. Labour's two-seat majority was very much a personal triumph for Nash, but he was equally responsible for the party's defeat three years later.

This other Eden.

Neville Colvin, *Evening Post*, ca 1953-56. ATL: H-705-014

Labour inherited a serious balance of payments after years of National largesse and Nash, still with vivid memories of his cap-in-hand journey to London in 1938 to fund the first Labour government's promises, was determined to avoid large-scale overseas borrowing. However, Nash and finance minister Arnold Nordmeyer seriously misjudged the New Zealand public with the principled, but politically naïve, June 1958 'Black Budget' that savagely taxed cigarette, liquor and petrol consumption.

If this was not damaging enough, two projects that were part of an attempt to build the country's industrial base – an aluminium smelter and cotton mill – proved particularly controversial. Even more damaging electorally was Nash's support of the Rugby Union's decision to send an 'all-white' team to South Africa.

Whether battling the enemy abroad or austerity at home – wartime dreams had been for a quiet, comfortable, normal suburban family life, and young couples hurried to marry and bring up children in the sunshine instead of the shadow of depression and world war. The media and films romanticised marriage, housewifery and child-bearing. A period of sustained prosperity, coupled with the family benefit and generous housing loans, meant that nuclear families in their own suburban bungalows became wood and brick reality and the birth rate in New Zealand came close to doubling between the late 1940s and the mid-1960s.

The baby-boom parents, their conservatism and preoccupation with the material things of life profoundly affected the 1950s. Their 'baby-boomer' children would be as influential, but in different ways, in later decades.

There was a discernible smugness about New Zealand in the 1950s. Edmund Hillary had, after all, climbed Everest; Yvette Williams jumped further than any other woman at the Olympics; Godfrey Bowen shore a world-record number of sheep; and the All Blacks defeated South Africa three tests to one during a home rugby series. The population had reached two million in 1952, and the staging of the Commonwealth Games at the beginning of the decade and the opening of the harbour bridge in 1959 were confirmation that Auckland was one of the world's great cities. To the vast majority of New Zealanders, the Tangiwai ('Weeping Waters') rail disaster on Christmas Eve 1954, during the visit of Queen Elizabeth 11, was an aberration, not a sign of the gods' displeasure as claimed by some Maori. They had been unhappy about aspects of the royal tour, the first by a ruling monarch.

If New Zealand is committed to any 'ism', it is surely materialism. And in the good times keeping up with the Jones has meant catching up with the new products available since export prices last peaked. Whether it has been motor cars or cellphones, New Zealanders have been early experimenters and often very quickly among the world's heaviest buyers and users. These 'league tables' probably say more about life in New Zealand than its place on the OECD standard-of-living list.

While time and labour-saving appliances in the home might have been luxuries before, women expected them in the prosperous early 1950s, even though most of them had returned to suburbia from their wartime jobs. By 1956, according to that year's census, more than half of all New Zealand homes now had washing machines, refrigerators and electric stoves. The same year New Zealand had the highest income per person in the world.

In the late 1930s about 80 percent of Maori lived in rural New Zealand. When there were 'manpower' shortages in the cities during the war, and after it, when the 'bright lights' contrasted with limited countryside opportunities, there was a sizeable and growing migration of mainly young Maori to urban centres, particularly Auckland. Housing was a particular problem as most of the new city-dwellers were in low-skilled, low paying jobs. Until 1947, Maori were not eligible for state housing, the unblushingly stated reasons being that they would 'lower the tone' and not be able to afford the rent. After 1947, when the government changed the rules, Maori families were 'pepper-potted' in pakeha areas, but as numbers swelled they increasingly concentrated together. These areas, ghettos to some, eventually nurtured a new and different urban culture and identity. But it was not an easy process for Maori: the culture shock was considerable and there was no extended family for support and advice. At the end of the war, about 25 percent of Maori lived in cities and towns; by the mid-fifties it was 35 percent with the pace accelerating.

In the 1940s adolescents did what was expected of them. Few thought of tertiary education when they left school. During the war, most young men joined the armed forces as soon as they could; young women went to work, contributing to the family's budget until they married and had children.

In the 1950s, however, a social revolution spread throughout the prosperous western world. Parents, who had been through depression and world war, wanted more for their children – more education, more leisure, more money to spend. Sensing a new phenomenon – a brand new, large and growing market with spending power – sharp-eyed advertising experts coined the term 'teenager'. Then, with the willing assistance of magazines, movies, record companies and radio, and newly powerful television, they fashioned the 'identikit' teenager – complete with his and her vocabulary, clothes, music and disturbing disregard for parental authority. The new teenagers liked what they were told, and 'rock and rolled' their parts with relish.

With technology's advances, the teenage phenomenon was replicated in New Zealand – disc jockeys playing rock and roll, juke boxes in milkbars, bodgies and widgies – at much the same time as the rest of the world. Parental controls weakened markedly. Radios had been solid, expensive pieces of furniture, plugged into the living-room wall with parents, usually fathers, often controlling the knobs and the family's listening patterns. When transistor radios arrived, they became as much a 1950s symbol of teenage independence as cellphones were a half century later. Parents struggled to understand their teenagers, the 'generation gap' becoming a reality. An increase in 'juvenile delinquency' was blamed on teenage culture and, after publicity about the sexual escapades of Hutt Valley secondary school students, a commission of inquiry blamed, in part, the corrupting influence of American films and pulp fiction. The 'Mazengarb Report' was mailed, in November 1954, to all 300,000 households receiving the family benefit and two films – *The Wild One* and *Rebel Without a Cause* – were promptly banned. Just as likely to have been contributory factors were the bleak, sprawling new suburbs without the facilities to occupy young people with time on their hands.

Television might have been on its way to New Zealand, with experiments and demonstrations beginning, but radio was at its most influential in the 1950s. The popular home entertainment was dominated by Selywn Toogood and Jack Maybury, presenters of programmes like *It's in the Bag* and *The 64 Hundred Show*, often recorded in filled-to-overflowing town halls. DJs like Neville Chamberlain and Des Britten appealed to the teenage market. More seriously, the Concert Programme began in 1950 and the first Mobil Song Quest, to be important to the careers of opera stars like Kiri Te Kanawa and Malvina Major, was held in 1956.

The NZBS's drama department had begun back in 1938, but in the 1950s and early 1960s – when radio's future was under increasing threat – it was the fertile training ground for a generation of actors and writers who would be successful on the stage, in television and, sometimes, film.

There had been hints of it for two decades, but there was, in the 1950s, an impressive outpouring of imaginative riches from novelists, dramatists and poets. Among fiction writers, Frank Sargeson with his 'realist' narrative style and blunt local idioms was the dominant force, but impressive novels were written by Dan Davin, James Courage, Janet Frame, Ruth France and David Ballantyne. Bruce Mason was the most important playwright. Not only did he meet head on the big issues of cultural identity and erosion of traditional values, but he pioneered solo performance at a time when professional theatre was in its tentative infancy. His *The End of the Golden Weather* became a New Zealand classic and he performed it nearly 1,000 times. Younger poets like James Baxter, Louis Johnson, Alistair Campbell and W H Oliver robustly challenged the views of their older colleagues.

Unlike their counterparts earlier in the century, painters who made a singular mark in the 1950s and beyond –

ELEVEN TOP AMERICAN TRAVEL AGENCY HEADS
WILL BE SHOWN THE NORTH ISLAND TOURIST RESORTS
BY A SENIOR OFFICER OF THE GOVERNMENT TOURIST BUREAU.
.........NEWS.
NEW ZEALAND

"THAT ?—NOTHING THERE BUT SCENERY."

Sid Scales, *Otago Daily Times*, January 14 1954. A-311-4-003

Colin McCahon and Toss Woollaston among them – produced their major work in New Zealand. Through the 1950s, Cubism's motifs and spatial ideas provided starting points for artists like McCahon, T A McCormack, Louise Henderson, John Weeks and W A Sutton. In 1954, McCahon painted *I am*, one of his first 'word' paintings. Later in the decade, a number of young Maori artists, trained in European techniques, began to impress. Some like Cliff Whiting and Para Matchitt used Maori motifs modified by western art styles; others including Ralph Hotere and Selwyn Muru, were more influenced by modern western art

Eating out was a possibility, if still limited, in the late 1950s. Before the war, some among the very limited number of European immigrants – Greeks in Wellington and some Jewish refugees – had opened grill rooms and milk bar/restaurants in the cities. The department stores appealed to their generally upmarket clientele with tearooms that made a feature of palm trees, silverware, white tablecloths, and waitresses in crisply starched black and white uniforms. However, returning soldiers and new migrant groups during the 1950s wanted more variety and eating out opportunities. By the end of the decade, major centres had at least one Chinese restaurant and the first coffee bars were appearing, but the old-style tearooms continued, male-oriented pubs closed at 6 o'clock and the few restaurants, all dry, had shut their doors by 10 o'clock.

Motoring was at full throttle again after the lack of cars and petrol in the 1940s. In 1950 the 'No Remittance Licence' scheme was introduced, with private funds held outside New Zealand eligble for use as new car deposits. This, and some easing of import licences in later years, meant new cars flooded into the country. By the end of the 1950s, car registrations had jumped to nearly 490,000 – a 114 percent increase – with only 39 percent of them now more than 10 years old.

Solid Sid

Sidney George Holland was the prototype National politician: shrewd, aggressive and much more a pragmatist than political theorist. A Christchurch businessman, and MP from 1935, he replaced Adam Hamilton as National's leader in 1940. Apart from a brief period in the war administration, Holland distanced himself from the government. With his aggressive politics-as-usual approach, he chipped away at Labour in 1943 – his manifesto marrying Labour's social welfare concerns with competitive free enterprise – and at the 1946 election. After winning a workable majority in 1949, Holland vigorously dismantled state controls and, in 1951, had no qualms about squaring up to and defeating the militant unions, then ramming the advantage home at a snap election. A period of rapid economic growth followed but was accompanied by cost-of-living increases that had seriously eroded National's support before Holland, seriously ill, finally stood aside late in 1957.

1. Holland, who was also minister of finance until 1954, advocated a change in the way tax was paid, but the move from annual tax payments to a Pay As You Earn (PAYE) system did not happen until shortly before the 1957 election. *Ye Olde Paye Daye Pilgrimage*, F D Choate, *NZ Observer*, March 22 1950. ATL: J-065-058
2. After the 1949 election National quickly removed a number of lingering wartime controls and reduced government subsidies. *"You ll have to walk, I want the carpet back!"*, Keith Waite, *Otago Daily Times*, May 18 1950. ATL: A-312-7-020
3. After a long period of comparative economic stability, living costs began to rise sharply which, in turn, raised the unfounded spectre of widespread unemployment. *Waiting for the Cue*, Fox, *Standard*, March 12 1952. ATL: A-313-2-060
4. At the 1954 election, National's majority was halved, Labour won back a handful of seats and Social Credit, fighting its first political campaign, took more than 10% of the popular vote. *Policy Pounding*, Sid Scales, *Otago Daily Times*, November 3 1954. ATL: A-311-4-004
5. Prime minister for eight years, Holland's greatest achievement was to turn the unpromising, newly-formed National Party into the country's most effective political organisation. *How Tall?,* Neville Colvin, *Evening Post*, Evening Post, June 15 1955. ATL: C-132-890

1

YE OLDE PAYE DAYE PILGRIMAGE.

2

"YOU'LL HAVE TO WALK, I WANT THE CARPET BACK!"

3

Waiting for the Cue

4

POLICY POUNDING.

5

HOW TALL?

The Sinking of the Watersiders

When National removed controls in 1950, inflation bit sharply and the watersiders, members of one of the unions in the militant Trade Union Congress, wanted more money. Early in 1951, shipowners tried to include an earlier award to watersiders in a 15 percent Arbitration Court wage order. When the angry watersiders banned overtime work, employers retaliated by laying off men and the dispute quickly flared into the longest, most costly stoppage in New Zealand history. Backed by employers, farmers, the press, and the Federation of Labour, the government proclaimed a state of emergency, imposing harsh regulations. The Waterside Workers' Union was de-registered and its funds seized, but the watersiders' leaders, Jock Barnes and Toby Hill, were slow to realize how completely isolated they were. The dispute lasted 151 days and there was considerable hardship, and some isolated violence, before the watersiders conceded defeat.

1 With a record 271,500 man-days lost to strikes in 1950 at the height of an export boom, and with ships queueing up to be loaded, Minister of Labour Bill Sullivan faced a critical industrial situation. *"What I need, Mr Sullivan ....",* Keith Waite, *Otago Daily Times*, October 28 1950. ATL: E-549-q-2-049

2. Under cold war pressure, the FOL changed its international affiliation to a US-backed confederation. When the watersiders left the FOL, but retained links with the Soviet-supported World Federation of Trade Unions, Holland and F P Walsh claimed – wrongly – that the 'wharfie' leaders were communists. "*Hands up all those ....*". Gordon Minhinnick, *NZ Herald*, February 27 1951. ATL: A-311-1-030

3. When Holland used wartime emergency powers still in force, and added others, to crush the watersiders, there was widespread concern at draconian moves against freedom of speech, assembly and other democratic rights. *"The country is right behind the government"*, JRC, *Here & Now*, May 1951. ATL: J-065-062

4. With media coverage universally and often violently opposed to them, the watersiders told their side of the story in crude cyclostyled pamphlets. *"The government could take over the port ..."*, Jack Manson, *illegal watersiders bulletin*, August 1951. ATL: J-065-065

5. After the 1951 dispute, many militants were never able to return to waterfront work; the more acquiescent who did, and ensured the smooth loading of frozen lamb carcasses, were well rewarded. *"Shed No. 6 at 5 o clock sharp, please Jenkins"*, Sid Scales, *Otago Daily Times*, September 30 1953. ATL: A-311-4-002

1

'WHAT I NEED, MR SULLIVAN, IS A BAZOOKA!"

2

"HANDS UP ALL THOSE WHO VOTE FOR A STRIKE!"

3

"THE COUNTRY IS RIGHT BEHIND THE GOVERNMENT."
Statement to Australia.

4

"the Government could take over the port AND RUN IT ITSELF!!" (Big Bill)

5

"SHED NO. 6 AT 5 O'CLOCK SHARP, PLEASE JENKINS."

On the Sheep's Back

National won power in 1949 on a private-prosperity platform. The government loosened controls and, with timely assistance from the Korean War wool boom, built up agriculture and a neglected infrastructure. For the next decade, and well beyond, pastoral production developed rapidly – largely due to widespread mechanisation and electrification, stock breeding and pasture improvements, war declared against rabbits and other pests and the daring young men of the new aerial topdressing industry. In addition, favourable terms of trade and regular overseas borrowing underwrote a mushrooming population's developing taste for affluence. In 1957 Holland's health was in decline, but when he announced his retirement it was too short a time for his deputy Keith Holyoake to sufficiently raise his prime ministerial profile before the election contest with Walter Nash, a long-time national institution.

1. National knew it would be political suicide, even in prosperous times, to turn back the social security clock. Under National, state spending even grew slightly on the 1949 level of 28 percent of gross national product. *Social Insecurity*, Keith Waite, *Otago Daily Times*, August 26 1950. ATL: E-549-q-2-020
2. The Korean War in the early 1950s generated a significant boost in the demand for, and price of, wool. Briefly, the wartime price of 12 pence a pound of wool rocketed to 160 pence or higher. Prices peaked in 1951 when, frustratingly, the waterfront dispute reduced the number of shipments. *Sensational Wool Values*, Keith Waite, *Otago Daily Times*, November 16 1950. ATL: A-312-7-019
3. One of the increasing signs of affluence was the number of cars on the road. Now considered more a necessity than a luxury for most New Zealand families, during the decade the number of cars increased to the point where there was one for every 4.8 people. *"…. And that s our Working Men s Club"*, Tom Mayne, *The Press*, ca 1952. ATL: J-065-061
4. F P Walsh, the powerful Federation of Labour president, was close adviser to governments of both stripes. In 1958, with dairy export prices collapsing, Labour reduced the guaranteed-price pay-out. *"Mr Walsh wants you on the telephone!"*, Gordon Minhinnick, *NZ Herald*, April 30 1958. ATL: A-311-1-032
5. In the 1950s, New Zealand's economy was dependent on one market and very few products. However, 'diversification', a new word to farmers, was beginning to be heard and applied more later in the decade. *"Talk about farmers vocabulary …."*, Murray Ball, *Manawatu Times*, May 1959. ATL: J-047-003

1

SOCIAL INSECURITY.

2

3

4

"MR WALSH WANTS YOU ON THE TELEPHONE!"

5

"Talk about farmers' vocabulary – I see you forgot to mention to Harry that you had decided to introduce a bit of African stock to diversify your herd…"

The Great Procrastinator

Walter Nash succeeded to the Labour leadership when Fraser died in December 1950. The next year, his natural sympathy for the watersiders, and his aversion to Holland's repressive tactics, conflicted with his concern that the 'wharfie' leaders were being unduly perverse. When Nash became prime minister, by the slimmest margin, six years later, 22 years after he first became a cabinet minister, he inherited a snowballing, balance-of-payments crisis. However, Labour's politically naïve over-reaction to it, immortalised in Nordmeyer's 'Black Budget', ensured that Nash had only one term as PM. Nash was leader of the Labour Party until 1963 and served his Hutt electorate until his death in 1968. Honoured and respected as the 'grand old man' of New Zealand politics, Sir Walter was one of the ablest ministers of finance the country ever had and remained, through his long political career, true to his own moderate brand of Christian socialism.

1

"WE HOPE HE'LL BE O.K. FOR THE BIG FIGHT"

2

1. Nash's neither-for-nor-against-the-watersiders stance was widely ridiculed and Labour lost more ground at the snap 1951 election. *"We hope he ll be O.K. for the big fight"*, Keith Waite, *Otago Daily Times*, July 27 1951. ATL: H-723-002
2. The 1957 election was so close – a wafer-thin two-seat margin – it was not certain on election night that Labour had won. *"All I want for Christmas ... "*, Neil Lonsdale, *Auckland Star*, December 1957. ATL: A-309-045
3. Nearing 80, Walter Nash was a bundle of peripatetic energy. As prime minister he bustled around the world discussing disarmament and other weighty matters with the leaders of Britain, the United States, India, USSR, and the United Nations. However, while respected internationally, his regular absences did not impress New Zealand voters. *"Same Seat?"*, Neil Lonsdale, *Auckland Star*, February 18 1959. ATL: E-549-q-13-060
4. Nash's 'a bob both ways' reputation, acquired in 1951, haunted him for the rest of his career. It was not helped by his indecision and procrastination when he finally became prime minister. *"No it doesn t! It means ...."*, Gordon Minhinnick, *NZ Herald*, March 20 1959. ATL: H-705-010

3

4

"No it doesn't! It means I'm mostly for, and only a teeny bit against!"

Short and not so Sweet

The planned introduction of PAYE income tax allowed National and Labour to promise tax concessions at the 1957 election. Their £100 tax rebate, coupled with the promise, duly honoured, to abolish compulsory military training and 3 percent loans for housing, resulted in a wafer-thin win for Labour. However, the government's reputation was effectively sunk after Arnold Nordmeyer's June 1958 'Black Budget'. While it grappled with serious balance of payments difficulties inherited from National and, although there might have been only sufficient overseas reserves for six weeks' imports, the public's attention, and anger, was focused on the budget's tax increases on beer, spirits, cigarettes and petrol. The 'Black Budget' was to cast a long shadow over Labour's term and obscure a number of achievements: negotiations to set up major industries to reduce dependence on imports; equal pay for equal work, regardless of sex, in the public service; and capitalisation of family benefits for house deposits or mortgage payments.

1. Labour's 1958 budget turned out to be an over-reaction as the country's terms of trade swiftly improved. *"There they go again ...",* Gordon Minhinnick, *NZ Herald*, May 13 1959. ATL: E-549-q-13-128
2. It was politically damaging when Nash sat on the political fence in 1960 – tacitly supporting the Rugby Union's decision to send an 'all-white' team to South Africa – after Eruera Tirikatene, associate minister of Maori Affairs, said Maori had been *whakamomori* (suffering in silence) too long. *Racial Issue*, Neil Lonsdale, *Auckland Star*, June 18 1959. ATL: A-316-4-006
3. The Social Security system had grown to a size not imagined, or intended, by Nash and his colleagues in 1939. *He s a big boy now!,* Sid Scales, *Otago Daily Times*, April 4 1959. ATL: A-311-4-006
4. After 1958, it was assumed that every Nordmeyer budget would 'fleece' the New Zealand taxpayer. *"Did you hear about the UK budget?"* Neil Lonsdale, *Auckland Star*, April 9 1959. ATL: A-316-4-005
5. It was difficult to find much 'socialism' practised by Nash's administration; in fact, there was considerable interest from overseas investors in new import-substitution industries including an aluminium smelter, gin distillery, glass works, steel-rolling mill, and oil refinery. *Poison Ivy*, Sid Scales, *Otago Daily Times*, July 25 1959. ATL: A-311-4-007

1

"THERE THEY GO AGAIN –SABOTAGING OUR POLICY!"

2

3

He's a big boy now!

4

"DID YOU HEAR ABOUT THE U.K. BUDGET?"

5

Poison Ivy.

Looking Up to Uncle Sam

For decades New Zealand had willingly clung to Britain's apron strings, studiously ignoring dominion status in 1907 and delaying ratification of the operational clauses of the Statute of Westminster which, in 1931, gave the dominions complete autonomy. Although it had disagreed with Britain at the League of Nations and insisted – rather more in theory than in practice – on the ultimate control of troops serving overseas in the Second World War, Labour took 12 years to ratify the provisions of the Statute of Westminster. After the war, even though unhappy about America's Pacific presence, New Zealand huddled gratefully under the United States' defence umbrella, adopting the Truman Doctrine's communist versus non-communist view of the world. There was no dissent in 1950 when New Zealand troops joined United Nations forces in Korea and the ANZUS pact, and the less durable SEATO treaty, gave substance to New Zealand's collective-security hopes.

1. At the beginning of the decade, New Zealand public sentiment still closely identified with Britain, but policy-makers had decided, with considerable regret, the strategic future was mostly with the United States. *It Must be a Bug*, Gordon Minhinnick, *NZ Herald*, February 23 1950. ATL: H-652-002
2. New Zealand's relations with the USSR through the 1950s were equivocating. There was fervent opposition to communism and support for the Hungarian uprising to the extent of welcoming refugees – yet the Soviet Union was a large market with a growing taste for New Zealand dairy produce. *Guns or Butter*, James Sanders, *NZ Observer*, August 19 1953. ATL: J-036-083
3. Holland, like Fraser before him, still thought of defence in Commonwealth terms. New Zealand fought alongside other Commonwealth contingents in Korea and, from 1956, supported Britain during the Malayan Emergency, yet it increasingly found its Southeast Asian concerns better catered for by ANZUS and the American-inspired South East Asia Treaty Organisation (SEATO). *"After You!"*, Keith Waite, *Otago Daily Times*, May 19 1950. ATL: A-312-7-021
4. The Korean War fostered the theory of Asia falling, like dominoes, to communism, persuading a previously lukewarm United States to join a mutual defence pact with Australia and New Zealand. ANZUS was to dominate New Zealand's defence thinking and debate for decades. *"What – no Chaperon?"*, Sid Scales, *Otago Daily Times*, September 27 1952. ATL: A-311-4-001
5. Nash, a devoted internationalist, was suspicious about the objectives of the World Bank and IMF. His National successors were in no hurry to sign up either. *"Everybody s out of step but me"*, Neil Lonsdale, *Auckland Star*, July 3 1958. ATL: E-549-q-11-084

1

IT MUST BE A BUG

2

GUNS OR BUTTER.

3

4

"WHAT – NO CHAPERON?"

5

"EVERYBODY'S OUT OF STEP BUT ME!"

Flexing some Sporting Muscles

A by-product of peace and prosperity is the time and opportunity for heroics on the sporting field, and New Zealand did not disappoint during the 1950s. Yvette Williams' long jump gold medal at the 1952 Olympics had symbolised New Zealand women's athletic prowess. Mountain climbing might have been a minority, if long-established, pursuit, but New Zealand was quick to trumpet Edmund Hillary's 1953 ascent of Everest as the ultimate achievement of the country's sporting manhood, nourished by a diet of meat and dairy products, fresh air and open spaces, and an indomitable pioneering spirit. In the 1950s the All Blacks were also on top of the world, even if rugby was played by barely more than a handful of countries. On a bigger canvas again, there were wins in walking and yachting at the 1956 Olympics and a cascade of gold at the decade's three Empire and Commonwealth Games, the first, in 1950, in Auckland.

1. In the 1950s, with more than 50,000 punters crammed into the stands at Ellerslie in Auckland, only rugby tests attracted larger, more diverse crowds than horse racing. Bookmakers, banned in 1911, had continued to operate 'off-course' until trumped by the Totaliser Agency Board (TAB), which opened for business in 1951. *"Who said Easter had lost its religious significance?"*, Sid Scales, *Otago Daily Times*, April 13 1955. ATL: A-311-1-005
2. There were two home cricket tests against England in 1955, fast bowler Frank Tyson contributing to the New Zealanders' heavy defeats. During the 1950s New Zealand teams, including a number of notable players, won one test, drew 10 and lost 21. *".... Tyson has measured his run ..."*, Neville Colvin, *Sports Post*, March 12 1955. ATL: B-154-122
3. Maori could not play – or watch – the Springboks in South Africa, but they could at home during the 1956 tour. *"You sell te family ticket ..."*, Neil Lonsdale, *Auckland Star*, July 20 1956. ATL: A-316-4-004
4. There was considerable pride at stake, not to mention anger, when the NZ Maori team played the visiting Springboks in 1956. However, Maori were excluded from the All Black tour party to South Africa in 1960. *"I think I ll take my name ..."*, Harry Dansey, *Taranaki Daily News*, August 27 1956. ATL: J-065-068
5. Visitors were, and remain, puzzled by the grip rugby has on the New Zealand psyche. *"By cripes, Dad ...."*, Nevile Lodge, *Evening Post*, 1959. ATL: J-065-063
6. With the number of courses keeping playing costs down, golf has been a much more egalitarian game than in other countries. But it did produce a worrying social phenomenon – the 'golfing widow'. *"Excuse the caddy ..."*, Charles Milne, *The Press*, 1959. ATL: J-065-060

1

"WHO SAID EASTER HAD LOST ITS RELIGIOUS SIGNIFICANCE?"

2

3

"YOU SELL TE FAMILY TICKET, EH?"

4

"I think I'll take my name off the Maori roll!"

5

"BY CRIPES, DAD, NATURE'S WONDERFUL THE WAY SHE WORKS THINGS SO WE DON'T HAVE SO MUCH TO DO AROUND THE FARM IN THE FOOTBALL SEASON."

6

'Excuse the caddy, fellows, a little wedding celebration for the wife.'

An In-Between Time

There was still a 'British-ness' about New Zealand in the 1950s. It would take television and the fast-food industry to further intensify the 'Americanisation' of the country that had been nudged in that direction by sojourning American soldiers during the war. At a time when the *NZ Woman's Weekly* sold many more copies when the young new queen was on the cover, royal visits rated alongside rugby tours as popular attractions. They were as important to the flag waving crowds at railway stations and along roadsides as to the select few invited to garden parties and other grand occasions. Britain-by-ship was the almost automatic destination of travelling New Zealanders. There would be many more destinations when the first commercial jets started flying in the early 1960s. South Islanders were also travelling, mainly to live in the North Island. By 1976, more than 70 percent of New Zealanders lived in urban areas, increasingly in suburbia and in Auckland.

1. With the south's declining population, there was spare hydro power generating capacity – and plans to siphon it off to the North Island. *"Now give it to poor little Johnny!"*, Keith Waite, *Otago Daily Times*, October 3 1950. ATL: E-549-q-2-037
2. During a month long royal tour, in the summer of 1953-54, the country's enthusiasm was matched by Sid Holland, the avowedly Anglophile prime minister. *From Auckland to the Bluff*, Neville Colvin, *Evening Post*, December 23 1953. ATL: C-132-868
3. Under the 'No Remittance Licence' scheme, fortunate New Zealanders could use overseas funds to import larger, more exotic cars. Less fortunately, the country's petrol octane rating – at 78 – was the lowest in the world; a higher octane fuel was not marketed until 1960. *"It s the best we can do at the moment!"*, Neil Lonsdale, *Auckland Star*, July 17 1957. ATL: A-309-200
4. There were television demonstrations by the mid-1950s with experimental TV broadcasts beginning in 1959. New Zealand life, including rugby, would never be the same again. *"So much for your brilliant ...."*, Murray Ball, *Manawatu Times*, May 1959. ATL: J-047-004

1

"NOW GIVE IT TO POOR LITTLE JOHNNY!"

2

FROM AUCKLAND TO THE BLUFF.

3

IT WILL BE AT LEAST A YEAR BEFORE HIGH OCTANE PETROL
IS MARKETED IN NEW ZEALAND . . . . . NEWS

STANDARD
STANDARD
STANDARD
STANDARD

HIGHER
OCTANE
PROMISE

LONSDALE

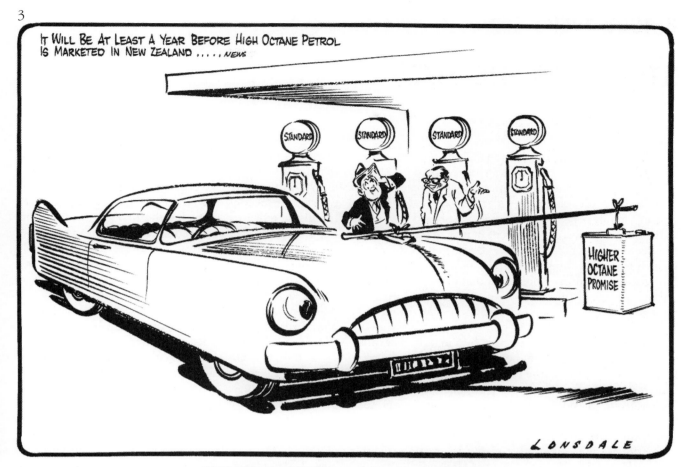

"IT'S THE BEST WE CAN DO AT THE MOMENT!"

4

"So much for your brilliant 'Let's get a close-up of this' idea..."

8: 1960-1969

STEADY AS SHE GOES

After Labour and National's long tenures on the treasury benches, the second Labour government lasted three unhappy years.

Labour could claim considerable achievements – housing, family benefit capitalisation, equal pay for women in the public service, development of new industries – but the electorate did not forgive the 'Black Budget' that was in such marked contrast to Labour's promises. And Keith Holyoake, consummate politician that he was, never let a debate or speaking opportunity pass without an impassioned denunciation of Nordmeyer's first, notorious budget.

National won the 1960 election by a margin that took years to erode. Ironically, although Nash and Nordmeyer had panicked in 1958, the economy had righted itself in time for National to be the grateful beneficiaries. Keith Holyoake now presided over a 'steady as she goes' economic approach, with Harry Lake, his finance minister, playing a carefully circumscribed role.

National's increasingly broad-spectrum support was nurtured by Holyoake's refinement of Holland's consensus style of politics. He rarely moved until he had studiously weighed public attitudes and he led from the safe middle ground of majority opinion. Holyoake presided over an able cabinet containing several strong personalities; among his most impressive achievements were his control in caucus, cabinet and the House and the heightened political instincts that led National to three more consecutive victories at the polls.

One of National's few initiatives, the decision to introduce decimal currency, gave a boost to the career of Robert Muldoon, appointed under-secretary of finance after the 1963 election. Holyoake was something of a mentor to Muldoon as Gordon Coates had been to him, and appointed him minister of finance when Lake died in February 1967. Decimal currency was launched, with few problems, the same year. In 1967-68 he showed his mettle by tackling the most serious of periodic balance-of-payments crises with stern, unpopular measures but, unlike Nordmeyer a decade earlier, he involved the electorate in the decision-making process. National had found a politician who could make the unpleasant palatable, or at least acceptable.

With liberally-minded senior ministers, and because of his own pragmatic approach, Holyoake's administration had few right-wing inclinations. National maintained and extended the welfare state and invested heavily in education at the secondary and tertiary levels. With a major contribution from Ralph Hanan, the government was also active in the civil rights area. An impressive list of achievements was chalked up: the first ombudsman office in the Commonwealth; the abolition of capital punishment that had been brought back in by the Holland government in 1950; the removal of censorship and broadcasting from direct political control; acknowledgement of the Security Intelligence Service (SIS) for the first time; the Hunn Report's telling catalogue of disadvantages faced by Maori in New Zealand. In addition, support for the 'No Maoris No Tour' view forced changes in the NZ Rugby Union's blinkered perspective and cancellation of the 1967 tour to South Africa.

There was also a more confident assertion of a distinct New Zealand identity, with the first locally born governor-general, Sir Arthur Porritt, appointed in 1967.

By the late 1960s, though, National's carefully measured approach was increasingly inappropriate. Involvement in the Vietnam War, as an ANZUS signatory, was debated at the 1966 election. The public accepted Holyoake's reasons: the threat of communism spreading through Asia, defence commitments and trade repercussions. But away from the public platform Holyoake had his doubts, and ensured New Zealand's participation was as limited as possible. At the same time the Holyoake government showed a degree of independence by declaring New Zealand a nuclear free country.

Despite this, the Vietnam War ended the bipartisan political approach to foreign affairs and was also the catalyst for a protest movement that took its environmental and moral concerns into the streets.

Until it had become clear by 1961 that Britain was committed to joining the European Economic Community (EEC), New Zealand governments had studiously ignored the possibility of one day losing Britain's safe and profitable primary produce markets. But now this top heavy trading dependence on one country, once a source of comfort and security, was seen, given the inevitability of Britain's eventual EEC membership, as the recipe for economic disaster.

Holyoake's calm and studied response, with most of the international legwork done by his deputy John Marshall, was to sign a free trade agreement with Australia (NAFTA), negotiate the best possible quotas into Britain for the post-EEC era and begin the business of developing new markets.

At the beginning of the 1960s, the balance of trade with Australia was 4:1 against New Zealand; after NAFTA was signed in 1965 the adverse trade balance was gradually corrected. France's Charles de Gaulle vetoed Britain's application to join Europe in 1963 and 1967 before 'third time lucky' success in 1971, and the lengthy lead-up period helped New Zealand gain support for its case for continued access to the British market. In the end, a five year transition period was agreed, allowing into Britain 80 percent of the country's butter and 20 percent of its cheese exports. There were also continued concessions for lamb exports.

In 1961, New Zealand also decided to join the International Monetary Fund (IMF), ending over a century's dependence on Britain as the primary source of loans. These initiatives combined to secure New Zealand against massive economic disruption.

National recorded comfortable wins at the 1963 and 1966 elections and scraped home in 1969 for two reasons – general, but gradually diminishing, satisfaction with the government's running of the country and Labour's poor performance in opposition.

Nash stayed on as party leader until 1963. His successor, Arnold Nordmeyer, an austere ex-Presbyterian minister and burdened with the legacy of his 'Black Budget', lacked the qualities to win back the middle ground National had so successfully occupied. In 1965, in a move more characteristic of National, a group of Labour MPs pushed Norman Kirk, a pudgy but impressive back-bencher, into the leadership. At 42 years old, he was the youngest ever Labour Party leader by more than a decade.

Kirk was a commanding figure during the 1969 election campaign, rising above the humdrum as he drew on his own practical experiences unencumbered by theory or doctrine. Although National won narrowly, Kirk outshone Holyoake on television, the powerful new medium that would become a key political tool in the 1970s.

It was nearly time for Kirk and Labour.

New Zealand's economy continued to boom resoundingly, with barely a hiccup through the whole decade. Few countries could boast more telephones, motor cars or practically anything else per thousand people. As a bonus, Peter Snell and Murray Halberg won four Olympic gold medals at Rome and Tokyo, proving there is something in the New Zealand water that favours longer distance runners. As a further bonus, in 1967 hotel drinking hours were extended to 10 pm, officially ending the 'six o'clock swill' that lasted half a century.

This, though, did not signify a quantum leap in sophistication. While it was legal to serve wine in restaurants from 1961, the nightlife in most cities and towns was usually limited to the new coffee bars which appealed to those with a taste for more than the traditional coffee and chicory essence. They provided a daytime meeting place for city workers and the growing number of university students and stayed open late into the night.

Tom Scott, *NZ Listener*, November 15 1980.
ATL: A-311-4-016

Toasted sandwiches were on the menu and some evenings a jazz trio or folk singer might perform. Coffee bars were dimly lit at night, the pseudo-European décor and fog of cigarette smoke providing, by New Zealand standards, an exotic atmosphere.

By the mid-1960s, the 'baby boomers' were beginning to make their presence felt. It is a moot point whether they have been more influential than other generations, but theirs was certainly larger than any before it, and has been an endless source of commercial interest to marketers and fascination to social scientists.

From the late 1940s, baby boomers had crowded maternity wards and then, in the 1950s, school classrooms. As they reached maturity from the mid-1960s onwards, against the backdrop of the 'cold war' and the lingering threat of nuclear annihilation, they rebelled against the conservatism, thrift and security-consciousness of their parents. In as much as it was a middle-class phenomenon, they were also rebelling against the orderly dullness of suburban life and the myth of the 'perfect family', a staple of American TV sit-coms, not to mention racism, war, inequality and hypocrisy.

Some baby boomers expressed their rebellion in the "make love not war" hippie 'flower power' counterculture which favoured 'new age' spirituality, and espoused free love and the use of mind expanding drugs as the path to revolution.

The 'Swinging Sixties' and the mini-skirt were

synonymous, but the swinging did not really get going until the second half of the decade, about the time the first baby boomers were making fashion choices. The 'Mod look' was an unusual fashion revolution that broke the established rules: centred in London, it was youth-orientated and controlled. Mini skirts, loud printed fabrics, bell bottoms and long hair launched a fashion trend that lasted two decades. In Carnaby Street, Mary Quant's boutique was selling skirts up to 18cm above the knee by 1966 and models like Twiggy were popular symbols of the little girl-woman androgynous look.

The generation's music – from blues-influenced rock 'n roll in the 1950s to the soul music and rebellious folk-rock and drug-culture acid rock of the 1960s – was to have a lasting influence.

In New Zealand, the baby boomer generation played a central role in the rising tempo of protest about playing rugby with apartheid South Africa and environmental destruction at home, and in the awakening of the long-quiescent women's movement.

One of the biggest protest movements in New Zealand history, opposed to sporting contacts with South Africa, had its beginnings in 1959, when it failed to stop an all-white All Black tour. But that was only the beginning. Growing protests against the Vietnam War included the 1968 blowing up of the Waitangi flagpole and subsequent bombings at a number of military bases. As well, Maori were angry about the paternalistic, if well-meaning, recommendations in the Hunn Report about coping with the stresses of rapid urbanisation. In 1968, there was large-scale opposition to government plans to raise the level of Lake Manapouri for hydro-electricity generation. The government seemed indifferent to the lake's national park status and the indigenous forests of outstanding beauty around its shoreline until forced to hold a commission of enquiry the next year and eventually agree not to raise the lake.

It was a good workout for the 1970s, the *real* protest decade.

There were disparate strands to the beginnings of the 'second wave' of feminism in the late 1960s. While young married women were having families in the suburbs, it had become more acceptable for their older married sisters to be in the paid workforce. Although women had continued to work in the public service after the war, the Government Service Equal Pay Act of 1960 providing additional incentive, most women were still in semi-skilled, low status occupations. About 26 percent of women were in the paid workforce in the early 1960s. However, 'the pill', a reliable oral contraceptive, in the early stages of revolutionising thinking about family size and population control, brought the baby boom screeching to a halt, and by the mid-1970s about 36 percent of women were in the paid workforce. The fact that by 1968 there were, for the first time, more women than men in the country, was certainly a spur to an increasing concern with a range of issues relating to equality.

In the early 1960s the migration of Maori to urban areas increased and, after the Hunn Report recommended a range of social reforms in 1961, the government provided more assistance with housing, employment and adjustment to a very different way of life. By 1966, about 62 percent of Maori lived in cities and towns; 20 years later it was to reach nearly 80 percent. There was now more social and work contact between Maori and pakeha and, inevitably, a significant increase in intermarriage. The children of these marriages, and those involving partners from different tribes, were the first urban generation. In time, the often long distance relationships with home marae weakened for many; some gained a sense of community from gang involvement and others joined urban marae.

As the desire and need for tertiary education grew, the larger secondary school rolls in the 1950s translated into a doubling of the number of university students in the 1960s.

While more girls qualified for university, only some of them continued with their education. Very few senior executives in either the public or private sectors had tertiary qualifications, but that began to change in the 1970s.

From the mid-1950s, there had been a steady increase in professional, administrative and managerial jobs and the growing numbers in the law and commerce faculties at universities confirmed the demand. There had been a rush of small businesses opening in the 1950s, dairy-grocer shops following new home owners into the suburbs and owner-operator manufacturing and building companies. Later in the 1960s, managers replaced proprietors in many sectors as businesses failed, grew or amalgamated. As retail competition intensified with the appearance of supermarkets – Tom Ah Chee opening Foodtown, the country's first in Auckland in 1958 – and shopping malls – the first at Auckland's New Lynn in 1963 – the number of dairy-groceries fell 10 percent between 1968-73.

In the 1960s there was no avoiding, good or bad, what the rest of the world had to offer, although New Zealand had certainly not raced helter-skelter to do so. A comparative trickle of new technology would become a torrent in the 1970s. In the decade when man landed on the moon, the cost of international tolls calls tumbled after the introduction of microwave transmission in 1963 and the use of satellites five years later. The first computer, a large cumbersome IBM machine, arrived in 1960. A random selection of other 1960s technology included the audio cassette, the compact disk, electronic fuel injection in cars, the first hand-held calculator, the ATM, and the bar-code scanner.

The gap between invention and everyday use was shortening all the time. However, television arrived fully 20 years late by international standards and jet aircraft had been flying other skies for almost as long before scheduled international services linked New Zealand with the rest of the world.

The first jet services began in 1963. In 1965, TEAL, having shed its Australian shareholding, became Air New Zealand and in 1966 the country had its first international airport at Mangere, Auckland. If New Zealanders had needed an excuse to travel they now had it. In 1960 there were 92,000 international flights coming and going; by 1970 the number had taken off vertically to 554,000. Many of these travellers were young people following the wartime boot-steps of their fathers and elder brothers in search of working holidays. 'Overseas experience' would soon be shorthanded to 'OE'.

Regular television programming began in 1960, initially for two hours on two evenings, but quickly increasing to four nights a week. It was a revolution even more profound in its effects than the teenage culture. In homes across the nation it rearranged furniture and changed eating habits; in offices and factories it became the principal topic of conversation. By 1968, 75 percent of New Zealand homes had a set. With its daily diet of violence, particularly graphic pictures of the Vietnam War, television was accused of de-sensitising the public; on the other hand, those same pictures strengthened the resolve of many New Zealanders that this was a war they wanted no part of. The big city movie theatres were now mostly empty and many suburban and small town picture theatres closed. The audience for evening radio was otherwise occupied. TV was not the great force for enlightenment some claimed it would be but, while the situation looked perilous for a while, neither was it the end of conversation, reading or visits to the theatre or art galleries either.

Radio made some of the decade's most entertaining news when a band of young 'pirates' took on the NZ Broadcasting Corporation monopoly and, in late 1966, after arrests and court appearances, set sail for international waters to broadcast from their *MV Tiri* 'station'. Radio Hauraki survived a shipwreck and groundings until, in January 1970 and back on dry land, it was granted one of the country's first private broadcasting licences. In time, New Zealand was to have one of the world's most crowded and cut-throat commercial radio markets.

The film industry carried on as before, slowly maturing. John O'Shea had made his first feature, *Broken Barrier*, with Roger Mirams in 1952. In the 1960s, he soldiered on, his Pacific Films making TV commercials while it trained bright young directors and put together the finance to make *Runaway* in 1964 and *Don't Let It Get You* two years later.

New Zealand's professional theatre had struggled in the 1950s when television was still a small cloud in an otherwise bright blue sky. The New Zealand Players, the inspiration of Richard and Edith Campion, had brought professionalism and daring to the concept of touring a mix of classical and more contemporary plays around the country. They survived from 1953 to 1960, finally beaten more by transport and labour costs than audience indifference. Television also seemed to stimulate professional theatre. The Downstage Theatre Society opened a theatre-restaurant in Wellington's Courtenay Place in 1964 and Auckland's Mercury Theatre staged its first play in 1968.

Several major British publishers opened offices and began publishing New Zealand books. Among new names, Bill Pearson, Ronald Hugh Morrieson, Errol Brathwaite, Graham Billing and Joy Cowley created considerable interest. Noel Hilliard's *Maori Girl* was the first novel to look at Maori migration to the cities; Barry Crump's *A Good Keen Man* broke bestseller records with its laconic recounting of a fast disappearing backblocks life. Among the growing number of histories, Keith Sinclair's *A History of New Zealand* was also a bestseller and, after 20 years of research and editing, J C Beaglehole's mammoth, critically acclaimed four-volume *Journals of Captain Cook* was finished in 1969.

There was much more acceptance of abstract art in the 1960s with the forms in the work of Gordon Walters, Milan Mrkusich and Don Peebles often quite severe. Ray Thorburn tempered the abstract with elements of 'Pop Art', which used images from the mass media, advertising and consumer products and was associated with 'swinging' London. John Drawbridge moved between abstract and the figurative; Phillip Trusttum's work contained semi-recognisable images; and Patrick Hanly brought a new perspective to figurative painting.

The Consensus Keeper

National clung to power through the 1960s, with diminishing majorities and in a swirl if dissent, because of prime minister Keith Holyoake's virtuoso political management and with continued prosperity funded by overseas borrowing. Holyoake, who left school at 12 to work on his parents' farm, was an MP nine years before becoming Holland's deputy in 1946. A successful minister for seven years before his first, brief prime ministership in 1957, he then won four successive elections. Since the 1960s were generally prosperous and Labour had recurring leadership problems, his 'consensus' style minimised conflict. And a master of delegation, he gave a talented and diverse line-up of ministers their heads in portfolios they usually held, and became expert in, over long periods. 'Consensus' and 'steady as it goes' were banal catchwords for Holyoake's skill at keeping public opinion just in front of government decisions, but for most of his 12 years in power, a largely conservative electorate wanted little political change and fewer surprises. It was a decade when there was going to be quite enough change in other aspects of people's lives.

1. Labour's two seat majority, courtesy of the Maori electorates, disappeared and National began another long period in government with a comfortable majority. *"I withdraw because I must"*, Gordon Minhinnick, *NZ Herald*, November 28 1960. ATL: B-056-105
2. While Holyoake presided over a generally prosperous economy, overall farm production began to level off in 1968 and by the end of the decade meat had replaced wool as the principal export earner. *The Wool Industry*, Eric Heath, *Dominion*, 1969. ATL: A-311-4-010
3. Holyoake did not master the powerful new TV medium: he came across as an aloof, pompous man, with a plum in his mouth and an inexhaustible supply of clichés. *Media Training for Sir Keith Holyoake*, Bob Brockie, 1969. ATL: A-341-065
4. Although generally genial, his staff learned to read one very obvious sign: if Holyoake sat down at his desk with his hat on it was going to be a difficult, demanding day. *The Dark Side of the Moon*, Nevile Lodge, *Evening Post*, 1969. ATL: B-133-888

1

"I WITHDRAW BECAUSE I MUST!"

2

3

MEDIA TRAINING FOR SIR KEITH HOLYOAKE

4

THE TWO HOLYOAKES

There's another side to Holyoake, too, that the public rarely sees. This is the forceful administrator who can, if he wants, put the fear of God into even senior public servants. Sometimes, when he is liverish in the mornings, he arrives at his office, takes off his coat and sits down at his desk, still wearing his hat. The first member of his staff who sees him in that condition quickly sends round word to all the other staff members: "It's a hats-on day, boys, watch out."

"Election '69"

THE DARK SIDE OF THE MOON

When Uncle Sam Hollers

Holyoake, who was also minister of external affairs, was lukewarm about the country's ANZUS involvement in the Vietnam War, but did not openly question the theory of an international communist conspiracy directed by Moscow with Asian nations falling like dominoes. National sent a small contingent of volunteers to fight alongside the puppet Saigon regime from 1965, but after 1967 visits from American officials, including General Maxwell Taylor, New Zealand nearly quadrupled its Vietnam commitment to about 550 troops. Over five years about 3,900 military personnel – artillery, infantry and SAS – went to Vietnam; 39 were killed. Small though this contribution was it profoundly influenced domestic politics. The war ruptured foreign policy consensus among politicians and gave birth to a protest movement that became increasingly vocal and aggressive.

1

1. Vietnam War opponents believed Holyoake unquestioningly supported Lyndon Johnson's war policies. *The Pentagon Papers* later showed a more independent line. *"I may be fat and going grey ...",* Bob Brockie, *Cock*, December 1967. ATL: A-311-4-013
2. The South East Asia Treaty Organisation (SEATO), a larger grouping than ANZUS that included Britain and France, was an expression of the United States' fear of a communist takeover in Laos, Cambodia and Vietnam. While the New Zealand Army was reorganized in 1964 to 'fit' with those of other SEATO signatories, there was no 'call to arms' from the organisation. *"The pressure of events has drawn us much closer together",* Gordon Minhinnick, *NZ Herald*, March 28 1961. ATL: E-549-q-13-177
3. For New Zealand, at least, the limited support of the United States in Vietnam was more calculated insurance against an uncertain South Pacific future than enthusiasm for an anti-communist crusade. Australia sent much larger numbers of conscripted troops to Vietnam. *The Strong Stand*, Gordon Minhinnick, *NZ Herald*, April 17 1964. ATL: E-549-q-13-204

2

"The pressure of events has drawn us much closer together."

3

THE STRONG STAND

In the Trenches Again

During the 1960s New Zealand fought another war in Europe; this time the country's very survival was at stake. New Zealand's secure British market – most of its dairy products and lamb and more than half of its total export income – was suddenly in jeopardy when, in 1958, the Rome Treaty gave birth to a European Economic Community committed to agricultural protectionism. There were product and price barriers to rapid market diversification, so the government concentrated – with British approval and through three entry bids – on securing special arrangements as a pre-requisite to Britain's EEC membership. During the final, tense negotiating sessions in 1971, New Zealand managed to improve the EEC's offer of access for dairy products. Britain also gave assurances that future sheep-meat regulations would not disadvantage New Zealand.

1. By the beginning of the 1960s it was clear that Britain saw its future linked, across the once stoutly defended channel, to Europe, old friends and enemies alike. *"What s she got that I haven t got?"*, Neil Lonsdale, *Auckland Star*, May 25 1961. ATL: A-310-032
2. John 'Gentleman Jack' Marshall, as minister of overseas trade, had the formidable and complex task of convincing countries with no ties of blood or history to give New Zealand 'special' consideration in Britain's eventual EEC agreement. *"It s a riddle within a mystery inside an enigma!"*, Gordon Minhinnick, *NZ Herald*, June 21 1962. ATL: A-311-1-035
3. Through the 1960s, Jack Marshall repeatedly visited Britain and EEC capitals to soft-sell New Zealand's case for continued access, EEC membership notwithstanding, to the British market. *Bop!*, Bob Brockie, *Cock*, 1968. ATL: A-311-4-014
4. Charles de Gaulle said "non" to Britain's application to join the EEC in 1963 and 1967. A third application, in 1971, succeeded; by then France was well aware of the case New Zealand was making for continued access. *"Proceed, then, to negotiate!"*, Gordon Minhinnick, *NZ Herald*. March 1 1968. ATL: A-311-1-039
5. Marshall had a particularly heavy workload during the second Holyoake ministry. As well as the deputy prime ministership and the critical overseas trade role he took on, after the 1969 election, the labour portfolio and attorney general role following the death of two senior colleagues. *"…. And now – this great feat ….",* Gordon Minhinnick, *NZ Herald*. December 23 1969. ATL: E-549-q-13-232

1

"WHAT'S SHE GOT THAT I HAVEN'T GOT?"

2

"It's a riddle within a mystery inside an enigma!"

3

4

"NEW ZEALANDERS SEEM AFRAID THAT THE COMMON MARKET IS BEING SET UP TO THEIR DETRIMENT... BUT IN THE FINAL ANALYSIS ALL THIS IS A QUESTION OF NEGOTIATION"
— FRENCH PARLIAMENTARY MISSION NOW IN NEW ZEALAND

MINHINNICK

"PROCEED, THEN, TO NEGOTIATE!"

5

"...and now – this great feat – never before attempted..."

Changing of the Guards

One of the drawbacks of the democratic system is that party leaders often outstay their welcome. Walter Nash, beaten at the 1960 election, carried on as Labour leader until 1963 – when he was 80 years of age. After an abortive 'coup' in 1954, his mana and the death of possible contenders had assured his position. Arnold Nordmeyer, a prominent minister in both Labour administrations, was unopposed early in 1963, but his lack of vote-catching appeal made him a stop-gap leader. Norman Kirk, the 20-stone party president, lost the deputy's post to Hugh Watt but his support built steadily and he easily defeated Nordmeyer in a caucus vote in late 1965. Keith Holyoake was safe while he won elections for National during the 1960s. He tired visibly after 1969, but had given no hints about stepping down by decade's end. The Social Credit Political League's leader didn't change, but the party's fortunes did when Vernon Cracknell won its first parliamentary seat in 1966.

1. Nash stayed on as Labour Party leader after the 1960 defeat; he and Nordmeyer had shunned the International Monetary Fund (IMF), preferring the long-established dependence on Britain for loans. *Bedtime Story for the Little Ones*, Gordon Minhinnick, *NZ Herald*, August 4 1961. ATL: E-549-q-13-184
2. Nash soldiered on, party because politics was his life, but also to stop Nordmeyer becoming leader. Finally, in February 1963, the party president precipitated a leadership vote and Nash resigned. *Double Entry*, Sid Scales, *Otago Daily Times*, February 1963. ATL: A-311-4-009
3. In December 1965, Kirk, with customary efficiency, successfully challenged a disbelieving Arnold Nordmeyer. He was 42 years old, and the youngest ever Labour Party leader. *"Why don t you look where I m going?"*, Gordon Minhinnick, *NZ Herald*, December 1965. ATL: A-311-1-037
4. After its 1966 success, Social Credit slumped at the 1969 election; Cracknell lost his seat and the party faced several years of internal strife and leadership changes. *"Excuse Me"*, Bob Brockie, *Focus*, 1969. ATL: A-311-4-015

1

BEDTIME STORY FOR THE LITTLE ONES

2

Double entry

3

"Why don't you look where I'm going?"

4

The Dark Eminence

The most powerful political figure in New Zealand through much of the 1940s, 1950s and into the early 1960s, prime ministers and their most senior colleagues aside, was the ruthless and devious Fintan Patrick Walsh. A Hawke's Bay farmer's son, he ran away to sea as a young man during the First World War. Back home, he changed his name from Tuohy, and was a member of the NZ Communist Party in the early 1920s. Walsh plotted the takeover of the powerful NZ Seaman's Union and was its full-time president from 1927 to his death in 1963. From this power-base, particularly secure after the introduction of compulsory unionism in 1936, his radicalism moderated. He feuded with the militant watersiders, its leaders his rivals for control of the union movement, and worked closely with Peter Fraser, during and after the war, to keep unions in line and their wages down. The culmination of Walsh's right-wing, anti-communist period was his support of the National government during the 1951 waterfront dispute; his reward was the leadership of a weakened union movement and presidency of the FOL until his death.

1. Fraser had been close to Walsh, but Nash disliked him intensely. The FOL president was critical of the 1957-60 Labour government, particularly Nordmeyer's 'Black Budget'. *The Glad Hand*, Gordon Minhinnick, *NZ Herald*, June 10 1960. ATL: A-311-1-034
2. It had suited Walsh to help Holland weaken the union movement in 1951; in the early 1960s, a challenge to compulsory unionism threatened his power. *The Revolution*, Gordon Minhinnick, *NZ Herald*, May 2 1963. ATL: E-549-q-13-201
3. National had stepped back from an earlier promise to abolish compulsory unionism, both Walsh and employers happy with the status quo, but the issue surfaced again in 1962. In the event, abolition had little effect as few unions wanted to change the way they operated. *Brinkmanship*, Gordon Minhinnick, *NZ Herald*, May 9 1961. ATL: E-549-q-13-180
4. The FOL grew stronger again; strikes, legal and otherwise, escalated and Walsh drove hard wage bargains with National. He sounded, in his last years, more like the radical of 40 years earlier. *Waterfront Calypso*, Gordon Minhinnick, *NZ Herald*, August 28 1962. ATL: E-549-q-13-194

1

THE GLAD HAND

2

THE REVOLUTION

3

BRINKMANSHIP

4

WATERFRONT CALYPSO

That Other Religion

Rugby had demonstrably been the country's national game since early in the 20th century, and possibly earlier. But it was more than sport. It gave meaning to abstract theories of egalitarianism: city barrister played bush lawyer; squatter played cow cockie; Maori played pakeha and shared a beer afterwards. Rugby expressed identity: belonging in an isolated settlement; regional differences in Ranfurly Shield challenges; north-south rivalries in inter-island matches; national pride in All Black victories. Most New Zealand males had two things in common – rugby, and talking about it in public bars. Rugby, with its controlled violence and athleticism, was a link to a more muscular colonial past. New Zealand has avoided a state religion, but rugby is the next best thing to a state sport – with cabinet meetings interrupted for All Black results. And the analogy with religion is not misplaced. How, for example, can New Zealand's crushing of the visiting 1956 Springboks be described as anything other than a crusade to avenge the 1949 'whitewash'?

1. In the pre-TV days, when test matches were played overseas, crowds flocked to cinemas to see lunch-time newsreels of the games. The 1960 tour of South Africa started with a 0-13 loss, followed by a win, draw – and series losing 3-8 defeat. *"More frightening than 'On The Beach …"*, Nevile Lodge, *Evening Post*, July 6 1960. ATL: B-133-070
2. Just days after the New Zealand Maori team lost to the visiting Springboks in 1965, South African PM Dr Verwoerd announced Maori players could not be part of the All Black touring party for the projected 1967 tour. (*Sarie Marais*, an Afrikaaners' marching song, was often sung at Springbok matches.) *"By cripes! He s right, eh?"*, Nevile Lodge, *Sports Post*, August 28 1965. ATL: B-137-286
3. To New Zealanders there's few things more satisfying than beating the Springboks; the 1965 home series was won three matches to one. *Big Game Trophy*, Nevile Lodge, *Sports Post*, September 18 1965. ATL: B-137-285
4. In 1967 the All Blacks toured Britain and France instead of South Africa. There were middle-of-the-night 'live' radio broadcasts of the four test matches – all won by New Zealand. *"I d say they all stayed up …."*, Nevile Lodge, *Evening Post*, 1967. ATL: B-133-572
5. A cartoonist anticipates the 1981Springbok tour with its ugly riots, and street and rugby ground violence. *"I ve invented a new game …."*, Murray Ball, *Stanley*, May 1964. ATL: A-305-078

1

"More frightening than 'On the Beach – with that film I only IMAGINED the world had come to an end!"

2

3

4

"I d say they all stayed up listening to the rugby broadcast last night and I d say that the All Blacks must have had a good win."

5

Protests to Order

Despite political stability, with Holyoake and National winning four elections in a row, the 1960s were a period of vigorous protest and dissent. In New Zealand, as elsewhere, the post-war generation of idealistic, well-educated students were anti-establishment. There was bitter opposition to the Vietnam War, and television, a late arrival in New Zealand, brought the conflict's horror and muddied morality into living rooms nightly – and dramatised the growing anti-war movement in the United States. Local protesters had their models and the medium for their message. The immediate influence of the anti-war movement was slight, but it rekindled popular involvement in political decision-making. Teach-ins, demonstrations and marches were subsequently used, with varying success, in campaigns to save Lake Manapouri; to forestall the Omega navigational tracking station; to halt French nuclear testing at Muraroa Atoll; and to end the country's sporting contacts with South Africa.

1. There were causes local, national and international to choose from. *"Which ll it be this week?"*, Nevile Lodge, *Evening Post*, 1965. ATL: B-133-314
2. The 'No Maoris – No Tour' movement did not succeed in 1960, but the mood had changed by 1967. There was now increasing pressure to end all sporting contacts with South Africa while it practised apartheid. *"He ain t dead, Sir ....",* Tom Scott, *Maskerade*, 1974. ATL: H-670-006
3. There was little opposition to the Springbok tour in 1965 – particularly as New Zealand won the series convincingly. Keith Holyoake walked to 'work' from his nearby house and was an easy target for early-bird protesters. *"Well, it must have been put in the wrong pile!"*, Gordon Minhinnick, *NZ Herald*, July 13 1965. ATL: E-549-q-13-208
4. Some protests were long-running, and in need of durable placards – the last New Zealand troops finally left Vietnam late in 1972. Other protest objectives were achieved more quickly. Holyoake's firm views on the subject forced the Rugby Union to abandon the planned 1967 tour of South Africa. *"Baked enamel should last a lifetime"*, Eric Heath, *Dominion*, August 29 1967. ATL: A-311-4-008

1

"Which ll it be this week?"

2

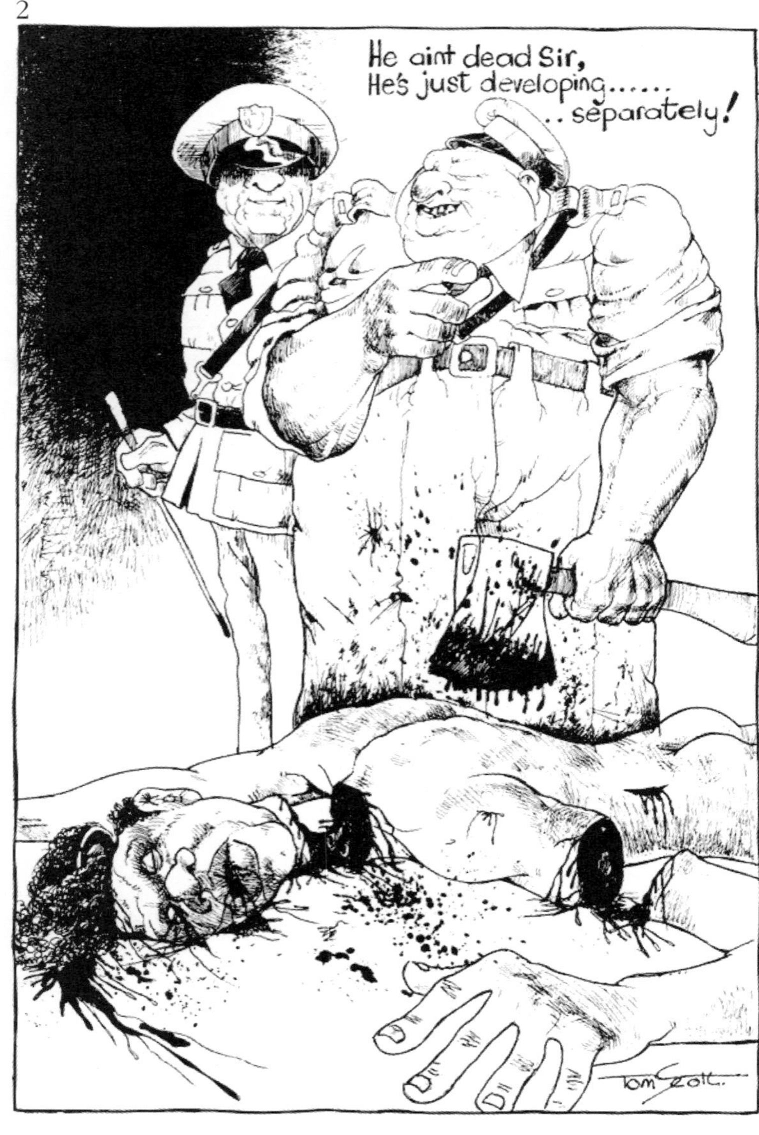

3

"Well, it must have been put in the wrong pile!"

4

"BAKED ENAMEL SHOULD LAST A LIFETIME."

A Brand-new World

The world arrived on New Zealand's doorstep in the 1960s, with opportunities and difficulties unimaginable less than a generation before. It was the beginning of an era of frenetic change that has not yet paused for breath. As new technologies began to change life patterns and jobs, it was exhilarating for some, terrifying for others. Television butted into people's lives with its addictive, but rarely satisfying, jumble of instant images and 'sound bites'. Increasingly busy airline schedules jetted the fortunate around the world to chase business opportunities or the winter sun. Calculators led to computers; very little would be the same again. The transistor radio gave even more freedom to teenagers. Plastics were the beginning of a 'disposable' society. The contraceptive pill gave women, and their partners, choices that tradition and value systems struggled to cope with. Equal pay in government departments helped nudge more women – up to one-quarter of them – into paid employment.

1. On a per capita basis, New Zealand continued to excel in international sporting arenas. There was disbelief and delight when Peter Snell and Murray Halberg ran away with their finals on one golden afternoon at the Rome Olympics. *"Well, at least with them all being Halbergs and Snells ...",* Nevile Lodge, *Evening Post*, 1960. ATL: A-349-004
2. High set-up costs and a small population meant TV advertising was inevitable from the beginning; few countries screen so much advertising per hour and most have non-commercial channels. *".... And now we interrupt the commercials for a programme,"* Neil Lonsdale, *Auckland Star*, April 5 1961. ATL: A-316-4-007
3. Modern tourism was off to a rocky start as new jet airliners flew in more visitors: regulations dogged the hospitality industry, 'service' was not a widely understood concept, and cities and towns 'closed down' at weekends and during holiday periods. *"Say! This is like that Wellington place ...",* Nevile Lodge, *Evening Post*, 1962. ATL: B-137-532
4. The TAB, or legal 'off-course' betting, introduced in 1951 spelt the end of 'bookies' who had been banned from racecourses in 1910; there was also apprehension felt by racing clubs worried about the effect on raceday crowds. *"Remember when he was a colt ...",* Nevile Lodge, *Evening Post*, 1963. ATL: J-065-069

1

"WELL, AT LEAST WITH THEM ALL BEING HALBERGS AND SNELLS, IT'LL BE EASIER ON THE WINDOWS THAN LAST TERM WHEN THEY WERE ALL DON CLARKES."

2

"...AND NOW WE INTERRUPT THE COMMERCIALS FOR A PROGRAMME."

3

THE ESTABLISHMENT OF A "GHOST TOWN" HAS BEEN SUGGESTED TO THE TOURIST AND PUBLICITY DEPT. IN AN EFFORT TO ATTRACT MORE TOURISTS TO WESTLAND
HOTEL
STORE
HARDWARE
HOTEL
BAR
NEW ZEALAND ROAD SER
NEVILLE LODGE
1/62

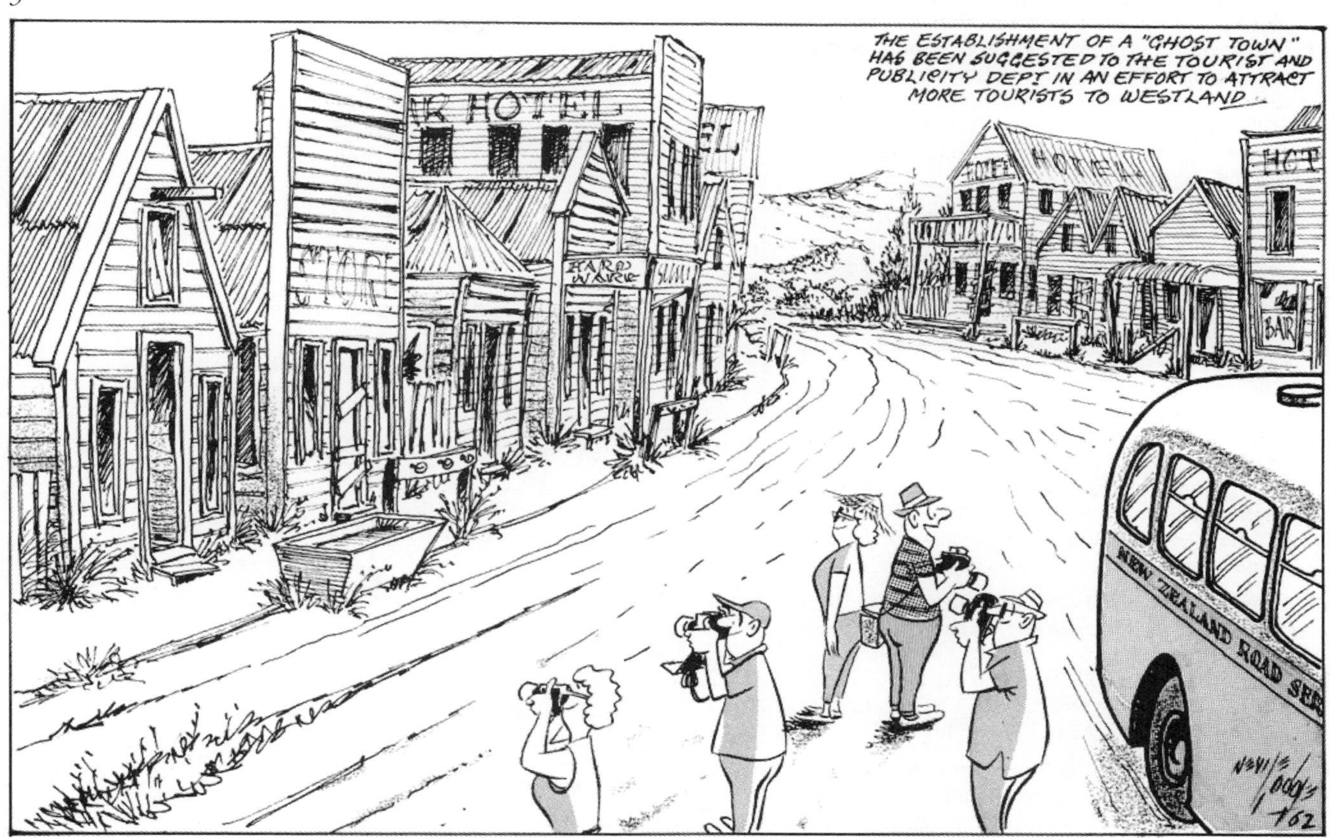

"Say! This is like that Wellington place on a Sunday!"

4

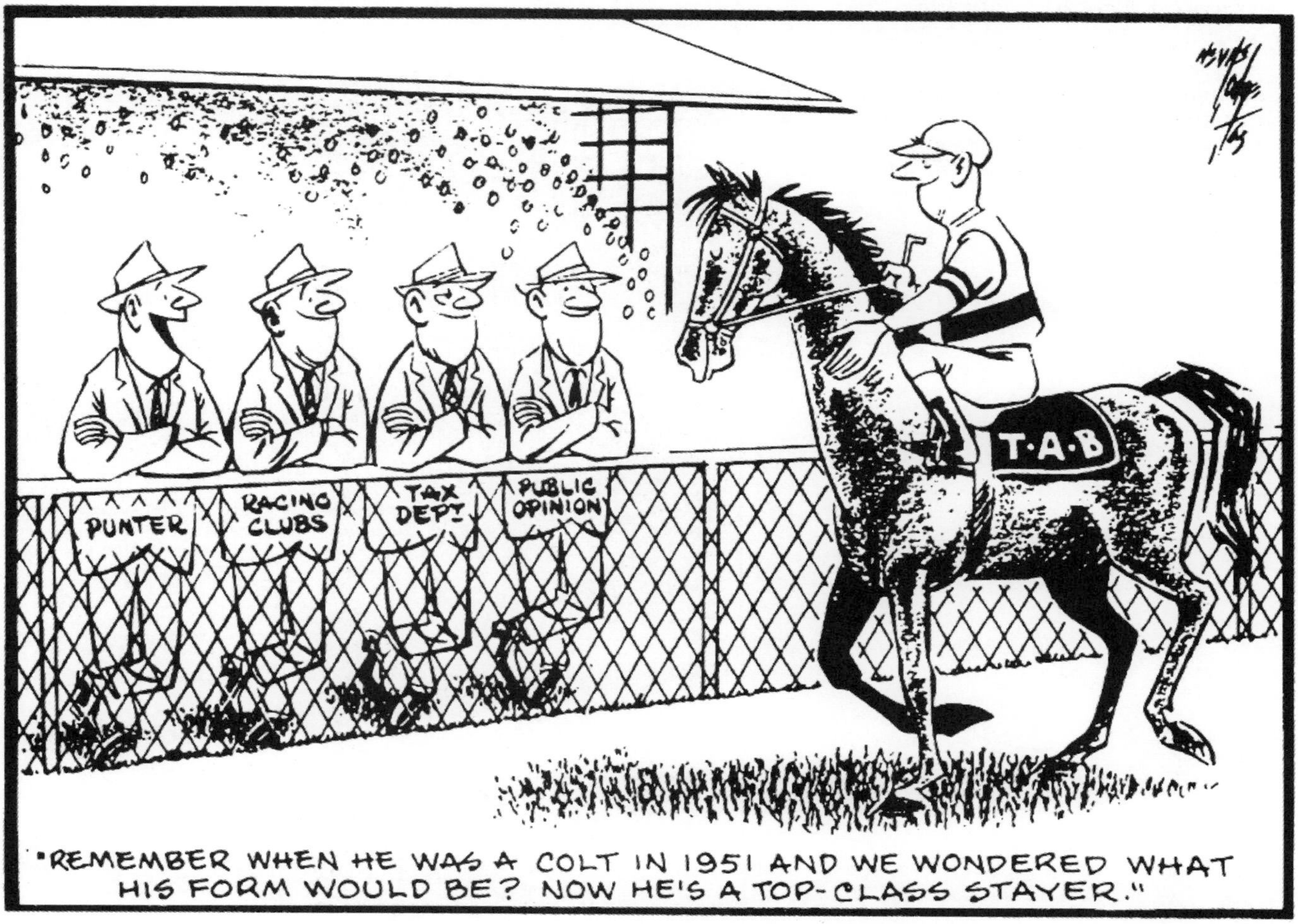

PUNTER
RACING CLUBS
TAX DEPT.
PUBLIC OPINION
T·A·B
"REMEMBER WHEN HE WAS A COLT IN 1951 AND WE WONDERED WHAT HIS FORM WOULD BE? NOW HE'S A TOP-CLASS STAYER."

5. With mass media and communications technology making the 'global village' a reality, the shock waves of UK prostitute Christine Keeler's simultaneous bedding of a British cabinet minister and Russian naval attaché soon washed up as far away as Wellington's beaches. *"I give up! Last year you thought this was a good name ....",* Nevile Lodge, *Sports Post,* 1963. ATL: B-137-266

6. The 'gardening revolution' had not yet arrived so, in the 1960s, there was an understandable tension between the weekend pleasures of a glass or two of beer and a round of golf, and digging over the vegetable garden –*"It s what I call my Labour Weekend Incentive Plan",* Nevile Lodge, *Sports Post,* 1968. ATL: J-059-003

7. As American marketing methods and willing consumers combined to turn shopping from a necessary chore to a 'leisure experience', 'muzak' was piped through larger shops to provide appropriate ambience. *"Wilkins! Quick! They ve had an overdose,"* Gordon Minhinnick, *NZ Herald,* September 30 1964. ATL: A-311-1-036

8. Newly discovered teenage angst had less opportunity to express itself – aside from surliness and scruffiness – while uniforms were standard in most schools, public as well as private. *".... And I don t have to look very far ....",* Nevile Lodge, *Evening Post,* 1965. ATL: B-133-349

9. A referendum said "yes" to 10'oclock closing in 1967 after the 6 o'clock 'swill' had been a fixture since 1917. It was the signal for a gradual 'night life' blossoming of cafés and bars and a wine and food industry of increasing sophistication. *"They haven t got used to the idea ....",* Nevile Lodge, *Evening Post,* 1967. ATL: J-059-016

10. After nearly two decades of unparalleled prosperity, with dollops of conspicuous consumption, New Zealanders were only slowly counting the cost of sprawling landfills and increasing pollution. *"Some day son, all this will be yours!",* Gordon Minhinnick, *NZ Herald,* January 9 1969. ATL: A-311-1-038

5

6

7

"WILKINS! QUICK! THEY'VE HAD AN OVERDOSE!"

8

"…and I don't have to look very far to find a reason why the royal family didn't consider sending Prince Charles to a New Zealand college."

9

"They haven't got used to the idea that it's legal to drink to 10 – they saw you coming and thought it was a raid."

10

"Some day son, all this will be yours!"

9: 1970-1979

BIG NORM AND LITTLE ROB

By the beginning of the 1970s, National was running out of steam; several able ministers had died in harness and others, including Keith Holyoake, were visibly wilting.

The politics of consensus, successful at first, were now bogging the government down in endless policy consultation with committees, commissions and conferences. Internationally, the cold war blocs were breaking up and, locally, women and Maori were more assertive, opposition to the Vietnam war had mounted and environmental concerns multiplied.

Under Norman Kirk's increasingly assured leadership, Labour stirred quiescent nationalistic feelings with an independent approach to foreign policy and, at home, offered positive programmes in areas such as health, housing, and regional development.

Holyoake stayed on too long as prime minister, doing what Holland had done to him, and handing over to his deputy John Marshall when the government's fortunes were in steep decline. When Holyoake finally stood down in February 1972, Jack Marshall tried, in some desperation, to revitalise National, but it was Norman Kirk, considerably fined down and spruced up by his PR advisers, who impressed.

Although he was an old-style, conservative 'law and order' man and distrusted conventional economics, Kirk had a passionate belief in a reforming government's ability to create a society of genuinely equal opportunity in New Zealand. He spoke from the heart, believing the electorate aspired to more than 'consensus'. In the television age, when impressions can carry more weight than arguments, it was the emotional response to Kirk's vision for New Zealand rather than enthusiasm for the party's policies that catapulted Labour into a massive, 23-seat majority at the 1972 election. The electorate was more than ready to endorse Labour's 'It's Time' slogan at the ballot box.

It was very much Kirk's personal triumph and 'Big Norm' was now an affectionate nickname. Labour set about the business of government with gusto. Norman Kirk had an additional reason to hurry – although few of his colleagues knew he had a heart complaint, his premonitions of an early death were to come tragically true 18 months later. There was an immediate Christmas bonus for pensioners, underlining Labour's social welfare commitment, and an injection of money for a stagnating house-building industry.

A full-scale economic boom, stimulated by soaring meat and wool prices and an expansionary budget in 1972, was further pushed along by Labour ministers jostling to introduce programmes involving large government expenditure or incentives. Material and labour shortages were countered by a surge of imports and immigration.

In 1973, parliament introduced a substantial body of significant legislation, some of it foreshadowed by National. Kirk also defused his first major problem, the cancellation of the Springbok rugby tour, with his public, step-by-step agonising leaving the still-dazed opposition little to exploit.

While the economy boomed, Kirk was preoccupied with foreign affairs. He had travelled widely as opposition leader and his views about New Zealand's role in the world meshed perfectly with those of his foreign affairs bureaucrats. If New Zealanders held their heads a little higher in 1973, it was largely because of Kirk's determination that small nations should assert themselves and attempt to modify great-power behaviour. In short order, he made a lasting impression at a Commonwealth PMs conference, his government established diplomatic relations with the People's Republic of China, and French nuclear weapon testing in the Pacific was challenged.

However, in 1974 the boom sputtered out as New Zealand's principal trading partners were caught in a recession complicated by the first oil shock – inflation rose dramatically, there were large wage increases and, belatedly, an ill-conceived Maximum Retail Prices (MRP) justification scheme. Abortion and homosexual law reform, which Kirk opposed, were divisive items on the legislative agenda. As Labour drifted through the first eight months of 1974, National sent its own adrenalin pumping when Rob Muldoon replaced John Marshall as leader in July, one month before Kirk died.

Kirk had returned from an Asian tour exhausted, depressed and ill; paranoia and suspicion of colleagues, noticeable before, was deepening. Complications followed an April operation for varicose veins and Norman Kirk died, 51 years old, on August 31 from congestive cardiac failure and heart disease.

Ironically, John Marshall, uncomfortable in opposition after 20 years as a minister, had resigned under pressure just a month earlier, his National colleagues believing his deputy Rob Muldoon would be more effective against Kirk. Bill Rowling who succeeded Kirk, rather than his deputy Hugh Watt, was much more in the Marshall mould.

By September 1974, the inflation rate was about 12 percent and climbing, with a trade deficit of more than $750 million as lower export prices fell further behind the increasing volumes of higher priced imports. In hindsight, Rowling should have called an election, seeking a fresh mandate after Kirk's death; the sympathy vote would almost certainly have given him another three years. As it was, he remained a caretaker, trying to keep alive the spirit of Kirk's vision as economic reality bit. He also remained consistent in his economic philosophy – borrowing heavily rather than retrenching, keeping people and industry at work.

Indefatigably, in the lead up to the 1975 election,

Muldoon repeated, on television and in packed halls, the memorable phrases that New Zealanders responded to. Labour's solution was to "borrow and hope"; only National could repair the country's "shattered economy". National, with Muldoon's dogmatic certainty about the uncertain future and the security of a generous, no-strings superannuation scheme, had found an election combination that transcended traditional party lines.

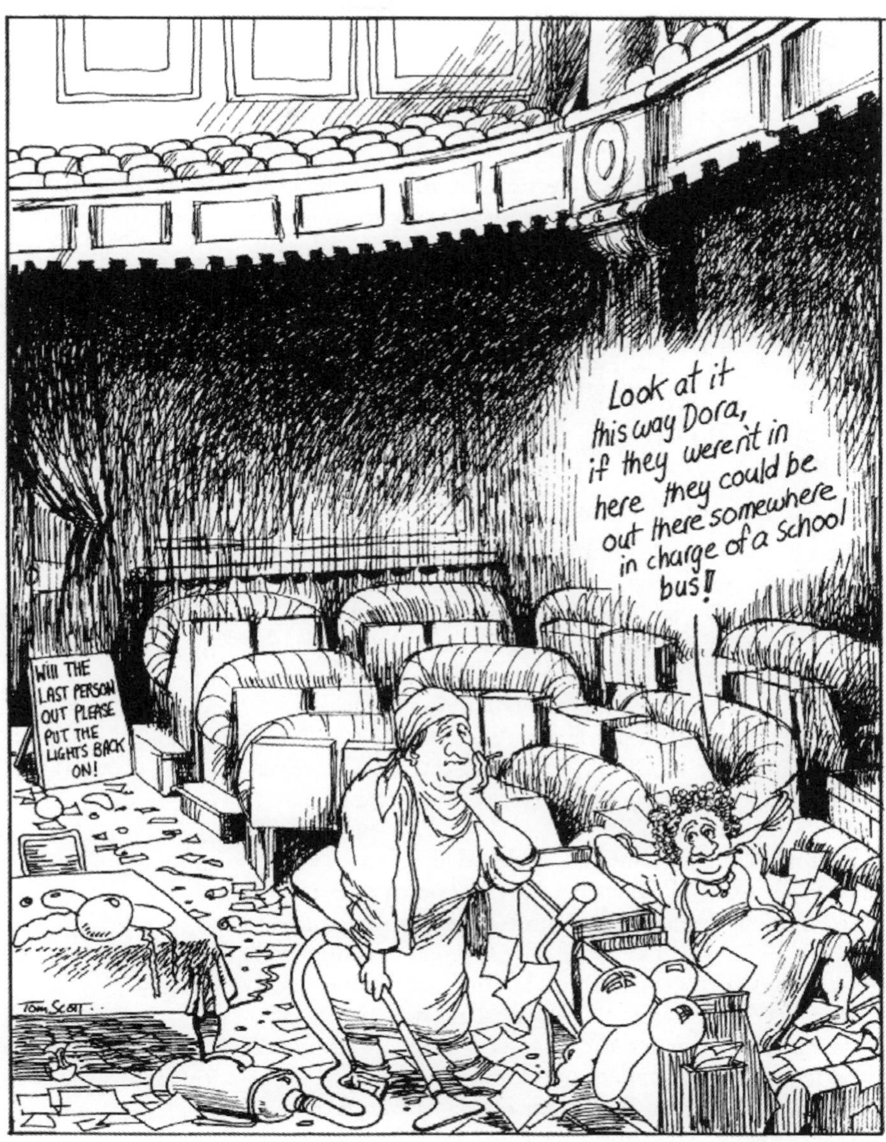

Tom Scott, *NZ Listener*, January 15 1977. ATL: A-312-4-005

Labour was beaten as comprehensively at the 1975 election as National had been humiliated three years before. National won 48 percent of the popular vote; the margin of 23 seats was its largest ever parliamentary majority.

Muldoon was now prime minister, arguably the most powerful ever. His combativeness was sufficient to subdue most colleagues and public servants; he enlarged the prime minister's department to get advice independent of treasury and foreign affairs mandarins; he interfered in his ministers' portfolios; and his staring down-the-camera-lens interview technique and ability to communicate with the 'ordinary decent bloke' produced mesmerising television performances. Most significantly, he continued as minister of finance as well.

Some saw him as the 'economic miracle worker'; others saw 'Piggy' Muldoon as a dangerous threat to the country's democratic tradition. Certainly, the prime minister's abrasive, divisive style encouraged a dormant strain of insensitivity and intolerance among New Zealanders.

For the rest of the decade Muldoon was rarely off the front pages of the nation's newspapers, often for unedifying reasons. The greatest cause célèbre, and a distasteful example of his penchant for 'counter-punching', was the angry exchange in the House in November 1976 that ultimately wrecked Colin Moyle's parliamentary career.

However, a populist demagogue on the one hand, Muldoon was cautious and conservative when it came to making decisions. He prevaricated for several years about closer economic relations with Australia; the fallout from the 1976 All Blacks tour of South Africa forced him to sign the Gleneagles Accord and, in theory at least, discourage such sporting contacts; his tinkering approach to economic management meant change was glacially slow.

Muldoon kept the economy on a short, closely guarded leash, 'fine-tuning' with mini budgets. He reined in economic activity, attempting to control inflation and reduce the overseas deficit, and engaged in wholesale state intervention to lessen dependence on imported oil and boost export income. Like his methods or not, they did lay the basis, particularly in the tourism, forestry and energy sectors, for a much broader-based economy in the future.

National won the 1978 election, its majority halved; Labour gained little satisfaction from winning the popular vote. The second oil shock, in 1979, showed Muldoon had no new ideas, but Labour was caught in its own time warp too. Bill Rowling survived, often precariously, as opposition leader after the 1978 election, but it was not until David Lange's election as deputy leader in November 1979, less than three years after he took Colin Moyle's place in the House, that Labour's fortunes looked considerably brighter.

This was the decade of protests, upping the tempo from the 1960s on a number of fronts, and now involving a growing number of middle class liberals and university students.

While opposition to the Vietnam War was generally more peaceful than elsewhere, there was a violent confrontation, and many arrests, in Auckland in 1970 during the visit of US vice-president Spiro Agnew, a fervent Vietnam War supporter. And in Christchurch in 1973, 500 police clashed with fewer anti-war demonstrators as they tried to break into a US naval support force base.

Anti-nuclear sentiment had hardened after France began weapons testing at Mururoa in 1966 and Greenpeace, newly arrived in New Zealand, sent a protest vessel to the nuclear test site in 1972. After its ramming by a French warship raised temperatures further, the third Labour government was sufficiently angered to send a New Zealand warship into the test area in 1973; this and the protests of other governments forced French testing underground in 1974.

By the 1970s, over 70 percent of Maori were living in cities and towns. Their fortunes tied to the Labour Party, they were increasingly frustrated by National's actions and attitudes during the long 1949-84 period when it dominated politics. Maori could not be ignored and were increasingly anxious and angry about the paternalistic pakeha approach to the growing poverty trap many low income urban Maori were caught in, the housing, health and education consequences leading, in turn, to street kids, drug abuse and crime.

The 1967 Maori Affairs Amendment Act, aiming to compulsorily 'improve' Maori land, became known as the 'last land grab'. The response to this and other policies was the Land March (Hikoi) of 1975, led by 80-year old Whina Cooper, which made a deep impression on many pakeha New Zealanders.

During Labour's brief 1972-75 return to power, Matiu Rata set up the Waitangi Tribunal to hear Maori claims and compensate proven treaty breaches. But the tribunal was more decorative than useful and National made sure it stayed that way. From 1971 the February 6 ceremonies at Waitangi were often the focus of anger and dissent and there were protests about land confiscation at Auckland's Bastion Point in 1977-78 and Raglan's golf course in 1978.

After protestors set fire to the Auckland Rugby Union headquarters and cut down goal posts at Christchurch's Lancaster Park, the All Blacks toured South Africa in 1970, Maori in the party deemed 'honorary whites'. In 1973, Norman Kirk banned a Springbok tour to New Zealand. After the Soweto massacre in 1976, there was an intensification of anti-apartheid feeling, powerfully articulated by Halt All Racist Tours (HART) and other organisations, but new PM Muldoon sanctioned the All Blacks touring South Africa the same year – a loss in the test series followed by a diplomatic crisis of embarrassing proportions.

During feminism's 'second wave' in the 1970s, street marches protested social issues, like safe abortions; *Broadsheet* magazine preached militancy; the Women's Electoral Lobby, begun in 1975, did what its name implied, aiming for more women in decision-making positions. The catch cry was "Girls Can Do Anything", and they were beginning to do so in previously male-dominated occupations; less happily, they also increasingly matched their male counterparts at drinking, smoking and other popular vices.

There were rarely more than four women MPs until the early 1980s, but the 1970s activists had the satisfaction of seeing remarkable increases after that. There was also considerable legislative progress: the Matrimonial Property Act 1976 provided for the equitable division of assets in separations and divorces and the Human Rights Act 1977 legislated against women's discrimination.

There were bitter battles with the Society for the Protection of the Unborn Child (SPUC) but legal abortions were much more readily available in New Zealand from 1979. Feminists brought domestic violence, with its long, silent history, into the open. From 1974, a fast-growing number of women's refuges, and related publicity, helped harden public and judicial opinion against perpetrators.

However, discrimination in the workplace was too deeply entrenched to provide any victories for the women's movement in the 1970s. The number of women in the paid workforce had risen substantially after 1961 – many of them married with older children – but whether in offices, shops, schools and hospitals, there were 'glass ceilings' firmly in place. In 1975, only 2 percent of lawyers in New Zealand were women. It was much worse for working-class women, including most Maori and Pacific Islanders, who found it almost impossible to break out of a cycle of low pay, part-time work and regular job loss.

Concern about the environment was no longer a quirky, minority interest. In 1970, a total of 264,907 New Zealanders, nearly 10 percent of the population, signed the 'Save

Malcolm Walker, *Sunday News*, January 18 1976. ATL: H-358-001

Manapouri' petition. Lake Manapouri was not raised and the Clutha Valley development plan was modified. The Values Party, precursor to the Greens, contested the 1972 election, contributing to the debate that forced the government to take the environmental movement more seriously. There was a minister for the environment from 1972 and a commission for the environment the next year. Nevertheless, old habits died hard and there was another storm of protest in 1973 when the government decided to sell South Island beech forests for chipping. In 1975 the newly formed Native Forests Action Council claimed the Forest Service's announcement of much reduced indigenous forest cutting targets did not go far enough. Two years later the council delivered a 341,159 signature forest protection petition to government. Also in 1977, the Queen Elizabeth II National Trust was set up to protect significant natural and cultural features on private land.

Going hand-in-hand with the challenges of protesting was the 'baby boomer' penchant for sometimes neurotic self absorption and self-improvement that ran the gamut from consciousness raising groups to self-help books. As the established health system came under scrutiny there was also an increasing interest in alternative health approaches including naturopathy, homeopathy and acupuncture.

Television became omnipresent during the 1970s. A night's news bulletins influenced opinions the next day; familiar TV faces became the country's first celebrities; the 1972 election was fought on 'the box' rather than in the nation's town halls. Colour transmission began in 1973; television was restructured into TV1 and TV2 in 1975; a succession of telethons raised millions for varied causes; drama ranged from the first, long-running 'soap' *Close to Home* to *The Governor*, a much grander production based, rather loosely, on the life of Sir George Grey.

Television music shows launched the careers of a number of entertainers and groups in the 1970s, none bigger than Split Enz, the group debuting in 1973 on 'Studio One'.

There was a flowering of theatres early in the decade: Four Seasons in Wanganui, the Court Theatre in Christchurch, Theatre Corporate in Auckland, Centrepoint in Palmerston North and the Fortune in Dunedin. And, in Wellington, Downstage moved into the impressive Hannah Playhouse, built on the site of its first Courtenay Place headquarters. The nutrient which was to enrich most of them was the fertile and funny pen of Roger Hall, his *Glide Time* in 1976 the first in a steady flow of box office successes.

In 1970, eight years after it was formed, dancers from the New Zealand Ballet performed at Expo 70 in Japan; in 1973 the Impulse Dance Theatre pioneered modern dance in the country.

A number of young directors – including Geoff Murphy (*Wild Man*) and Roger Donaldson (*Sleeping Dogs*) – unveiled their first feature films in 1977, the year before the New Zealand Film Commission was set up; now the country's small independent film-makers had the opportunity to top up their modest budgets from public funds. Hollywood, badly hit by television, was fighting back with blockbusters like *Jaws* (1975) and *Star Wars* (1977).

There was a confident air to the work of New Zealand novelists as the range of themes were expanded by James McNeish, C K Stead, Maurice Shadbolt, Albert Wendt, Maurice Gee and Fiona Kidman. There was also a steady increase in New Zealand histories, with Dick Scott, Keith Sinclair and Michael King making diverse, authoritative contributions, and Margaret Mahy was beginning to earn a reputation as one of the world's most imaginative children's writers. In the early 1970s, Witi Ihimaera's *Pounamu, Pounamu* and *Tangi* were, respectively, the first published short story collection and novel by a Maori writer. The NZ Authors' Fund, begun in 1973, to compensate authors for the use of their books in libraries, was welcome news for those struggling to live from their writing.

The two 'oil shocks' in the 1970s were just that in a country that had become so dependent on the petrol engine. In 1973, the government reduced the open road speed limit to 80km/h, banned weekend petrol sales, and encouraged engine conversion to alternative fuels; in 1979, a 'carless day' scheme kept all vehicles garaged one day week. The crisis passed, but it was virtually the end of gas guzzling' six-cylinder models and definitely the beginning of the 'small' Japanese car era.

Time to Go

National won narrowly, and somewhat surprisingly, in 1969. But fast-rising prices and an immediate defeat in the Marlborough by-election rocked National as much as it boosted Labour's confidence. The 'steady does it' formula of reacting to situations when public pressure demanded was no longer adequate. National's caucus was increasingly divided between Marshall and Rob Muldoon as Holyoake dithered about retirement, and an ageing cabinet staggered from one crisis to another: Lake Manapouri, unmanageable inflation, unpopular taxes and ineffective price and wage restraints. Labour was firmly ahead in political polls until Marshall became PM. However, although his 'new look' cabinet gave a temporary fillip to party morale and National's poll standing, the country was clearly of the opinion that it was time for a change of government.

1. Jack Marshall was the obvious successor to the prime ministerial mantle, but Holyoake's tactic to delay the day was to weigh his deputy down with more and more heavy ministerial responsibilities. *The Prime Minister has "no present proposals ....",* Nevile Lodge, *Evening Post*, 1970. ATL: B-137-098
2. Although they were very different – in background, education and personality – Holyoake and Marshall had worked well together for many years. But by now, as Marshall made it clear he wanted the top job, there was much more tension in the relationship. *1972 Happy Holiday Snaps No 1*, Peter Bromhead, *NZ Truth*, 1972. ATL: A-314-1-006
3. Rob Muldoon thought he could win the leadership vote after Holyoake stepped aside.. In the event, Marshall won easily but Muldoon, appointed his deputy, was perfectly positioned to move after the new prime minister lost an increasingly unwinnable election. *Old Story under New Management*, Deighton, *Auckland Star*, 1972. ATL: A-297-009
4. External pressures on the economy forced National to experiment with indicative planning, but performances fell embarrassingly short of the targets set by the National Development Conference in 1968-69. *Marking at the Butts*, Gordon Minhinnick, *NZ Herald*, March 10 1972. ATL: A-311-1-041
5. Marshall was not at ease on the hustings. He did not have the common touch, nor could he stir an audience with rhetoric – two talents Norman Kirk had in abundance. *The Election*, Deighton, *Auckland Star*, October 31 1972. ATL: A-297-007

1

The Prime Minister has "no present proposals for any changes in Cabinet."

2

3

OLD STORY UNDER NEW MANAGEMENT.

5

4

MARKING AT THE BUTTS

The Short Reign of Big Norm

Norman Kirk had a varied carreer before becoming Labour's leader in 1965. He had left school in Christchurch before his 13th birthday, worked at labouring jobs, qualified as a boilerman, became mayor of Kaiapoi, then MP for Lyttelton in 1957 and Labour Party president in 1964. Although Kirk lost narrowly in 1969, his increasingly assured leadership gave focus to nationalistic stirrings with an independent approach to foreign policy and, at home, offered positive programmes in areas such as health, housing and regional development where National's performance had been mediocre. Before the 1972 election, Kirk stumped the country, quoting from a policy document, detailing promises and their costs, like an evangelist finding inspiration in his bible. The electorate was converted – and Labour won a stunning victory.

1. A political pragmatist, Kirk knew he could not lose three elections in a row – so he submitted himself to a complete makeover. He lost weight, let his curly silver hair grow and dressed in snappy new suits. The difference – and result – was electrifying. *"It s Time, Gentlemen Please!"*, Eric Heath, *Dominion*, November 27 1972. ATL: A-311-4-017
2. The Maui gas field, 35km off the Taranaki coast, was discovered in 1969 and, after the 1973 'oil shock', was developed by a consortium of oil companies and the government. Full production began in 1979. *Maui*, Gordon Minhinnick, *NZ Herald*, April 5 1973. ATL: A-311-1-042
3. Labour was slow to react to the slowing of the world economy following the 1973 Arab-Israeli war and first 'oil-shock'. Inflation rose dramatically and there were large wage increases to compensate for higher prices. *Price Regulations*, Peter Bromhead, *Auckland Star*, December 1 1973. ATL: A-314-1-007
4. As inflation worsened, a poorly conceived MRP price justification scheme was introduced, bringing industrial strife with it. *"Can you hold on a bit?"*, Peter Bromhead, *Auckland Star*, December 5 1973. ATL: A-314-1-008
5. Labour's campaign to stop French nuclear testing in the Pacific included the despatch of a frigate to the Mururoa test area. Further, Kirk was the first New Zealand politician to advocate a South Pacific nuclear free zone. *"Is there some reason ...?"*, Eric Heath, *Dominion* February 27 1974. ATL: C-132-124

1

2

3

4

5

"IS THERE SOME REASON WHY WE CAN'T SUPPORT A NUCLEAR FREE ZONE, GENTLEMEN?"

Big Shoes to Fill

Bill Rowling, finance minister and then Kirk's successor in August 1974, was a cautious economics graduate caught between the rational need to systematically invest in faltering economic growth, after years of 'stop-go' policies, and the new Labour government's impatience to implement its social agenda. Rowling's attempts to dampen down fast rising prices and inflation achieved little, even before the massive oil price hikes following the Yom Kippur war in October 1973. Before long, the record overseas reserves were gone, with import costs sky-rocketing and export prices sagging, and New Zealand signed up for the largest single overseas loan in its history. The underlying fragility of the economy had been exposed, but Rowling rejected the traditional, knee-jerk, retrenchment option and attempted to juggle Labour's promises, like holding government charges, while encouraging economic growth. Although inflation reached 15 percent and unemployment and prices shot up, New Zealand weathered the global crisis of a threefold increase in oil prices better than most other countries.

1. With his mild manner, light voice and short stature, Bill Rowling was unlucky to have been preceded by Kirk and facing Muldoon on the opposition benches – two of the all-time larger-than-life prime ministers. *Prime Minister*, Bob Brockie, *Sunday Times*, September 1974. ATL: H-705-028
2. One bright spot – as export prices fell behind increasing volumes of higher priced imports – was the trading position with Australia. *"Please sir, I don t want any more!"*, Bill Wrathall, *NZ Truth*, September 23 1975. ATL: A-289-54
3. Trade and industry minister Warren Freer had the unenviable job of trying to make the MRP scheme work. To try to slow inflation, all retail items displayed an MRP shield showing a maximum price. In fact, the rate of inflation resulted in constantly changing maximum prices and the eventual collapse of the scheme. *Can I have my horse back please?"*, Peter Bromhead, *Auckland Star*, August 12 1975. ATL: A-314-1-011
4. At the 1975 election, the 'Citizens for Rowling' campaign – with its 'Clergy for Rowling' and 'Lawyers for Rowling' offshoots – backfired, the elite roll call not impressing heartland New Zealand. *All God s chillun got left wings …*, Sid Scales, *Otago Daily Times*, November 20 1975. ATL: A-319-025
5. There was not time to turn the economy around before the 1975 election and Rowling's economic strategy was, according to Rob Muldoon, "borrow and hope". It was a phrase that stuck, along with an array of other slings and arrows. *The Martyrdom of Saint Wallace*, Bob Brockie, *National Business Review*, 1975. ATL: A-314-2-065

1

2

3

4

"ALL GOD'S CHILLUN GOT LEFT WINGS . . ."

5

The Martyrdom of Saint Wallace

The Tamaki Terror

Mistakenly, Rob Muldoon, Auckland cost-accountant and the aggressive, 'counter-punching' minister of finance since 1967, thought he had the numbers to succeed Holyoake in early 1972. But Muldoon had underestimated National's debt to Jack Marshall, Holyoake's loyal deputy for 14 years. In the event, the deputy leadership, coupled with Marshall's low-key style and his crushing defeat in 1972, eventually strengthened Muldoon's position. A consensus emerged while Marshall was overseas in April-May 1974 that Muldoon's more combative style was essential to National's comeback. Marshall stood above the lobbying and went quietly in July when the caucus finally made its feelings clear. Just a month later, Norman Kirk died and with him went one of the more compelling reasons for Muldoon's bloodless 'coup'. In 1975, National, with pinpoint accuracy, pitched its promises and its 'New Zealand the way you want it' slogan – and exactly reversed a massive 23-seat deficit. Muldoon had barnstormed around the country for 18 months before the election, ridiculing Rowling, offering strong leadership and promising, more tangibly, voluntary unionism, play-where-you-like rugby and a better superannuation deal.

1. The oil shock and dropping export returns turned boom-time into grim recession and Muldoon's aggressive election campaign, linked to scare-tactic TV commercials, hammered away at this and traditional Labour bogeys. *"Beauty is in the eye of the beholder ...",* Peter Bromhead, *Auckland Star*, December 6 1975. ATL: A-314-1-018
2. Muldoon clung to wholesale state regulation and public investment to keep New Zealanders in work. Later, his support for welfare state security had right-wing opponents branding him a 'socialist'. *"Hi-ho! Hi-Ho!",* Bob Brockie, *National Business Review*, May 12 1976. ATL: A-314-2-066
3. National pushed voluntary unionism at the 1972 election, but Muldoon's rhetoric spoke louder than his actions. The 1976 amendment to the Industrial Relations Act legislated for union ballots to assess the movement's support for compulsory unionism. Voluntary unionism finally arrived in early 1984. *"As you have heard, delegates ..."* Tom Scott, *NZ Listener*, May 29 1976. ATL: A-312-4-003
4. The irony seemed to escape Muldoon, but at National's 1978 conference he spoke out against challenges to sitting members. *"By and large, the tradition ....",* Peter Bromhead, *Auckland Star*, July 29 1976. ATL: H-745-003
5. Constitutional experts and opposition MPs tut-tutted when Sir Keith was appointed governor-general, the first politician in this non-political and largely ceremonial position. Some saw Holyoake's appointment as a further consolidation of Muldoon's power. *The king-maker*, Bob Brockie, *National Business Review*, March 16 1977. ATL: H-705-013

1

2

3

As you have heard, delegates, this is the sawdust Caesar who has attacked the living standards of the working man!
— this is the little Hitler who has viciously libelled the Trade Union movement!
— this is the fascist who wants to introduce voluntary unionism to smash the unions!
— it won't happen however, thanks to this living Saint who has unified us as never before!
29.5.76

4

BY AND LARGE, THE TRADITION OF THIS PARTY IS NOT TO TACKLE SITTING MEMBERS...
BROMHEAD

5

THE KING-MAKER
Brockie

Bags of Economic Tricks

National claimed the new prime minister's restoration of 'the shattered economy' would be remembered as the 'Muldoon Economic Miracle'. Unfortunately, Muldoon's formidable image was built mostly on his public aggressiveness, his ability to persuade the public to accept the unpalatable, and well-publicised 'mini-budgets'. His underlying caution, and an over-riding political expediency, delayed the essential and fundamental restructuring of the New Zealand economy strongly recommended by the NZ Planning Council he established. The second 'oil shock', following the Shah of Iran's overthrow early in 1979, quickly showed that Muldoon's interventionist, reactive, tinkering approach no longer worked. When New Zealand's oil bill doubled virtually overnight, Muldoon retreated to his old formula of incentives and imposed counter-productive sales taxes. He also introduced a massive programme of diversification and import substitution projects, the most grandiose of them energy-related. Inflation rocketed to nearly 18 percent; there was no economic growth; unemployment was at its highest level since the 1930s; and more New Zealanders left the country than ever before.

1. Muldoon was probably most successful in the 1976-78 period. He largely shielded New Zealanders from a worsening situation, controlling economic activity to check inflation and the overseas defecit, with state intervention to reduce imported oil requirements and push up export income. *Hard Times – Kiwi Style ...*, Peter Bromhead, *Auckland Star*, October 2 1976. ATL: A-130-031
2. What Muldoon pulled out of the hat before the 1978 election was primarily a restructuring of the tax system – giving relief to both low and average wage earners – that persuaded the electorate National was, as the campaign slogan said, keeping its word. National's majority was cut to 10 seats; Labour won the popular vote. *The hat trick*, Gillian Fraser, *PSA Journal*, June 1978. ATL: J-065-070
3. There had been a lengthy slide in agricultural commodity prices through the 1970s and, despite 'special treatment', Britain was taking barely half as much produce as previously. It was a major challenge for overseas trade minister Brian Talboys to 'milk' traditional markets for additional income to ease the serious balance of payments crisis. *Farmer Brian*, Malcolm Evans, *NZ Herald*, July 21 1977. ATL: B-124-012
4. After decades of complacent reliance on Britain, it took time to develop new markets in Japan, North America, mainland Europe and the Middle East, particularly as frozen carcasses were of limited appeal. At the end of the 1970s, millions of unsold carcasses were being rendered down into blood and bone fertiliser. *"They might be rich ....?"*, Bob Brockie, *National Business Review*, July 26 1978. ATL: A-314-2-068

1

2

3

FARMER BRIAN

4

The Also-Rans

After National's astonishing 1975 comeback, the parliamentary Labour Party and its morale were in tatters. With Rowling making little impact in parliament, in the press or the polls, and with the party's preoccupation with its own internal problems, the most effective protests against Muldoon bluster sometimes came from his own caucus – particularly a group of independent-minded Hamilton MPs. In May 1978, two MPs rejected by their parties – one National and the other Labour –finished their terms as the first independents for many years. Bruce Beetham, Social Credit leader and MP for Rangitikei since a February 1978 by-election, was also in parliament. Further opposition to the government came from several 'National' alternative candidates who contested National-held seats in 1978 for a variety of reasons.

1. Labour struggled after its crushing 1975 defeat. Rowling was not a sufficiently assertive opposition leader, he had to deal with a sometimes rebellious caucus, and he did not handle the 'Moyle Affair' well, finally persuading his close friend to resign. *".... This is getting monotonous",* Peter Bromhead, *Auckland Star*, January 27 1977. ATL: A-130-034
2. Following his resignation from parliament, Colin Moyle finally decided against contesting the by-election in his Mangere seat. A number of hopefuls, including Mike Moore, sought selection, but rank outsider David Lange was selected and romped home at the by-election. Colin Moyle returned to parliament in 1981. *"Cheer up lads ....",* Malcolm Walker, *Sunday News*, February 20 1977. ATL: A-316-2-018
3. In 1978, Labour narrowly won the popular vote but National was comfortably ahead, 51 seats to 40. *"Wait for it! ....",* Gordon Minhinnick, *NZ Herald*, November 27 1978. ATL: A-311-1-047
4. Bruce Beetham retained his seat but, although Social Credit doubled its share of the vote to over 16 percent, it was not enough to give the party a second member of parliament. *"Only room for one of you",* Bob Brockie, *National Business Review*, December 7 1978. ATL: A-314-2-069
5. To Muldoon, the Federation of Labour was of more concern than the parliamentary opposition. Muldoon had a pragmatic working relationship with FOL president Tom Skinner, as Holland had with Walsh. Skinner's successor, Jim Knox, was more of an ideologue and, at a time when a wage-tax trade-off was critical, Muldoon could not get him to work to their mutual advantages. Ironically, Muldoon and FOL secretary Ken Douglas, a communist, understood each other better. *"Safe as Fort Knox!",* Bill Wrathall, *NZ Truth,* May 15 1979. ATL: A-317-2-001

1

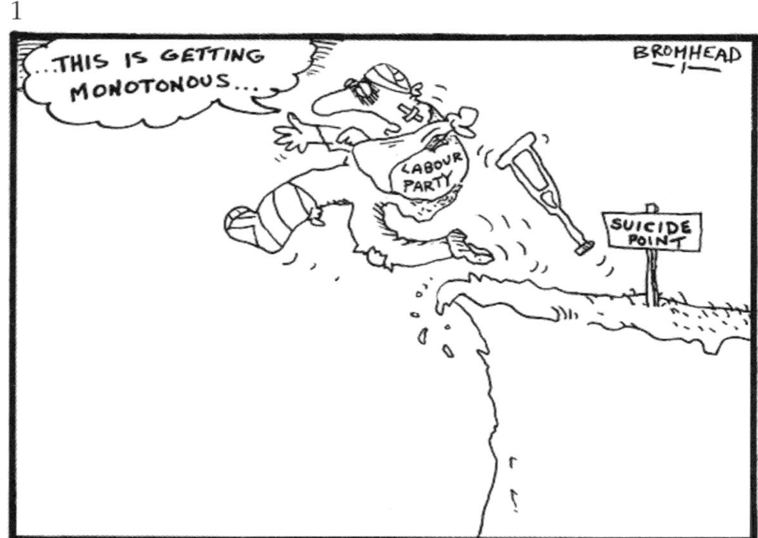

2

3

"Wait for it! Wait for it!"

4

SOCKED
only room for one of you
full
PARLIAMENTARY PACK
Brockie

5

F.O.L.
PRESIDENT
SECRETARY
DOUGLAS
S.U.P.
ETC.
SAFE AS FORT KNOX!

Lots of Lip

Muldoon's combativeness was always sufficiently close to the surface to subdue most people and there seems little doubt that his abrasive aggressiveness encouraged the same qualities in some New Zealanders. His tough, name-calling style was novel and effective while he was minister of finance and opposition leader. As prime minister, Muldoon not only continued to bait and bludgeon his favourite local targets as if he was in opposition, but his boots-and-all performance internationally sent shivers down many diplomatic spines. Abraham Ordia, from the Supreme Council of Sport in Africa, was told to "stew in his own juice", and the remark that New Zealanders emigrating to Australia raised the IQ in both countries was neither original nor likely to warm Muldoon's frigid relationship with Malcolm Fraser. Locally, the most notorious incident, a vicious exchange at the end of the bitter 1976 parliamentary session, with the prime minister ruthlessly pursuing contradictory responses to homosexuality allegations, led to the resignation from parliament of Colin Moyle, a potential Labour Party leader.

1. When Muldoon visited China in late April 1976, his audience with Chairman Mao was purely symbolic as the Chinese leader was too frail to talk trade or anything else. *"....and if you welsh ....",* Bob Brockie, *National Business Review, May 5 1976.* ATL: A-314-2-079
2. After the initial parliamentary incident, Muldoon persisted with the unbalanced judicial enquiry that precipitated Moyle's resignation. *"Now how on earth did that happen?",* Peter Bromhead, *Auckland Star*, February 12 1977. ATL: A-328-036
3. After disparaging remarks about Jimmy Carter's peanut-farming background, Muldoon found it hard to arrange a White House audience with the new US president. *Greetings*, Gordon Minhinnick, *NZ Herald*, November 7 1977. ATL: A-311-1-046
4. Muldoon's views on communism and the USSR were well known, but there was also the need to make up the shortfall in meat, wool and dairy produce sales to Britain. *Bearable*, Malcolm Evans, *NZ Herald*, August 11 1976. ATL: A-315-5-002
5. Muldoon's approach to diplomacy before the signing of a fisheries agreement with Japan in 1978 was typically tough-talking. *The Battle to Control the Sun*, Nevile Lodge, *Evening Post*, 1977. ATL: B-135-165

1

2

3

GREETINGS

4

BEARABLE

5

THE BATTLE TO CONTROL THE SUN

The Unhappy Country

With Norman Kirk's death, something else seemed to die in New Zealand. Politically, freshly-minted hope was soon replaced with a mean-spirited divisiveness that seeped through to everyday life. In 1976, the country was split when the All Blacks toured South Africa with National's blessing. But it was the resulting international furore that forced Muldoon to bow to mounting Commonwealth pressure and sign the Gleneagles agreement, undertaking to actively discourage sporting contact with South Africa. Back home, he blurred the agreement's meaning and went to tortuous lengths to avoid outright bans. It was International Women's Year in 1975, but the government allowed the 'free conscience' vote in parliament which tightened the grounds for abortion to the point where rape was excluded. Concern about civil liberties grew: the chief justice found against the prime minister for advising employers to flout superannuation legislation; the contentious Security Intelligence Service legislation did not go to a select committee; and the government's attitude to Pacific over-stayers and Maori land protesters was worrying.

1. A number of early Muldoon decisions, some based on National's election manifesto, were particularly unpopular among younger New Zealanders. *The Young Vote in 78*, Peter Bromhead, *Auckland Star*, August 7 1976. ATL: A-344-073
2. Muldoon invited visits by US nuclear-powered warships in the name of ANZUS obligations and an expressed concern about an increasing Russian presence in the region. He claimed opposition – including protest flotillas and industrial stoppages – were inspired by Moscow-aligned communists. *"Hello again, Sailor ...!"*, Malcolm Walker, *Sunday News*, October 3 1976. ATL: A-316-2-017
3. With Muldoon's personality and policies so divisive, he was routinely blamed for things he could not, in all fairness, be responsible for! *"Rain, rain, rain ....", Malcolm Evans, NZ Herald*, September 21 1977. ATL: B-124-008
4. For many, the 1976 All Black tour of South Africa caused more pain than pleasure. The test series was lost three matches to one but, more significantly, the government's support of the tour resulted in 29 African nations boycotting that year's Montreal Olympics because of New Zealand's participation. Muldoon tried to blame the HART and CARE protest organisations for the country's sudden notoriety, claiming their "propaganda" was bordering on treason. *"As a bridge-building exercise ....",* Tom Scott, *NZ Listener,* October 9 1976. ATL: A-312-4-008
5. Despite a confusion of ministerial denials, police randomly checked Pacific Islanders during a migrant over-stayer crackdown. Police minister McCready explained: "If you have a herd of Jerseys and two Friesians, the Friesians stand out." *"I said WOGS, not dogs",* Bob Brockie, *National Business Review*, November 3 1976. ATL: A-314-2-067

1

2

3

"Rain, rain, rain – that Muldoon's got a lot to answer for, Ethel."

4

As a bridge-building exercise I still say it was worth it!
In spite of— the Olympic boycott! the racial violence! the biased refereeing! the rough play! —what are you.. a madman?
No, a dentist!
down, Fang!

5

I said WOGS Not Dogs!
Brockie

Protest Lines

In many ways, 'protest' defined the 1970s. Economic uncertainty and a less secure future gave a third political party, Social Credit, a higher percentage of 'protest' votes than it could have reasonably expected in balmier times. There were protests and anger about the rugby relationship with South Africa, and the reversal of New Zealand's nuclear-free status. In 1970, nearly 10 percent of the population signed the 'Save Manapouri' petition in response to politicians' and industry's indifference to the environment. In the 1975 Land March (Hikoi), from Cape Reinga to parliament, 35,000 marched in a peaceful protest at the loss of Maori land. Women marched in support of safe abortions. However, protests about discrimination bore fruit when the Human Rights Commission Act, in 1977, gave practical expression to the 'Girls Can Do Anything' catch-cry – with women applying to be engineers, firefighters, train drivers, prison officers, mechanics, meat inspectors, traffic officers, air force pilots, and jockeys. Dairy farmers complained about daylight saving, parents were angry with their teenagers, South Islanders were sick of being exploited by northerners, Nigeria boycotted the Commonwealth Games because of New Zealand.

1. The first of a series of United Women's Conventions was held in Auckland in 1973. It helped define the goals the women's movement could agree on – and showed up some areas where there were major differences. *"Er .... Is there a man in the house?"*, Peter Bromhead, *Auckland Star*, September 15 1973. ATL: A-314-1-009
2. It was the 'permissive society', but the moral guardians made sure there was no place in the curriculum for sex education in New Zealand schools. *".... How dare you disgust me when I m eating!"*, Peter Bromhead, *Auckland Star*, August 4 1977. ATL: A-335-064
3. Research showed reading suffering as television tightened its grip on New Zealanders' leisure time with the introduction of colour in 1973 and a second channel two years later. *Book Week*, Peter Bromhead, *Auckland Star*, October 3 1978. ATL: A-314-1-013
4. The Human Rights Commission Act in 1977 prohibited discrimination on the grounds of sex in employment and a number of other areas. In 1978 Linda Jones, credited with being the country's first woman jockey, and other women, campaigned successfully to have the NZ Rules of Racing changed to allow female riders. *"Ladies first!"*, Malcolm Evans, *NZ Herald*, November 1 1977. ATL: A-315-5-004
5. The 1975 Royal Commission on Contraception, Sterilisation and Abortion deliberated for 21 months before producing, in March 1977, a conservative, controversial report. Although not satisfying either abortion reformers or 'right to lifers', the report was the basis of legislation passed in December. *"I wonder what HER choice would be?"*, Malcolm Walker, *Sunday News*, May 1 1977. ATL: A-316-2-019

1

2

3

4

"LADIES FIRST!"

5

6. Daylight saving, which had been in force between the two world wars, was re-introduced in the mid-1970s. Many dairy farmers hated the idea, but the public response was generally favourable and a period was set from the last Sunday in October each year to the first Sunday in March the following one. *"He s all steamed up about daylight saving ....",* Nevile Lodge, *Evening Post*, 1975. ATL: B-134-843

7. In 1977, the Anglican church in other parts of the world was very divided when five female priests were ordained in New Zealand. *Lady of the Cloth*, Malcolm Evans, *NZ Herald*, December 16 1977. ATL: B-124-007

8. Teenagers, and how to live with them, were now a perennial media topic and of growing concern to parents worried about 'teen culture' and the 'peer pressure' accompanying it. *"Did you remember to put the cat out?",* Peter Bromhead, *Auckland Star*, August 8 1978. ATL: A-314-1-015

9. The Edmonton Commonwealth Games was not one of New Zealand's most successful: Nigeria stayed away because of the South Africa sporting contacts issue and the medal haul was half as good as in Christchurch four years before. But there could well have been other podium possibilities when the competitors arrived home. *Welcome Home*, Eric Heath, *Dominion*, August 15 1978. ATL: B-157-026

10. The Cook Strait cable link was supplying the North Island with a vital 30 percent of its electricity in the late 1970s, with the South Island apparently getting very little in return. The South Island's complete independence had been put to the vote in parliament in 1865; now there was considerable popular sentiment to do so again. *Unplugged*, Simon Darby, *Auckland Star*, June 6 1979. ATL: A-313-1-046

6

"HE'S BEEN ALL STEAMED UP ABOUT DAYLIGHT SAVING EVER SINCE THEY BROUGHT IT IN, BUT TO MAKE THINGS WORSE HE GOT ALL MIXED UP AND PUT HIS CLOCK ON ANOTHER HOUR INSTEAD OF PUTTING IT BACK!"

7

A LADY OF THE CLOTH

8

DID YOU REMEMBER TO PUT THE CAT OUT?
Mmm
WHAT ABOUT THE KIDS?
DAMN!
HERE..GO FIND YOURSELF A DISCO OR SOMETHING..
$
BROMHEAD

9

1
2
3
ERIC HEATH

10

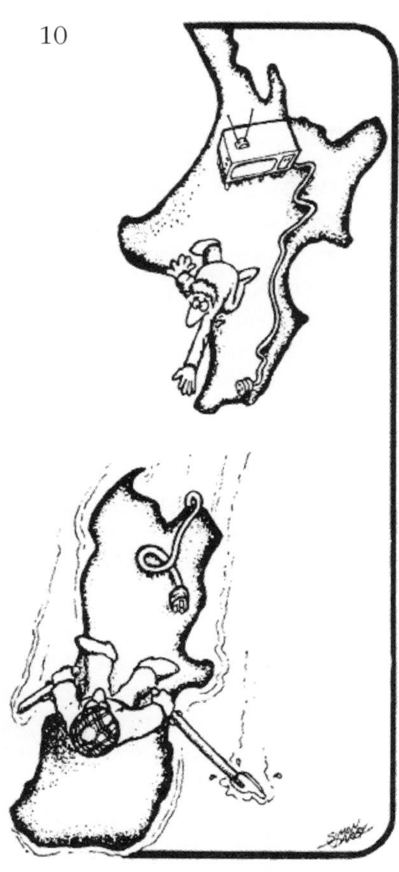

10: 1980-1989

LABOUR VEERS TO THE RIGHT

At the beginning of the 1980s, Robert Muldoon was becoming as unpopular within the National Party as he was in the electorate at large.

The last straw for Muldoon's caucus, already frustrated by his increasingly dictatorial behaviour and unwillingness to open up the economy, was the shock loss, in September 1980, of the East Coast Bays seat to Social Credit after he allowed the sitting member, a personal friend, to resign and take up a diplomatic post with a year of the parliamentary term to run.

The next month Muldoon had to use all his political guile to turn aside the 'colonels' coup', engineered by a quartet of middle-level but respected cabinet ministers. The coup leaders had the numbers to defeat Muldoon, but both he and his deputy, and likely successor, Brian Talboys were overseas. On his return Muldoon fought tenaciously, including a television appeal to the 'Rob's Mob' admirers of his populist politics. Talboys procrastinated and the crisis passed. The unforgiving Muldoon promptly forced Talboys' resignation. He then backed loyal friend Duncan MacIntyre, seriously compromised in a loan controversy, for the deputy leadership.

Labour had not made the most of its opportunities when, after the 1978 election, the deepening fuel crisis forced the government to make longer term, controversial economic decisions. On the positive side, they elected businessman Jim Anderton as party president and replaced deputy leader Bob Tizard with David Lange, but harmony was stretched by Roger Douglas's 'alternative budget' in July 1980 and Matt Rata's resignation.

While nearly all economic indicators were in retreat, National stayed ahead in the polls only because Labour and Social Credit split the growing opposition support. 'Think Big' and the cynical exploitation of the internally divisive and internationally damaging Springbok rugby tour gave Muldoon the 1981 election – losing the popular vote again but scraping in by a one seat margin.

The National Party generally revered winners, and Muldoon had been a three-time winner but he was going too far for some members of his caucus. A welcome to nuclear-armed warships from the United States and a frigate offered to Britain during the Falklands war, voluntary unionism and special legislation to circumvent Clyde High Dam holdups troubled National's more 'liberal' back benchers, notably Marilyn Waring and Mike Minogue. Cabinet minister Derek Quigley was forced to resign when he questioned the government's growth strategy. Muldoon was several times saved the indignity of legislative defeat by Social Credit votes and Labour defections.

Meanwhile, an indication of the electorate's frustration was the decision of property magnate Bob Jones, once a Muldoon confidante, to form the New Zealand Party and contest the 1984 election in protest at interest rate controls and the lengthy, back-to-the-wall wage and price freeze imposed in June 1982.

The election was held four months earlier than it might have been, triggered by Muldoon's claim that he could no longer rely on Waring's support. His justifications were largely spurious, but weariness, serious health problems and increasing evidence that his band-aid economic tinkering was failing contributed to his snap election decision.

Labour was in better shape for the 1984 election than National. After Bill Rowling stood down as opposition leader in February 1983, the much slimmer David Lange, in his well-fitting suits and carefully styled hair and fashionable spectacles, looked and sounded every inch the moderate, consensus-seeking prime minister elect. Labour's polling had shown the electorate's contradictory desire for reconciliation and strong leadership, and these were the key themes from Lange's inspirational opening address through to the remarkable TV confrontation between the two party leaders a few days before the poll.

The election was a crushing loss for Muldoon and National, the party securing just 36 percent of the vote. The New Zealand Party did not win a seat but its vote splitting contributed to Labour's overall 17-seat majority. In a final act of defiance, Muldoon brought New Zealand to the edge of an unprecedented constitutional crisis when he briefly defied the incoming Labour government's instructions to devalue the dollar.

The 20 percent devaluation, to stop the run on currency reserves precipitated by the snap election, was heaven-sent for new finance minister Roger Douglas, who had been developing a 'monetarist'–small government, low inflation – agenda for several years, and he seized the opportunity to set in train a seemingly irreversible series of decisions. The goal, that Douglas shared with like-minded Treasury bureaucrats, was a radically deregulated economy driven by market forces and in a few short months, and with minimal consultation, New Zealand was transformed from one of the most restriction-riddled western-style economies to one of the least regulated.

Lange and Douglas were, in 1984, the perfect political team. Lange was fully committed to the government's economic reforms during its first term. The apparent rationality of Douglas's ideas appealed to him; his Methodist puritan streak reconciled him to the need for 'pain' before 'gain'; his most senior colleagues were young and receptive to new ideas and change; and he was evangelical about 'selling' policies that were the antithesis of 'Muldoonism'.

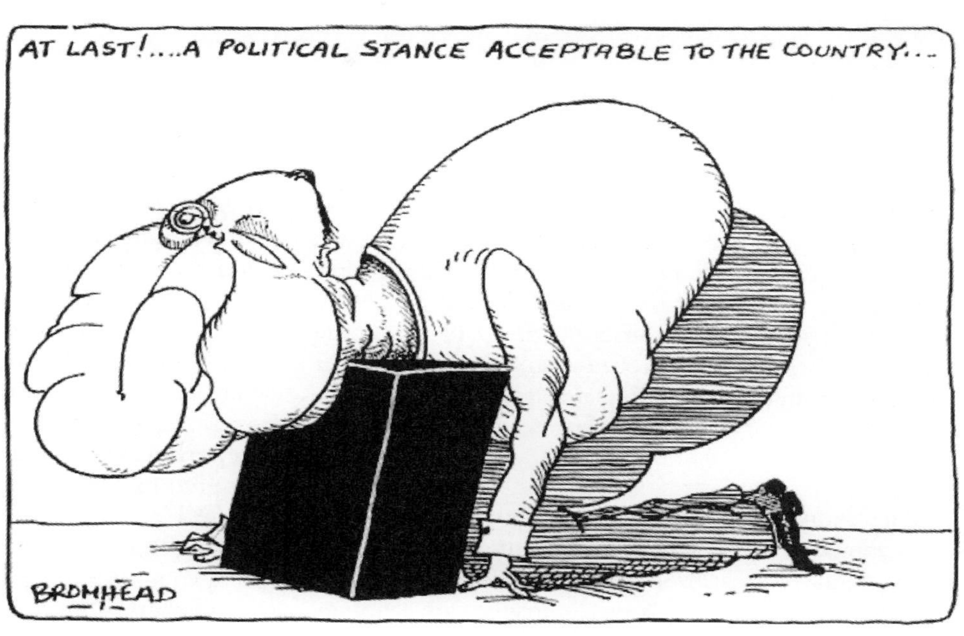

AT LAST!....A POLITICAL STANCE ACCEPTABLE TO THE COUNTRY...
BROMHEAD

Peter Bromhead, *Auckland Star,* October 18 1980. ATL: A-330-029

Economic crisis management was Douglas's justification as Labour removed restrictions on banks, overseas borrowing and foreign exchange purchases and, in March 1985, floated the New Zealand dollar, introduced radical tax changes (including a goods and services tax, now embedded in the language as GST), eliminated agricultural subsidies and removed much of the manufacturing sector's protection.

The 'efficiency' catch-cry was also behind the creation of nine state-owned enterprises (SOEs) carved out of former government trading departments. Staid economic predictability had vanished and everyone struggled to cope with the see-sawing ups and downs of inflation, interest rates, share prices and the Kiwi dollar as local and international 'market forces' buffeted the country.

Appalled by the government's conservative, market-led economic policies, the party faithful welcomed its radical foreign policy. David Lange, as foreign minister, was an eloquent advocate for the total ban of nuclear-powered and armed warships from New Zealand ports, pushed for a nuclear-free South Pacific, strengthened diplomatic contacts with Asia and Africa and upheld the Gleneagles agreement with more vigour than the previous administration. The ultimate ANZUS break, when the United States was unbending with its 'neither confirm nor deny' policy about the nuclear status of its warships, strengthened anti-nuclear feeling and American threats were resented. The sinking of Greenpeace's *Rainbow Warrior* by French agents in Auckland harbour in July 1985 drove bad economic news off the front pages and was a long-running saga that fascinated and distracted New Zealanders.

All the while, Labour's eager-beaver cabinet was committed to other initiatives – a Bill of Rights, legal clout for the Treaty of Waitangi, official language status for Maori, a new environment ministry, homosexual law reform, and the restructuring of local government. Despite growing economic concerns, the government's overall dynamism, coupled with National's stumbling performance, including three leaders in 18 months, resulted in Labour winning again in 1987, and even increasing its majority.

Roger Douglas, and his ideological parliamentary lieutenants, saw the election result as a signal to speed up the 'reform' process. The next stage of 'Rogernomics' included a flat-scale tax system (an article of faith among 'supply-side' economists) deregulation of labour unions and state sector privatisation. David Lange, however, could no longer ignore the detail of its consequences. The October 1987 sharemarket crash, barely two months after the election, was a dramatic and ugly confirmation of the dangers of the totally unfettered market. With reverberations from the crash and the elimination of low-skilled jobs as the SOEs tidied up their bottom lines, there were soon over 100,000 out of work.

Increasingly concerned that 'pain' had swamped 'gain' among Labour's core constituency, Lange halted flat tax planning early in 1988, but Douglas went ahead with plans to sell state corporations – believing the 'new right' tenet that private enterprise was always more efficient than state ownership. He also had social spending cuts in his sights. Lange tried to rein in Douglas by appointing two associate finance ministers in a September 1988 reshuffle; SOEs minister Richard Prebble was fired in November; and Douglas followed him from the cabinet table a month later.

The prime minister, a stranger to backroom politicking, was now increasingly isolated. Over the next seven months he weathered a motion of no confidence and, in June 1989, a Douglas challenge for the parliamentary party leadership. The final straw, in early August, was caucus voting in favour of Douglas's reinstatement to cabinet. A week later New Zealanders were astonished when David Lange resigned, publicly anointing loyal deputy Geoffrey Palmer his successor.

Palmer had been a particularly effective backroom operator, controlling an ambitious legislative programme and a large, sometimes dysfunctional caucus, but he was not the larger-than-life prime minister New Zealanders had become accustomed to. Nevertheless, as the 1980s ended he, Lange and the government could take some satisfaction from two parliamentary terms that had produced as much far-reaching change as the Liberals in the 1890s or the first Labour government elected in 1935.

The changes after 1984 were painfully dislocating for many thousands of New Zealanders. Hundreds of farmers lost all equity in their properties; businesses turned from manufacturing to importing to survive; government employees were corporatised out of jobs; young homeowners could no longer manage steeply climbing mortgage interest rates; the wages of lower-paid workers fell further behind as inflation accelerated again.

Hypnotised by 'new right' mantra, Rogernomics celebrated private enterprise success and wealth regardless of how it was acquired, and the government appointed a number of multi-millionaire entrepreneurs to key SOE posts. New knights included corporate raiders like Ron Brierley and, presumably for political favours rendered, Bob Jones, who greatly exaggerated his role in ending the Muldoon era.

The New Zealand business world quickly gained a 'wild west' reputation with ruthless, irresponsibly leveraged takeovers of old-established companies. It was smarter to make a fortune from shuffling other people's money than from old-fashioned roll-up-the-sleeves work. Traditional values, already under immense pressure, were further skewed. Consequently, and ironically, it was of some comfort that Transparency International routinely rated New Zealand as one of the three least corrupt nations in the world.

Nevertheless, the economic gap between rich and poor in New Zealand widened considerably. In 1956, New Zealand had the highest income per person in the world; by the 1980s the country had slipped to about 17th place. But there were a great many more millionaires.

Although most of the country's export income still came from primary production, Rogernomics accelerated the workforce's shift to the service sector. At the beginning of the 20th century, 11 percent of New Zealanders worked in service industries; in 1981 it was 62 percent. With the euphoria of unbridled economic reform there were even far-fetched suggestions about New Zealand's future as the financial centre of the South Pacific.

'Consumerism' was dominant, the Consumers' Institute and long-running TV programme *Fair Go* had plenty to do and, as foreign exchange controls disappeared, the country's shops were piled with imported goods, providing mind-numbing choice and driving local businesses to the wall. Middle class 'baby boomers', particularly those born in the late 1940s and early 1950s, had moved on from their protest and counter-culture days into high-paying 'white collar' jobs. The media dubbed these young urban professionals 'yuppies' or 'dinks' (double income no kids) when they were couples. Their new passion was conspicuous consumption and the 'me generation' indulged its self-absorbed collection of 'labels' and status symbols. In New Zealand, as elsewhere, it only made starker the yawning income gap between the well-off and those the market economy had identified as surplus to requirements.

Black and white sets were practically universal, and by 1981 67 percent of households had colour television. The same year, there were 1.7 million motor vehicles, more than one for every two people in the country. Later in the decade there was a flood of used car imports. A total of 12,000 used cars were registered in 1987 – and just two years later, with 52,000, New Zealand had the doubtful distinction of being the world's largest importer of second-hand Japanese cars, some of very uncertain origin.

The women's movement added significantly to its 1970s list of achievements: the Family Proceedings Act (divorce following two years' separation) in 1980; the 1982 Domestic Protection Act (non-violence and non-molestation orders); the Ministry of Women's Affairs was established in 1984; there was an enquiry into serious failure in cervical cancer screening in 1987-88. Before the Second World War less than 4 percent of married women were in paid work; by 1981 35 percent – or 310,000 – were in full or part-time employment.

In 1985, the incoming Labour government gave the Waitangi Tribunal more muscle, allowing it to hear claims dating back to 1840. An important court ruling the next year stated that the Treaty of Waitingi, and Maori interests, had to be considered in the sale of any state assets. The fast growing backlog of claims encouraged Labour, and then National, to begin negotiating directly with tribal groups, reaching some significant and far-reaching agreements.

One of the by-products of rapid Maori urbanisation was the loss of language. In the early 1950s about 50 per cent of Maori children spoke the language fluently; by the mid-1970s only a fraction of that number had any words at all. The impressive turn-around in the 1980s was spearheaded by kohanga reo, or 'language nest' pre-schools, conducted in Maori. In 1987, the Maori Language Act made Maori an official New Zealand language and established a commission to promote its use. The number of Maori leaving school without any qualifications began to drop and, in tandem, there was a steady growth in university enrolments.

However, there was a bleaker picture as well. In 1985 Maori were imprisoned at 12 times the pakeha rate; half the country's prison population was Maori. For many young urban Maori, most vulnerable to economic blips and busts, the 'street culture' – ranging from 'street kids' to 'patched' gangs – was a substitute for traditional tribal links, but an environment in which there were few, if any, constraints against crime, drugs and violence.

It might have picked up the 'permissive society' tag from Britain, where there were huge shifts in attitudes to sex and sexuality, but New Zealand was much more circumspect in sensitive areas. Decriminalisation of homosexuality was recommended by the Wolfenden Report in Britain in 1957; in New Zealand, up to 1961, sodomy was punished with life imprisonment. Homosexuality was legalised in Britain in 1967; there was considerable and passionate opposition to similar legislation in New Zealand in 1986, even though lesbian women were a prominent strand of the 'second wave' of feminism in the 1970s.

The churches saw themselves as the protectors of moral standards, the holders of the line against the unspeakable and, to some from the new fundamentalist sects, the unimaginable. Even token adherence to the traditional churches – Anglican, Presbyterian, Methodist and Roman Catholic – continued to drop, nearly halving between the early 1960s and late 1980s for some of them. Legislation like the Homosexual Law Reform Bill rallied both the traditional conservatives and the fundamentalists, whose Pentecostal church congregations had grown rapidly since the mid-1960s.

The 1980s was a lively decade environmentally. Protestors, including those who established the 'Independent State of Aramoana' with its own passports and postage stamps, managed to stop a large aluminum smelter being built at the head of Otago harbour, but the Clyde Dam was unstoppable. The fourth Labour government declared New Zealand nuclear-free in 1984 and recognised the growing importance of the environment and conservation, setting up: a ministry for the environment, an independent parliamentary commissioner for the environment and a conservation department. In 1986, a quota management system was introduced to conserve fish stocks in New Zealand's exclusive economic zone, and the West Coast Accord protected areas of native forest from logging.

There was a growing, widely-based cultural confidence in the 1980s. On stage, Greg McGee's *Foreskin's Lament* probed the rugby playing psyche and Murray Ball's 'Footrot Flats' strip cartoon morphed into a musical. Geoff Murphy's 1981 *Goodbye Pork Pie*, a Hollywood-sized blockbuster in per capita terms, proved there could be successful films about New Zealand. Peter Jackson's splatter movie, *Bad Taste*, in 1987 gave little indication of what was to come. Charles Brasch, Sylvia Ashton-Warner, Janet Frame and Frank Sargeson wrote autobiographies; Michael King was chided for writing Maori biographies. Keri Hulme's novel *The Bone People* won a number of awards, including the prestigious Booker Prize in Britain in 1985. The *Collected Poems* of James K Baxter, who had died in 1972, were published in 1980. The biennial NZ International Arts Festival in Wellington began in1984, the year the Royal NZ Ballet toured China, sponsored by a meat exporting company. The same year *Te Maori*, an exhibition of traditional art and craft, made a triumphal tour of major American art galleries. The enterprising Flying Nun label was busy recording local bands and Tim Finn went his successful solo way, his group Split Enz finishing with a memorable Australasian tour in 1984. The NZSO Chamber Orchestra and NZ String Quartet took bows for the first time in 1987. However, architecturally it was not the best of decades, with many fine old buildings knocked over in favour of bland office towers.

The 1980s was a decade when New Zealand-Australian relations reached a new low with the 'underarm' bowling incident at the end of a nail-biting one-day cricket match; Judge Mahon made his famous "litany of lies" comment about Air New Zealand's defence at the enquiry into the Erebus air disaster that killed 257 in Antarctica in 1979; eight gold medals at the 1984 Los Angeles Olympics was the best haul ever – seven on the water (canoeing, rowing, yachting) and one on a horse (Charisma); the first locally contracted case of AIDs was reported in 1985; the much travelled John Paul 11 was, in 1986, the first pope to visit New Zealand; 'power dressing', with shoulder-padded jackets, was in vogue as women started to climb corporate ladders; the All Blacks won the 1987 World Cup, a winning streak that lasted for two more years; New Zealanders proved once again they like a 'flutter' when Lotto, based on a weekly draw of numbers, started in 1987. And, in 1989, it was a sign of things to come when Sunday trading got underway, the third TV channel began competing with the state-owned ones – and Tim Berners-Lee invented the World Wide Web.

Saved by the Whistle

By 1981 the Muldoon cabinet was looking jaded. The prime minister had just survived the 'colonels' coup'; there were record internal/external deficits and unemployment, rising inflation and zero economic growth. Nevertheless, National went into the November campaign comfortably ahead in the polls because of its cynical manipulation of the Springbok rugby tour, which made a crucial difference in wavering provincial seats, and its inflated promises about the 'Think Big' energy projects. Labour narrowed the gap with a professional campaign and strong performance by leader Rowling, but Social Credit was as much a beneficiary of the increasing disquiet about National's performance and policies. On election night National did not have an overall majority, winning 46 seats to Labour's 44 and Social Credit's two. It appeared that Social Credit might hold the balance of power until a voting error correction gave National another seat and a narrow margin. Once again, Labour won the popular vote.

1. New Zealand's export receipts were dipping at the same time as fuel costs were surging upwards. *You want concessions ...?,* Peter Bromhead, *Auckland Star*, May 17 1980. ATL: A-314-1-003
2. Muldoon took a particular interest in, and expressed opinions about, the trials of Dr W B Sutch and Arthur Alan Thomas. Earlier, when he was ordered to pay costs in the court case that found he had advised employers to ignore superannuation legislation, Muldoon claimed the chief justice had "misunderstood" the situation. *"This is fun – what is the next case?",* Gordon Minhinnick, *NZ Herald*, February 7 1980. ATL: A-311-1-049
3. In December 1980, Labour's Bill Rowling survived – on his casting vote – a leadership challenge organised by David Lange supporters. About the same time, Muldoon forced Brian Talboys, his deputy, to retire, replacing him with close friend Duncan MacIntyre. *"Don t look now ....?",* Eric Heath, *Dominion*, January 30 1981. ATL: B-145-613
4. New Zealand's overseas debt was certainly reaching new heights as Muldoon borrowed more to keep the economy from collapsing like a pack of cards. *"Our credit rating has never been higher,"* Bob Brockie, *National Business Review*, April 13 1981. ATL: A-311-4-021
5. As Muldoon's election year woes compounded he attacked Labour, already vulnerable from publicly aired caucus disagreements about economic and Maori policy. *"Beware the Labour Party!",* Murray Ball, *New Zealand Times*, May 1981. ATL: A-313-1-047
6. Social Credit, which won over 16 percent of the vote in 1978, was a worry to both National and Labour at the 1981 election. *Beetham*, Malcolm Walker, *Sunday News*, December 6 1981. ATL: A-316-2-009

1

2

"This is fun – what is the next case?"

3

4

our credit rating has never been higher
NZ NEGOTIATES $500 MILLION LOAN — NEWS
Brockie

5

The world of QUENTIN HANKEY Murray Ball
"BEWARE THE LABOUR PARTY!"
Profit
Tax Dodgers
SIS
racists
The unemployed
dole queue
OVERSEAS OWNERSHIP
FOREIGN CONTROL
I KNOW — IT'S FULL OF COMMIES AND UNDESIRABLE PEOPLE...
Murray Ball

6

WALKER
BEETHAM

Riotous Rugby

After months of acrimonious debate, New Zealand reeled under an unprecedented state of siege in July-August 1981 during the tour of the South African rugby team. While many debated the Springboks tour issue on moral grounds – from opposition to apartheid to the rights of New Zealanders – it was also obvious that Muldoon, cannily aware of provincial attitudes, used the tour to firm up support in a number of the country's conservative, rugby heartland, marginal electorates. There were ugly riots, street and ground violence, and police using paramilitary tactics. One game was cancelled; another was shortened after the field was flour-bombed by an airborne demonstrator. There was widespread bitterness in the community – family members turning against each other, a loss of trust between police and public – and a severe bruising of the country's reputation internationally.

1. Muldoon equivocated over the projected Springbok tour in 1981, sending uncharacteristically mild messages to the Rugby Union, before deciding, to widespread disbelief overseas, there was nothing in the 1977 Gleneagles agreement to justify denying New Zealand sportsmen and women contact with South Africa. *"Our policy ….",* Bob Brockie, *National Business Review,* March 16 1981. ATL: A-311-4-020
2. Internationally, and to many New Zealanders, the Muldoon government and Rugby Union were seen as the last defenders of the apartheid system. *Kiwi s Last Stand*, Gordon Minhinnick, *NZ Herald*, May 26 1981. ATL: A-311-1-050
3. At Hamilton, the match was cancelled when protesters invaded the playing area after pulling down a fence, and the authorities considered the risk of violence and injury unacceptable. *"Right Jan ….",* Peter Bromhead, *Auckland Star*, July 28 1981. ATL: A-314-1-016
4. Despite the difficulties, the three test matches were played. The All Blacks won the first and third narrowly and lost the second by a wider margin. *"Keep the protesters out?",* Eric Heath, *Dominion*, August 12 1981. ATL: B-144-108
5. As the level of anger and protest rose during the tour, Muldoon tried to shift the debate from apartheid in South Africa to law and order in New Zealand. *The love affair,* Peter Bromhead, *Auckland Star*, August 13 1981. ATL A-314-1-023
6. In 1985, an All Black team was about to leave for South Africa, the Rugby Union having ignored the new government's specific request not to tour. After an interim court injunction prevented the team leaving while a case brought against the Rugby Union by two Auckland lawyers was still being heard, the Union, with bad grace, cancelled the tour. Some of the players toured South Africa in the unofficial 'Cavaliers' team the next year. *Rugby and apartheid*, Trace Hodgson, *NZ Listener*, May 11 1985. ATL: A-317-3-026

1

2

KIWI'S LAST STAND

3

4

BOKS
NZ
1ST. TEST
NO – THE BOKS!
KEEP THE PROTESTERS OUT?
ERIC HEATH

5

... THE LOVE AFFAIR ...
THE TOUR
NZ
BROMHEAD

6

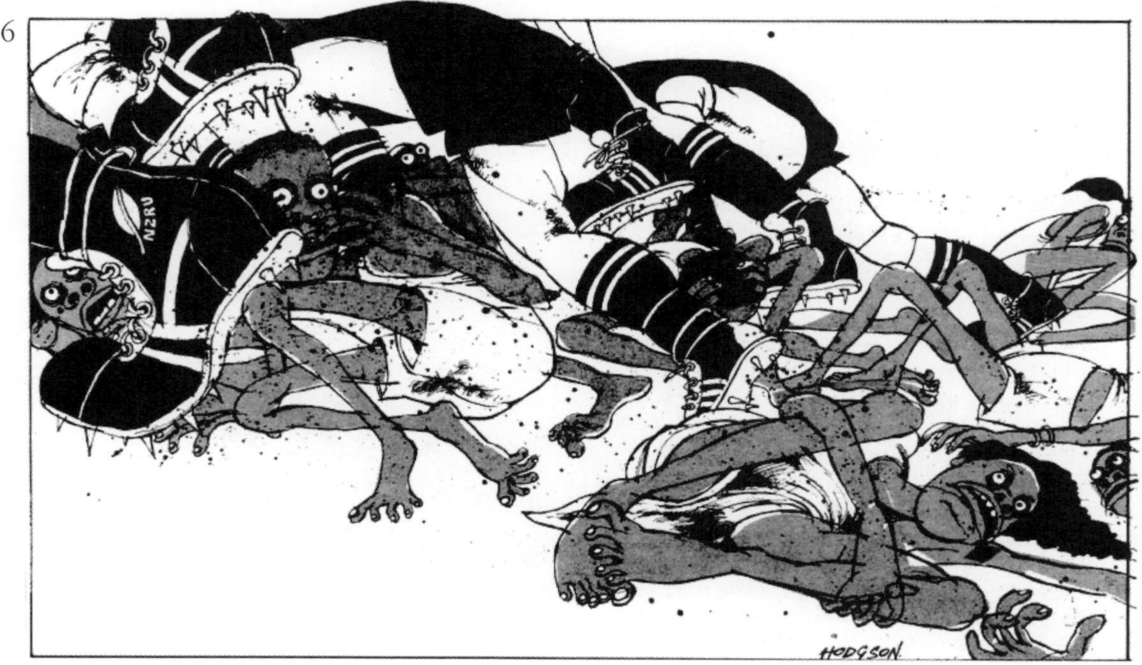
NZRU
HODGSON

Knight Errant

The Labour and Social Credit opposition did not seriously challenge National's tenuous one-seat majority. Social Credit lost its political virginity, its main asset, when it sided with the government over controversial legislation. Labour dithered over the leadership of three times loser Bill Rowling through 1982 and lost the support of two MPs in 1983. Muldoon tightened his caucus grip by firing Derek Quigley from cabinet for questioning the 'Think Big' strategy; he imposed on an intransigent economy a year-long wage and price freeze, later extended to early 1984. In classic style, he also tried to boost flagging popularity with foreign adventures – the loan of a frigate to the British during the Falklands campaign and tireless, doom-laden odysseys to international economic forums. Muldoon's knighthood – usually bestowed after retirement – was one more issue for negative public debate. More positively, a new era of trade with Australia began with the signing of the Closer Economic Relations (CER) treaty. In one of the early signs of growing Maori assertiveness, the Treaty of Waitangi was successfully invoked to stop Taranaki synfuels plant effluent being discharged into coastal fishing grounds.

1

2

3

1. The National government set up the Commission for the Future in 1976 but Muldoon disbanded it in 1981, more concerned with the next election than looking the 30 years ahead the commission had been charged with studying. *"…. But with me around …?",* Malcolm Walker, *Sunday News*, April 4 1982. ATL: A-316-2-010
2. During the Falklands War, and after the sinking of *HMS Sheffield*, Muldoon persuaded cabinet that a New Zealand frigate should be provided to free up a British warship in the Indian Ocean. The gesture, appreciated by Margaret Thatcher, was done with half-an-eye to future negotiations over primary produce access to Britain. *"It s good to know he s behind me ….",* Bill Wrathall. *NZ Truth*, May 25 1982. ATL: A-317-2-002
3. To reverse a planning tribunal denial of water rights to the Clyde high dam, Muldoon needed Social Credit's support to push through special legislation that eliminated the rights of affected property owners. *"What the hell Bruce …",* Bob Brockie, *National Business Review*, July 19 1982. ATL: A-311-1-022
4. The price and wage freeze was part of Muldoon's armory of devices to avoid economic reality. Originally for a year from June 1982 it was extended into early 1984. *"The freeze is one today ….",* Nevile Lodge, *Evening Post*, May 22 1983. ATL: B-136-184
5. In OECD terms, New Zealand was performing poorly on a number of economic fronts. In particular, the inflation rate was much higher than in other countries, but a strong anti-inflationary approach would have sent unemployment climbing at an even higher rate. *"Now, which bucket of cold water ….",* Peter Bromhead, *Auckland Star*, May 30 1983. ATL: A-314-1-017

4

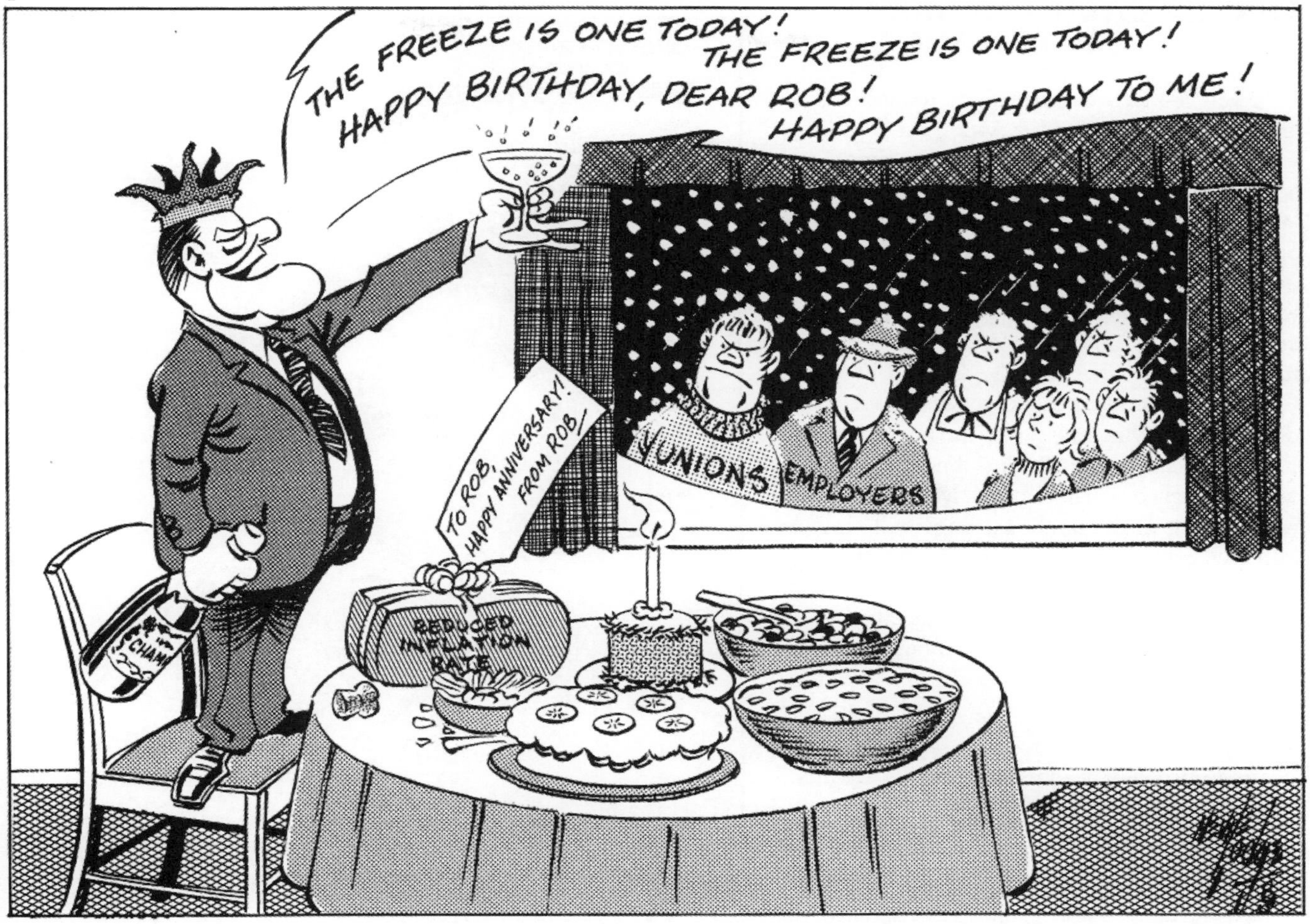

THE FREEZE IS ONE TODAY!
THE FREEZE IS ONE TODAY!
HAPPY BIRTHDAY, DEAR ROB!
HAPPY BIRTHDAY TO ME!
TO ROB, HAPPY ANNIVERSARY! FROM ROB.
REDUCED INFLATION RATE
UNIONS
EMPLOYERS

5

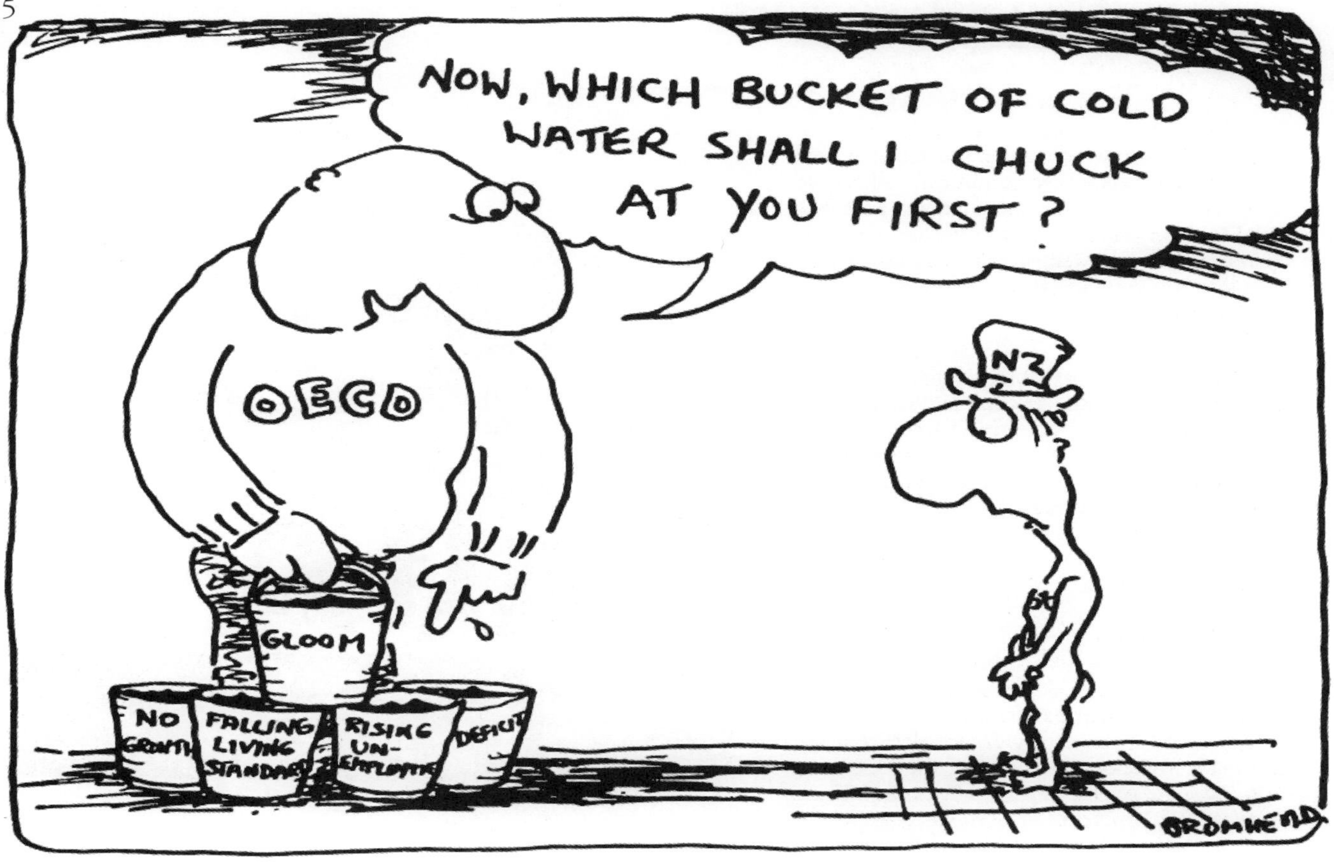

NOW, WHICH BUCKET OF COLD WATER SHALL I CHUCK AT YOU FIRST?
OECD
NZ
GLOOM
NO
FALLING LIVING
RISING UN-
DEFICIT
BROMHEAD

One Election Too Many

The 1984 election campaign probably began, and certainly started going wrong for Muldoon, when property magnate Bob Jones, one-time friend and later outspoken critic of the prime minister, launched the New Zealand Party in August 1983. Sitting on a knife-edge majority and a large number of marginal seats, Muldoon could not afford an erosion of right-of-centre support, but by year's end the 'Jones' Party', as the prime minister habitually called it, had edged ahead of Social Credit in the polls. Belatedly, National replaced deputy leader MacIntyre with the much younger Jim McLay in March 1984. Just three months later, Muldoon called a snap election. Muldoon looked weary and defensive on the hustings while Labour leader David Lange barnstormed the country with few promises but a powerful emotional undertaking to 'bring New Zealand together again'. As the polls predicted, Labour crushed National.

1. Jones, who founded, financed and later tried to dissolve the New Zealand Party, had one main target, Muldoon, who was attacked for his abrasive, all-controlling leadership and his frequent intervention in, and tight control of, the economy. *The New 'Profit* , Chicane, *Southland Times*, December 21 1983. ATL: A-316-3-009
2. The New Zealand Party siphoned off sufficient votes in National-held marginals for Labour to win them more comfortably than they might otherwise have done. Bruce Beetham lost his Rangitikei seat, but Social Credit won Pakuranga to retain a two-seat parliamentary presence. *Class of 1984*, Bob Brockie, *National Business Review*, June 25 1984. ATL: A-311-2-023
3. By 1984 National's cabinet was in poor shape. Senior members were planning to retire, several were, or had recently been, seriously ill, others had tendered resignations Muldoon had not accepted. Yet Muldoon was not prepared to bring in 'new blood' and he had wanted Bill Birch rather than McLay as his deputy. *"All of you that agree with me* ....", Tom Scott, *NZ Listener*, May 5 1984. ATL: H-312-4-012
4. The National Party that Muldoon committed to an election three months before the due date was divided, dispirited and increasingly at odds with the prime minister's regulatory, interventionist approach. *"Don t shoot, men, until I give the order ....",* Tom Scott, *NZ Listener*, July 7 1984. ATL: H-312-4-013
5. Sir Robert Muldoon had no intention of going quietly. As a delaying tactic, he suggested the leadership should be reviewed at the first caucus meeting in February 1985, and that he was unlikely to stand again. He quickly changed his mind and was a candidate when the vote was brought forward to the end of November. McLay was elected on the first ballot; Muldoon was a decidedly graceless loser. *"I ve decided to go gracefully ....",* Peter Bromhead, *Auckland Star*, November 23 1984. ATL: A-330-138

1

2

3

All of you who agree with me that there is no need for a Cabinet reshuffle please raise your right arm or press your buzzer...
R.D.M.

4

Don't shoot, men, until I give the order...
N

5

I'VE DECIDED TO GO GRACEFULLY...
BROMHEAD

Front-man for a Revolution

David Lange had a meteoric rise in politics. In his early thirties, with his considerable bulk, ballooning suits and lengthy list of cases, he became the dominant legal personality at the Auckland Magistrate's Court, representing the poorest, least-likely-to-pay clients. A year after contesting the National-held Hobson seat at the 1975 election he was, to general surprise, selected for the safe Mangere seat after Colin Moyle's resignation from parliament. With his physical presence, booming voice and compelling way with words Lange made an immediate impact on the national political scene. In 1979, aged 37, he became Labour's deputy leader. Deeply weary after the 1981 election, Lange tackled his weight problem with risky but successful stomach by-pass surgery. Bill Rowling stood down in February 1983 and an increasingly assured Lange led Labour to a stunning election victory in 1984. A new, sleeker, silver-tongued prime minister now poured healing balm on a badly bruised electorate, his broad-brush, inspirational style of leadership capitalising on the ANZUS issue and the *Rainbow Warrior* affair to keep country and caucus united while finance minister Roger Douglas beavered away at restructuring the economy.

1. Labour replaced National's comprehensive wage and price controls with direct union-employer wage bargaining and only limited state involvement. It radically changed industrial relations in both private and public sectors. *"The Labour government appreciates this opportunity ....",* Tom Scott, *Auckland Star*, May 11 1985. ATL: H-312-4-014
2. Lange had a 'nightmarish' start to his prime ministership: Muldoon briefly defied instructions to devalue the dollar; the United States applied ANZUS pressure; and the Rugby Union was determined to tour South Africa. *"What a nightmare!",* Trace Hodgson, *NZ Listener*, 1984, ATL: H-480-006
3. It seemed at times, and even to some members of Lange's caucus, that the only connection with the Labour party of Michael Joseph Savage was its name. *Mickey who?,* Gordon Minhinnick, *NZ Herald*, November 28 1985. ATL: A-311-1-053
4. At first, Lange was convinced necessary economic changes could not be achieved without some 'pain', but that the 'gain' would soon be apparent. *"Don t get too comfortable, folks ....",* Trace Hodgson, *NZ Listener*, February 8 1986. ATL: A-317-3-017
5. Labour brushed aside its own left wing and ignored possible political repercussions with a single-minded rush to deregulation and restructuring. *"Oops! That s the rough draft....",* Tom Scott, *Auckland Star*, February 1986. ATL: H-752-003

1

2

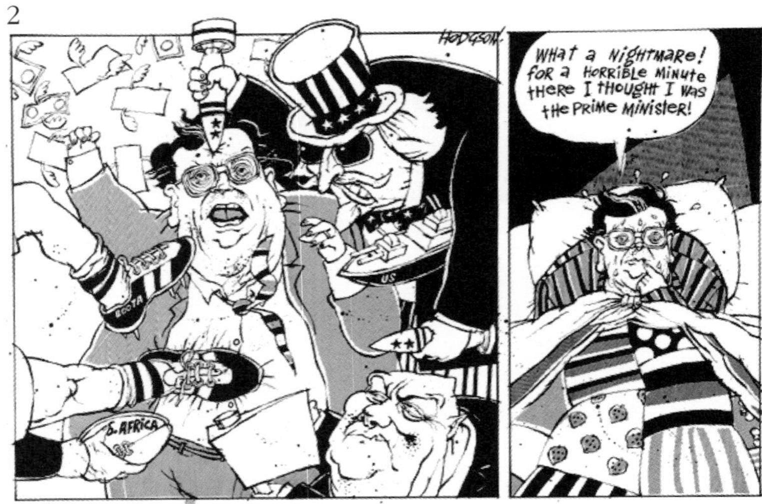

3

Mickey who?

4

DON'T Get too COMFORTABLE, FOLKS... THIS Year's GONNa Be TOUGH!
HODGSON

5

OOPS! THAT'S THE ROUGH DRAFT...
THE GOVERNMENT WILL CONTINUE WITH ITS PLANS TO RE-STRUCTURE THE N.Z. ECONOMY, AND ADVISES ALL OPPOSED TO THIS COURSE TO GO TAKE A RUNNING JUMP IN THE...
AAH THIS IS MORE LIKE IT..
THIS IS AN OUTRAGE!

Rogernomes at Work

Labour's finance minister Roger Douglas capitalised on the 20 percent devaluation crisis to make a number of 'free market' moves that resulted in a major and very rapid restructuring of the economy. 'Rogernomics', as the government's economic policy was popularly (or unpopularly) known, deregulated the money and foreign exchange markets, introduced radical tax changes, eliminated agricultural subsidies and removed much of the manufacturing sector's protection. 'Efficiency' justified the nine new state-owned enterprises (SOEs) created from former trading departments. Companies and individuals fought to survive see-sawing inflation, interest rates, share prices and the Kiwi dollar as 'market forces' battered New Zealand. After three years it was generally agreed Rogernomics had produced a leaner, better managed, more realistic and innovative economy, but that serious inflation and interest rate problems remained and the ballooning overseas debt was a deep-seated problem.

1. Roger Douglas's 'honeymoon' period did not end with his first budget. As he continued to make sweeping economic changes, he won extraordinary accolades overseas and support from unlikely sources, including Bob Jones and Derek Quigley, at home. *"You gotta pick a pocket of two ....",* Chicane, *Southland Times*, November 9 1984. ATL: H-752-001
2. Douglas and his colleagues progressively eliminated nearly all controls on the money and foreign exchange sectors – and in March 1985 they floated the New Zealand dollar. *"And God bless all who sail in her!",* Peter Bromhead, *Auckland Star*, March 4 1985. ATL: A-314-1-019
3. The 10 percent Goods and Services Tax (GST), introduced on October 1 1986, operated more smoothly and generated far more revenue than expected. *"Roll up, roll up ....",* Trace Hodgson, *NZ Listener*, July 20 1985. ATL: A-317-3-036
4. Farmers were probably hardest hit. Incomes crashed, with low prices on depressed international markets and an all-too-buoyant floating dollar, while costs and interest rates soared and farm values fell. *And From the Rural Sector ...,* Malcolm Walker, *Sunday News*, June 8 1986. ATL: A-316-2-014
5. Commercial world high-flyers like Ron Brierley greatly expanded their enterprises, particularly overseas. A flurry of takeovers concentrated a major part of the New Zealand economy in a few giant companies. *"We like to think of ourselves ....",* Trace Hodgson, *NZ Listener*, March 14 1987. ATL: A-317-3-051
6. The October 1987 stock market crash showed graphically the dangers of a completely unregulated economy. *The Unknown Investor*, Tom Scott, *Evening Post*, November 25 1987. ATL: H-670-007

1

2

3

4

WALKER'S
Believe It or Not!
AND FROM THE RURAL SECTOR . . .
8/6/86
MY GOD, IT'S NOT A NEW KIND OF SHEEP– IT'S A BLEATING COW COCKIE . . .
BAA! BAAA!
M.A.F.

5

HODGSON
WE LIKE TO THINK OF OURSELVES AS THE MOST UPWARDLY MOBILE GANG IN THE COUNTRY...
MONEY
CAPITALIST SWINE
PRES. FILTHY RICH RON.

6

THE UNKNOWN INVESTOR
Tom Scott.

Rainbow's End

Prime minister David Lange enhanced his reputation, and the public was diverted from economic problems, with his outraged David v. Goliath pursuit of France during the *Rainbow Warrior* affair. On July 10 1985, French secret service agents bombed and sank the *Rainbow Warrior* in Auckland harbour, killing one crew member, before the Greenpeace organisation's flagship could protest against French nuclear testing at Mururoa. In August, the French government appointed Bernard Tricot to investigate secret service involvement in the bombing; his whitewash report absolved the DGSE agents of blame, but after two 'bit players' in the saga had been caught and charged with murder, the French government finally admitted responsibility and fired defence minister Hernu and DGSE chief Admiral Lacoste. The two agents were sentenced to 10 years in prison after pleading guilty to manslaughter, but in July 1986, after arbitration by the UN secretary-general, the agents were moved to a French military base on an isolated South Pacific atoll for three years.

1. Far from being subdued by France's lofty disdain and the United States' anger, Lange's confident performance as foreign minister built on New Zealand's image as a gutsy, independently-minded and staunchly anti-nuclear nation. *"David", by Michael Langelo*, Gordon Minhinnick, *NZ Herald*, September 17 1985. ATL: A-311-1-052
2. To most New Zealanders the drama of the Rainbow Warrior affair – murder, the hunt for the killers and a war of words with France – was much more absorbing than the planned introduction of GST, even though this comprehensive, broad-based consumption type, value added tax was part of the seismic shift in economic policy. *"Just keep yer eye ....",* Peter Bromhead, *Auckland Star*, September 25 1985. ATL: A-334-050
3. The decision to attack the Greenpeace vessel in Auckland and the literal trail of evidence – oxygen cylinders, outboard motor, dinghy – suggested the French had scant respect for either New Zealand sovereignty or the local police. *"Bonjour, bonjour, bonjour ....",* Bob Brockie, *National Business Review*, September 2 1985. ATL: A-311-4-024
4. As the extent of French arrogance and apparent lack of concern about what had happened became clearer there was, in New Zealand, a largely spontaneous boycotting of French wine and other products – even when there was only a remote association with France. *"I reckon your anti-French feelings ....",* Bob Darroch, *Christchurch Star*, October 7 1985. ATL: A-316-161
5. France finally apologised to the New Zealand government and paid $3 million compensation. *"President Chirac has given me ....",* Malcolm Walker, *Sunday News*, July 13 1986. ATL: A-316-2-015

1

"DAVID" BY MICHAEL LANGELO

2

3

4

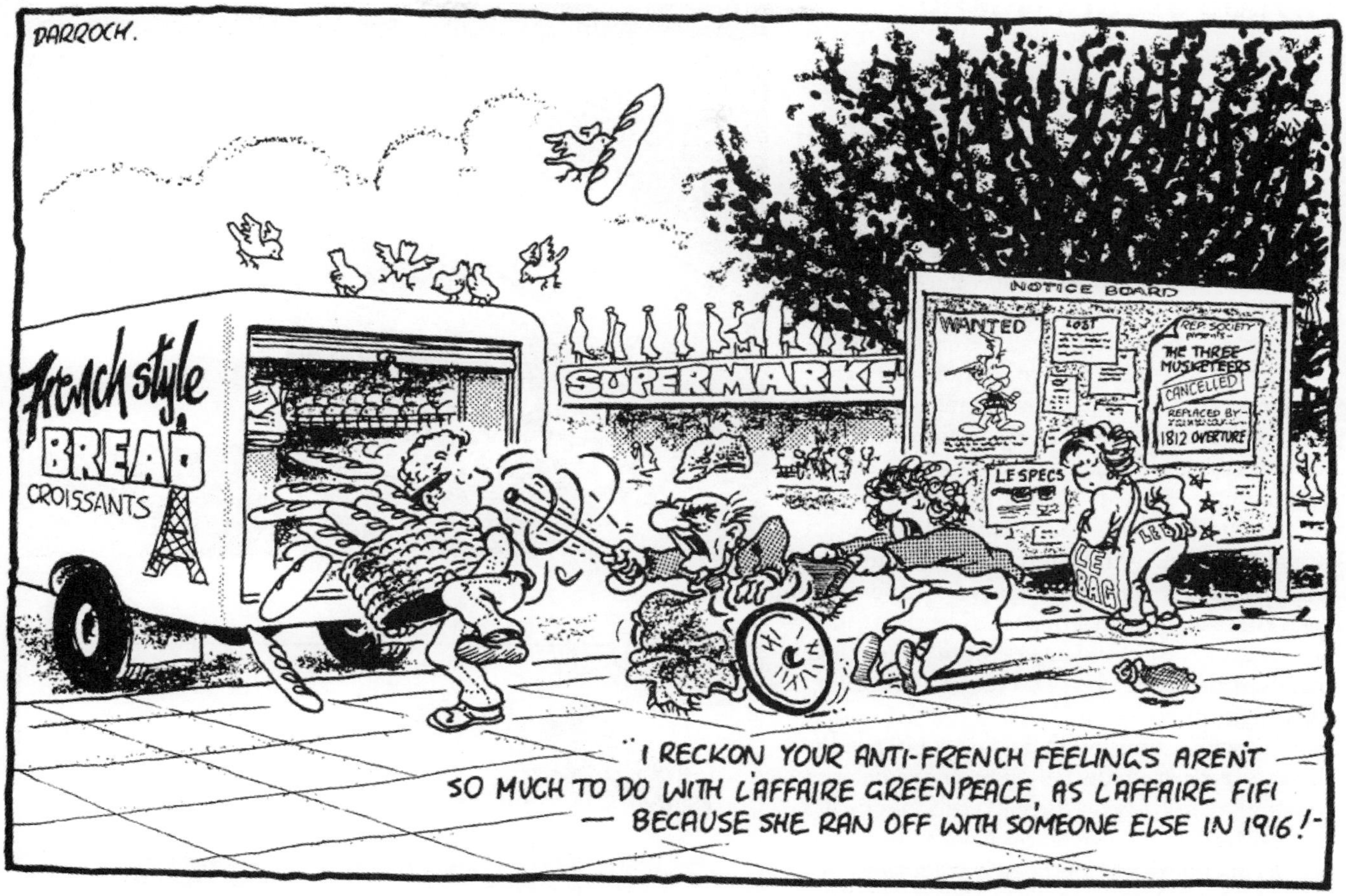

DARROCH.

"I RECKON YOUR ANTI-FRENCH FEELINGS AREN'T SO MUCH TO DO WITH L'AFFAIRE GREENPEACE, AS L'AFFAIRE FIFI — BECAUSE SHE RAN OFF WITH SOMEONE ELSE IN 1916!"

5

ANZUS Treaty Nuked

The banning of nuclear-powered and armed vessels from New Zealand ports was an act of faith for the Labour Party – and a convenient carrot for 'left-wingers' worried by Rogernomics. At the same time, Labour policy and public sentiment also favoured continued membership of ANZUS. The American view was simple and direct: ANZUS could not function unless all US ships, some of them nuclear-powered and armed, had access to New Zealand ports. For six months, David Lange sought compromises, but the Americans were not interested in verbal subtleties. Finally, in early 1985, the United States proposed, and the New Zealand government declined, a warship visit. When it became obvious that neither persuasion nor threats would change New Zealand's mind, Washington announced the end of ANZUS as a three-partner pact. But, congressional threats aside, the United States carefully differentiated between defence and trade sanctions and the NZ Nuclear Free Zone, Disarmament and Arms Control Act was passed in 1987 without further incidents. Subsequently, the government conducted an extensive defence review that emphasised self-reliance, a South Pacific role and greater co-operation with Australia; defence spending was increased considerably.

1. From the American perspective, any relaxation of its 'neither confirm nor deny' policy about whether ships were nuclear-armed or powered could threaten the operation of military pacts around the world. *"Okay, Holland, Denmark ....",* Tom Scott, *Auckland Star*, March 2 1985. ATL: H-312-4-017
2. To the Americans, accustomed to running ANZUS on their terms, New Zealand's ships ban was the unilateral torpedoing of a military alliance by a misguided ally. *"Good morning ....",* Al Nisbet, *New Zealand Times*, March 10 1985. ATL: A-315-4-001
3. To American military and foreign policy-makers, it seemed that anti-nuclear and anti-American were synonymous. *"There s no chip on our shoulder!",* Trace Hodgson, *NZ Listener*, September 6 1986. ATL: C-133-133
4. The majority of New Zealanders were pleased the country had managed to avoid any involvement with nuclear power and the risks associated with nuclear-powered or armed vessels entering local ports were unacceptable. *"Can t understand all this fuss....",* Eric Heath, *Dominion*, March 8 1985. ATL: H-302-00X
5. David Lange searched for a compromise, arguing it was possible for a nuclear-free New Zealand to partner the United States in a defence treaty, but the Americans flatly disagreed. *"As we no longer have any friends ....",* Peter Bromhead. *Auckland Star*, August 17 1986. ATL: A-314-1-021
6. The passing of the nuclear-free legislation was morally uplifting, but a fast-rising overseas debt implied a worrying level of economic dependency. *"We re free!",* Chris Slane, *NZ Listener*, June 7 1987. ATL: A-317-1-001

1

2

3

4

CAN'T UNDERSTAND ALL THIS FUSS THEY'RE MAKING OVER RADIATION!
DANGER
NO NUKES
USS BUCHANAN
ERIC HEATH

5

AS WE NO LONGER HAVE ANY FRIENDS, YOU WILL HENCEFORTH SAY, - HALT! WHO GOES THERE, FOE OR FOE!
NZ
BROMHEAD

6

$48 BILLION OVERSEAS DEBT
WE'RE FREE!
NUCLEAR FREE ACT
SLANE

Party Games

After the 1984 loss, National was burdened with both unwanted politicians and outdated notions. Although deputy leader Jim McLay replaced Muldoon four months later, more than a year passed before he attempted to strengthen the opposition's front bench with younger, less tarnished MPs. The move came too late and antagonised sufficient senior caucus members to allow new deputy Jim Bolger to topple McLay at the end of March 1986. In August 1985, after National won the Timaru by-election, Bob Jones decided to end the New Zealand Party in the same spontaneous way be began it, claiming that Labour were implementing many of his policies. The party lingered on but its electoral significance ended with its founder's resignation. Social Credit slumped to fourth place in the 1984 election and Pakuranga MP Neil Morrison replaced ex-MP Bruce Beetham as leader in 1986.

1. Muldoon retained a hard core of supporters, upset at the way he had been unceremoniously dumped by National. The Sunday Club, begun in February 1985 as a Muldoon support group, sprouted branches which he addressed at overflow meetings around the country. Calls for Muldoon's return to the leadership further weakened a prevaricating McLay. *"Careful now .... we need him ....",* Chicane, *Critic*, April 15 1985. ATL: A-316-3-008
2. The thought of retirement did not occur to Muldoon after losing the party leadership; politics was, after all, his life. When denied a front bench position, he retreated to the back benches, as intent on destabilising McLay's leadership as opposing Labour. *The Rise & Fall ....,* Eric Heath, *Dominion*, June 18 1985. ATL: B-128-001
3. In 1985, younger Social Creditors, attempting to forge a liberal centralist party out of a movement traditionally dedicated to monetary reform, succeeded in the adoption of a new 'Democrats' name. *".... Yeah, but it s still a Skoda ....",* Trace Hodgson, *NZ Listener*, June 8 1985. ATL: A-31-7-3-037
4. McLay had finally banished Muldoon to seat No 38 on the opposition benches; new leader Jim Bolger tried the opposite approach, elevating Muldoon to No 8 and appointing him foreign affairs spokesman. It would not to make life with Muldoon significantly easier. *"Come with me delegates ....",* Tom Scott, *Sunday Star*, August 10 1986. ATL: H-312-4-018
5. In 1987, Winston Peters joined National's front bench as Maori affairs, employment and race relations spokesman. His relationship with National would be complicated and chequered. *New 'N to be unveiled ....,* Klarc, *NZ Herald*, August 4 1988. ATL: H-725-010

1

2

3

4

5 NEW 'N' TO BE UNVEILED AT NATIONAL PARTY CONFERENCE–NEWS

More 'Pain' than 'Gain'

Labour cobbled together a strange coalition of interests – from commercial high rollers to traditional blue collar support – that won the party another term in office with an increased majority. National was left wallowing; three leaders in 18 months and difficulties developing credible alternative policies. Yet Labour unity was starting to crumble. Fearing that social spending was now at risk, Lange tried to slow down the 'new right' juggernaut. Early in 1988, he stopped flat tax planning and appointed associate finance ministers in an attempt to rein in Douglas, but the government unraveled along with further radical economic restructuring ambitions. There were firings and, in August 1989, Lange fired himself, handing over to his deputy Geoffrey Palmer. At decade's end, Palmer was unable to bring together the two feuding caucus camps, counter the growing perception that the reforms had not lived up to their ambitious expectations, or project the sort of prime ministerial 'image' the media and public had come to expect.

1. Lange's second thoughts about Rogernomics would fracture the close working relationship irreparably. "*Well, Rog, we ve cracked it!,* Trace Hodgson, *NZ Listener*, September 5 1987. ATL: C-133-162
2. The government's wide-ranging economic reforms could be compromised by too much rigidity in the industrial relations framework, but radical wage-setting changes could also seriously damage Labour's relationship with its industrial wing. *"How s she looking, Richard ?"*, Anthony Ellison, *Auckland Star*, May 26 1988. ATL: A-313-1-049
3. The Bank of New Zealand lent recklessly to 1980s 'corporate cowboy' entrepreneurs. After their over-hyped companies collapsed following the 1987 stock market crash, successive Labour and National governments bailed out the bank to the collective tune of $1.3 billion. *"Saved you!"*, Peter Bromhead, *Auckland Star*, March 15 1989. ATL: A-225-178
4. For Lange, the final straw, in early August, was caucus voting in favour of Douglas's reinstatement to cabinet. *"Struth! If they are made of clay ....",* Tom Scott, *Evening Post*, June 29 1989. ATL: A-312-4-019
5. After the 1987 election, Douglas was readying his next wave of economic reforms when Lange announced colloquially and publicly, and much to the surprise of his colleagues, that it was time for "a cup of tea and a breather". *"Aaah .... At last a chance for a cup of tea ....",* Trace Hodgson, *NZ Listener*, August 5 1989. ATL: H-725-013
6. Palmer gained most satisfaction from the environment portfolio, retaining it after he became prime minister. Among his achievements were the outlawing of driftnet fishing in the South Pacific and ozone layer legislation. *"I m off again ....",* Tom Scott, *Evening Post*, October 18 1989. ATL: A-312-4-020

1

2

3

4

STRUTH!! IF THEY ARE MADE OF CLAY IT'S DRIED AWFULLY HARD...
RATA-TAT-TAT-TAT-
Tom Scott

5

AAAH... AT LAST A CHANCE FOR A CUP OF TEA AND A BREATHER
ROGER
HODGSON

6

I'M OFF AGAIN TO OUTLAW DRIFTNETTING, FIX THE HOLE IN THE OZONE LAYER, AND REVERSE THE GREENHOUSE EFFECT...
IF YOU HAD THE IMPOSSIBLE TASK OF SAVING THE LABOUR PARTY, YOU'D LEAP AT THE CHANCE OF SAVING THE PLANET...
VIP
TOM SCOTT.

The 'Anything's Possible' Decade

The defeat of the Muldoon government in 1984 was liberating in a number of ways. Much more than the economy was let out of its straight-jacket. There was an unprecedented sense of freedom, an 'anything's possible' exuberance. Lange's witticisms said as much about the 1980s as Muldoon's aggressive dourness had about the 1970s. There was an extraordinary alchemy in the air, with key members of cabinet and many high-flyers in business, government service and the media, belonging to the same risk-taking generation unscarred by memories of war or depression; in their forties, they were younger decision-makers than at any time since the early days of European settlement. But a lifting of spirits and regulations led to over-exuberance, from excessive 'me-centred' consumerism to the corporate cowboy behaviour of some entrepreneurs, making the 1987 stockmarket crash all the more resounding. As well, contrasts between rich and poor were starker, and social stresses more worrying.

1. Women were making steady progress in many areas – the Domestic Protection Act provided for non-violence and non-molestation orders in 1982 – but it was not until 1984 that the new government 's Rape Law Reform Act extended the definition of rape and gave protection to complainants. *"It says here ....",* Eric Heath, *Dominion*, March 24 1983. ATL: H-719-023
2. The very occasional shooting of a police dog prompted more media headlines and public outrage than grisly murders; it was part of a phenomenon that saw SPCA appeals raise more money and concern than those for needy children. *"God! A policeman has been accidentally shot ....",* Malcolm Walker, *Sunday News*, November 20 1983. ATL: A-316-2-011
3. The celebration of Anzac Day, and its meaning, was in stark contrast to the behaviour of some young, disaffected New Zealanders escaping their troubled lives into temporary, and occasionally permanent, oblivion. *They Died So You Can Live*, Peter Bromhead, *Auckland Star,* April 27 1986. ATL: A-314-1-020
4. There were no Old Testament consequences, predicted by a growing fundamentalist movement, when a massive 800,000-signature was ignored and homosexual law reform legislation passed on a conscience vote in 1986. *"Bloody poofters!",* Trace Hodgson, *NZ Listener*, March 30 1985. ATL: C-133-105
5. In Auckland particularly, schoolboy rugby was less popular among middle-class pakeha parents. Concern about injuries was one reason, as larger, stronger Maori and Pacific Islanders began to dominate teams. *Delinquent for Today*, Gordon Minhinnick, *NZ Herald,* April 30 1985. ATL: A-311-1-051

1

2

3

4

5

DELINQUENT FOR TODAY

6. In the professional Olympics era, with fortunes to be made from winning, beating the 'drug police' had become, for some, as important as defeating rivals. At the 1988 Olympics in Seoul, the men's 100-metre winner, Ben Johnson, lost his gold medal after testing positive for steroids. *Olympic Highlights*, Peter Bromhead, *Auckland Star*, September 28 1988. ATL: A-333-120

7. From 1989, shops could open on Sundays – in fact, any days except Good Friday, ANZAC Day and Christmas Day. Shopping and Sunday sport further dented already dropping church attendances. By the 1980s about 10 percent of New Zealanders worshipped on a regular basis, with about a quarter belonging to Pentecostal or evangelical churches. *"….. and we of the church ….",* Eric Heath, *Dominion*, March 14 1989. ATL: A-313-1-048

8. Although research studies from 1981 showed the harmful effects of passive smoking, the tobacco industry managed to blur the issue for years. Reputable research shows passive smokers are 20 to 30 percent more likely to develop lung cancer than people not exposed to smoke. *"Mind if I smoke passively?",* Klarc, *NZ Herald*, July 8 1989. ATL: A-317-077

9. There was now more than one TV set in most New Zealand homes. Approval for the first privately-owned TV channel was granted in 1988 and TV3 began broadcasting the next year. Two years later Sky introduced pay TV. *" …. You are in my power ….",* Trace Hodgson, *NZ Listener*, July 23 1988. ATL: C-128-022

10. For the health conscious, research results regularly presented challenges about what was and wasn't safe to eat and drink. *"What the hell!",* Bill Paynter, *National Business Review*, March 20 1989. ATL: A-313-1-048

11. Among western nations, growing concern about child abuse, particularly with sexual emphasis or aspects, were encouraged by 'recovered memory syndrome', influential in the later Christchurch Civic Creche child abuse case. *"They caught him giving …..",* Tom Scott, *Evening Post*, April 17 1989. ATL: H-670-009

12. To shore up its defence relationship with Australia after the effective demise of ANZUS, the government embarked, in 1989, on the ANZAC Ship Project with its Australian counterpart, agreeing to buy two of 10 new guided missile frigates to be built over a 17 year period at the cost of $A7 billion. *"We can t afford to replace ….",* Tom Scott, *Evening Post*, September 6 1989. ATL: A-312-4-021

13. Just as office workers were getting used to computer terminals on their desks, there was another electronic leap forward. The relatively portable prototypes of the notebook-style laptop computer, now almost an executive fashion accessory, were first available in the early 1980s. By 1983-84 Microsoft, with Radio Shack, and IBM had more recognisable laptops competing on the market. *"Now this is a lap-top ….",* Peter Bromhead, *Auckland Star,* January 10 1990. ATL: A-314-1-022

14. There was growing public criticism of the treatment, considered too lenient, of hardened, repeat offenders by social service agencies and the justice system. *"It s okay lads ….",* Al Nisbet, *New Zealand Times*, October 14 1984. ATL: A-315-4-004

6

7

8

9

10

11

12

13

14

11: 1990-1999
YEARS OF ADJUSTMENT

The last year of the fourth Labour government was an anti-climax after the roller coaster ride of major economic reforms at home and an adventurous, nose-thumbing foreign policy.

Geoffrey Palmer, prime minister more by accident than design, had an unhappy 13 months in the job after David Lange stood down in early August 1989. There were two feuding – pro and anti-further reform – camps in the Labour caucus, a growing popular perception that the reforms had not lived up to their ambitious expectations and Palmer's struggle to talk in the generalised sound bites that often blur the truth and offended his belief in moderate, balanced discussion of issues.

At the same time, opposition leader Jim Bolger, was growing in confidence. After taking over from Jim McLay, Muldoon's successor, in March 1986, he had performed creditably at the 1987 election with National climbing back to a respectable 44 percent of the vote. With Don McKinnon as his deputy and Ruth Richardson as shadow finance minister, he was ready for the 1990 election.

Labour clearly wasn't and as the government sagged at the polls during the early months of 1990, Mike Moore, the fiercely ambitious No 3, positioned himself as a more populist, alternative leader. Worried caucus members in marginal seats saw Moore as their last, slim chance of political survival. While Palmer was in Australia, deputy PM Helen Clark polled her cabinet colleagues about a leadership change; it was a hint the prime minister chose not to ignore. Moore, his colleagues now reasoned, had the 'good Kiwi bloke' image that worked across party lines, and was a skilled campaigner. It was desperate stuff. In early September, with just 59 days before the 1990 election, Labour had its third leader in 13 months.

Predictably, National won at a canter, finishing with a massive 39 seat majority. But after the brief euphoria of the biggest electoral swing since 1935, Bolger had a number of problems to deal with. There was the insolvency of the Bank of New Zealand and the $620 million bailout that led to cuts in social spending and a backdown on the election pledge to remove the unpopular superannuation surcharge Labour had imposed in 1985. Denied a cabinet place, Robert Muldoon brooded on the back benches before precipitating a nail-biting by-election in the Tamaki electorate; the highly volatile Winston Peters lasted a year as Maori Affairs minister, later using his Tauranga bulwark as the first building block in the creation of New Zealand First; Ruth Richardson, whose economic ambitions were labeled 'Rogernomics on steroids', led an enthusiastic 'razor gang' assault on the ballooning deficit; her 'mother of all budgets' in 1991 was to haunt National for some time to come.

There were, of course, some positives. Jim Bolger took Mike Moore to GATT talks in Brussels early in 1991, both a calculated act of bi-partisanship and recognition of the important trade role his predecessor had played during the 1980s. The Uruguay Round, finally concluded in December 1993, was critical to the transformation of the New Zealand meat industry – and the trebling of sheepmeat's income over the next decade to $3.1 billion. After the Employment Contracts Act was passed in 1991 industrial stoppages fell away spectacularly and New Zealand climbed the world competitiveness charts. Bolger was committed to settling major Treaty of Waitangi claims and the first, the Sealord deal, was signed in September 1992. The Fiscal Responsibility Act in 1993 eliminated unpleasant financial surprises for incoming governments.

At the beginning of 1993, National's poll performance was as bad as it had ever been, but Bolger stumped the country brandishing Treasury reports suggesting the economy was on the mend. It was just enough to squeak back again. Mike Moore had been an energetic opposition leader and the election had been a close run contest, but the two-time loser was now swiftly replaced by Helen Clark.

The ultimate political pragmatist, Jim Bolger promptly dumped Ruth Richardson, deciding her rigidity and divisiveness were increasing liabilities, particularly with MMP (Mixed Member Proportional) representation in the wings. His close friend Bill Birch subsequently delivered a run of budget surpluses.

MMP had been recommended by a royal commission in 1986 but it was Bolger who took up the issue, admitting there was an inherent unfairness in the 'first past the post' system, and promising to hold two referenda. The first, in September 1992, showed New Zealanders wanted change, with MMP the preferred option. In the second referendum, at the 1993 election, MMP nosed out the status quo. There would be an MMP election in 1996.

Jim Bolger's second term stretched his considerable management and negotiating skills as parliamentarians attempted to shore up their post-MMP futures. A major new political grouping – the United Party – included four National MPs and two from Labour. Keeping all conceivable coalition options open, National agreed not to stand a candidate against United's Peter Dunne in Ohariu-Belmont and ensured ACT representation in the House by giving Richard Prebble a clear run in Wellington Central.

It took over seven long weeks to decide the outcome of the 1996 election. When New Zealand First emerged as the 'king-maker', negotiating with both Labour and National, it was assumed that the personal antipathy between Bolger and Winston Peters would stop them joining forces. The final outcome was a victory, of sorts, for Bolger's patience and flexibility.

Winston Peters would be deputy prime minister in the National-NZ First coalition government and, with the title of 'treasurer', run finance with Bill Birch.

The unlikely coalition survived minor personal scandals, a ministerial resignation, the Cave Creek tragedy and the referendum on compulsory superannuation during 1997. Nevertheless, Jim Bolger returned from a Commonwealth heads of government meeting in Edinburgh at the beginning of November to find that Jenny Shipley, then transport minister, had convinced sufficient caucus colleagues that it was time for a leadership change, and to be more assertive with New Zealand First. Bolger went quietly, negotiating a term as New Zealand's ambassador in Washington.

The change of leadership was a mixed blessing for National. The electorate had little affection for Jenny Shipley personally and her elevation did not reassure those hoping for a move back to more centralist politics. Shipley, New Zealand's first woman prime minister, enjoyed a 'honeymoon' period of about eight months, with National climbing steadily in the polls, and her focus, in the spirit of early 1990s radicalism, on micro-economic reform. But then the unraveling began.

In August 1998, the sale of Wellington Airport ended the increasingly brittle alliance, New Zealand First ministers walking out of cabinet and Shipley sacking Peters, her deputy PM, for flouting the concept of collective responsibility. National's junior coalition partner fragmented, leaving Shipley with a minority government dependent on a ragtag collection of miniature parties and independents.

There was automatic kudos from chairing the annual Asia-Pacific Economic Co-operation (APEC) forum in Auckland in September 1999, and Jenny Shipley did not lightly concede the election two months later, but she and National had made too many mistakes.

Labour, and Helen Clark, who increasingly had the look of a prime minister in waiting, secured a comfortable victory, with the Maori seats that had deserted to NZ First in 1996 back in the fold.

There had been massive, unrelenting change during the 1980s, and this continued into the new decade, with scores of thousands of lives turned upside down. It was a time, for some, to reflect and take pause, but the inequalities in New Zealand life were now in starker relief with the gap between the rich and the poor widening.

For decades up to the 1980s, the share of total personal income pocketed by top earners actually shrank; from the early 1980s it expanded rapidly. By 1999, 10 percent of top earners accounted for 32 percent of all personal income; the top 1 percent for 9 percent. There were similar gains in the purchasing and real spending power of the wealthiest 20 percent during the 1990s – and always at the expense of the poorest. Surveys suggest that, in the early 1990s, a senior executive in a major company earned 27 times the average worker's wage; by 1999 the differential had blown out to 77 times. Treasury grudgingly admitted that up to 8 percent of New Zealanders might be living in relative poverty – or unable to pay for an unexpected doctor's visit – but some commentators put the figure as high as 20 percent. However, the 'market' did not take prisoners and people had "to get over it" even if the number of unemployed surged over 200,000 for the first time ever.

Meanwhile, the rich had lost most of their inhibitions. Traditionally, New Zealand's wealthy had been circumspect about overt conspicuous consumption; in the nineties there was no embarrassment about multi-million dollar mansions, massive yachts, and huge salaries and severances based on doubtful international comparisons and, at times, regardless of performance.

The 'baby boomers' were older and starting to think retirement, but with age expectancies on the up and up, at least for comfortably off pakeha, declining years would be spent more robustly and with wallets full of credit cards. Marketers were now trying to get under the skin of Generation Xers, their grunge music expressing, it was said, their frustration at living in the shadow of the more numerous and influential baby boomers.

In 1984 more people lived in Auckland than the whole of the South Island; by 1990 the dominance of the 'City of Sails' generated degrees of arrogance and resentment. The expression, "New Zealand stops at the Bombay Hills" meant one thing to Aucklanders and something rather different elsewhere. Aucklanders tended to view the rest of the country as slow-paced and lacking in enterprise, and Wellington a synonym for 'restrictive bureaucracy'. Aucklanders or Jafas (Just Another F ****** Auckland) were characterised as brash, crass, hedonistic, boat-obsessed, self-centred, and politically naïve by those on the other side of the Bombays divide. There was, of course, an element of truth to all of it. Provincial rivalries, except on the rugby field, fizzled out with the abolition of the provinces, but Auckland versus The Rest still has an edge to it.

Any city with over one million people experiences growing pains, but geography and sprawl have made Auckland's more acute than for many much larger conurbations elsewhere. In the 1990s, water and power crises, harbour pollution and seemingly insoluble traffic congestion took some of the gloss off Auckland's physical attractions and benign climate. In recent years Auckland's population increase has come less from the 'drift north' in search of sun, jobs and markets than from new migrants. Certainly, Pacific Islanders and the Asian community have a clear preference for the Auckland area.

The country's plodding overall population growth has camouflaged the fact that nearly a million people migrated to New Zealand between the end of the Second World War and the century's end. A great majority, particularly in the earlier years, were of British or European ancestry, but that changed dramatically more recently.

The country's Pasifika population, mainly from the tiny island nations that share NZ citizenship, was barely 10,000 before 1960 when much greater numbers began arriving. By 1976, there were about 60,000, almost all in Auckland for family and climatic reasons, the numbers sparking infamous dawn raids searching for 'overstayers' with expired entry permits. After a temporary lull, numbers built steadily again to over 200,000 by the end of the 1990s. Many are now locally born, half are Samoan, with Tongeans the next most numerous. By 1999 about 13 percent of Auckland's population had Pasifika ancestry.

There were Indians in Northland from the early 19th century and Chinese, mainly in the south, from the 1860s goldfields era, but New Zealand's covertly racist immigration policies largely limited new East Asian arrivals to a restricted acceptance of members of already established families. In the mid-1980s, there had been a radical change of policy with the active encouragement of middle-class, well-heeled Asians. By the end of the 1990s there were over 180,000, mainly Chinese, but also Korean, Vietnamese and Indonesian. They have greatly added to the range of Auckland's, and the country's, culinary experiences, and done nothing to dent house prices in several more expensive suburbs, while their children have swelled rolls at the city's two universities.

In one of the little ironies history abounds in, as the voting age came down – from 21 to 20 in 1969 and to 18 in 1973 – tertiary students became less activist and politically involved. In the 1990s there were vastly more of them but, for vocational and financial reasons, they kept their heads down. The Student Loan Scheme, introduced in 1992, focused young minds on getting through courses and degrees as soon as possible. In the early 1960s, there were only about 20,000 students at the country's universities; in 1992, in addition to 90,000 university students, there were over 100,000 more tertiary students at the 25 polytechnics dotted around the country. The loan scheme was, in theory, to provide open access to higher education but, as total numbers reached a quarter million by the end of the decade, the amounts of money involved and debt levels being incurred were turning it into a political hot potato.

Gambling – a sport or last throw of the dice, literally or not, for the desperate – has been popular in New Zealand since the first race meeting in the Bay of Islands in 1835. Until major changes in the late 1980s, the horses had their noses out in front in terms of money won and lost with little competition, except for lotteries like the 'art union' and the 'Golden Kiwi' . However, 'Lotto', a game based on a weekly draw of numbers, began in 1987 and produced a very different gambling landscape. During the 1990s the game was regularly played by over 60 percent of the population, with the Saturday night TV draws watched by up to 400,000 people. In 1988, electronic gambling machines or 'one-armed bandits' were allowed into a range of sporting and other clubs, and in 1989, parliament voted in favour of casinos, with the first up and playing in Christchurch in 1993. In the late 1980s, about 85 percent of gambling money was spent on horses; by 1999 racing and other sports betting accounted for less than 20 percent. The big winners have been gaming machines (about 35 percent), casinos (25 percent) and the Lottery Commission's games (over 20 percent).

Auckland might be getting bigger, but there was increasing diversity in the way and where New Zealanders lived. The 'holy grail' of home ownership was not being pursued so vigorously and percentages were beginning to drop, house prices and lifestyle reasons contributing. Apartment living was a much more attractive option after city and town centres responded to liquor licensing changes in 1989 with a rush of restaurants, bars, intimate movie art houses and massive multiplexes.

However, there was also a small, but fascinating, reversal of the relentless depopulating of rural areas. In the 1980s and 1990s, in reaction to corporate and social excesses, and helped by booming city real estate prices, thousands of New Zealanders began moving to the countryside or small towns. It was a chance to re-establish values, bring up children in a healthier environment, get one's hands in the soil. A western world, middle-class phenomenon, it was boosted by two trends: the shift in work patterns to more self-employment and contract work, particularly in the ever-growing and mutating service industries; and technology's advances – with the fax machine, personal computer, then email and internet it was feasible, even sensible, to work from the rural smallholding or small town villa with only occasional forays to company or client in the city. Hand in hand with this trend was a return to the garden, solace for some, a necessary diversification income-earner for others; it sparked a countrywide retail boom in plants, manure, mulch and all the tools of the trade as well as numerous 'gardens open to the public' plus TV and radio programmes.

Between 1991-96 there was a solid 9 percent increase in the numbers living outside city boundaries. There are now well over 100,000 smallholdings on the peripheries of cities and towns and deeper in the countryside; they have breathed

Garrick Tremain, *Otago Daily Times*, February 16 1994. ATL: H-150-021

new life into rural communities and smallfarmers have been among the most innovative and successful farming experimenters. Dairy and fibre goats, emus and ostriches, alpacas and llamas, exotic sheep and cattle breeds, chestnuts, olives, herbs and lavender all began their sometimes chequered histories on smallholdings.

During the 1990s there were a number of Treaty of Waitangi settlements but aspects of these, together with the government's attempt to negotiate a $1 billion 'fiscal envelope' settlement for all outstanding claims, caused considerable Maori anger, frustration and resentment of 1970s proportions. The formal ceremonies at Waitangi on February 6 1995 were cancelled after disruptive protests; Wanganui's Moutoa Gardens protest later in the year was inspiration for the subsequent occupation of a number of public buildings, including a courthouse and police station, in various parts of the country.

In the 1990s, New Zealand made a particular point of celebrating its winners; to do one's best was no longer the virtue it used to be. Team New Zealand won yachting's premier prize, the America's Cup, in 1995 and retained it in 1999-2000; watching interminable hours of heaving seas on TV was a small price to pay. New Zealand's sauvignon blanc wines won numerous international awards through the decade. The Black Ferns, the women's rugby team, won the world championship in 1998 – which was just as well as the All Blacks didn't in 1991, 1995 or 1999. Te Papa, which opened in 1998, was rated the world's most innovative museum. Anna Paquin won an Oscar in 1994 for her performance in *The Piano*. In 1991, the Resource Management Act was lauded around the world as unique, pioneering and a totally new approach to environmental management, although some New Zealand individuals, companies and local bodies wished they had never heard of it.

In an increasingly competitive and, with the sale of the *NZ Herald* in 1995, foreign-owned media world, with its penchant for personality-driven stories, women got a good press for a lengthy list of 1990s firsts: eclectically and all in 1990, Dame Catherine Tizard, the first woman governor-general, Dr Penny Jamieson, first Anglican woman bishop in the world and Ruth Richardson, first woman finance minister in the country; Silvia Cartwright, first female high court judge and Helen Clark, first woman opposition leader in 1993; Jenny Shipley, first woman prime minister in 1997 and Helen Clark, first *elected* PM in 1999.

Labour Lingers On

As the new decade began, Geoffrey Palmer, a polished performer at No 2 in the government, was finding the prime ministership heavy going. The one-time law professor was not adept at the glib half truth; to him – although he was accused of being naïve and unworldly – truth and honesty were important. Labour sagged in the polls, and well-intentioned Maori initiatives worried pakeha more than they helped Maori. Palmer resigned when he was told a majority of caucus wanted Mike Moore as leader at the 1990 election, just two months away. With a cynicism that dismayed Palmer, his colleagues, including his deputy Helen Clark, were more concerned about Moore's ability to claw back a few marginals than his prime ministerial credentials. Moore lost the election as comprehensively – perhaps even more so – than Palmer might have done.

1. Caucus wanting Douglas back in cabinet had been the final straw for Lange. Douglas's return, under Palmer, in August 1989 as police and immigration minister satisfied neither his supporters nor his opponents inside and outside government. *The Albatross*, Peter Bromhead, *Auckland Star*, January 23 1990. ATL: A-314-1-024
2. Palmer's election year reshuffle had a desperate look about it. In early February 1990, some of the most senior and experienced ministers – Douglas, Stan Rodger, Michael Bassett, Russell Marshall and Colin Moyle – who were retiring later that year, resigned – with few of the replacements as capable. *"I ve got a few surprises ....",* Anthony Ellison, *Auckland Star*, January 22 1990. ATL: A-313-1-050
3. Colleagues, and the public, were confused by Moore's seemingly irreconcilable political views and the torrent of ideas that spilled out in speeches and interviews. It was widely thought his woolly rhetoric was too insubstantial and unfocused for him to be prime ministerial material. *"Who says this man has no depth ....",* Bill Paynter, *National Business Review*, September 11 1990. ATL: J-065-071
4. Teenage Mutant Ninja Turtles – which had mutated from comics to merchandising to TV and, in 1990, a movie – were very popular among the young. *"What s with this teenage mutant ....",* Bob Brockie, *National Business Review*, June 1 1990. ATL: A-314-2-074
5. Although Palmer had beaten him decisively for the leadership after Lange resigned, by the beginning of 1990, as Labour faltered, Moore was positioning himself as a more populist, alternative leader. Even if only briefly, he wanted to sit behind the big desk on the ninth floor of the Beehive. *"Mike seems to be taking ....",* Trace Hodgson, *NZ Listener*, July 30 1990. ATL:A-314-3-057

1

2

3

4

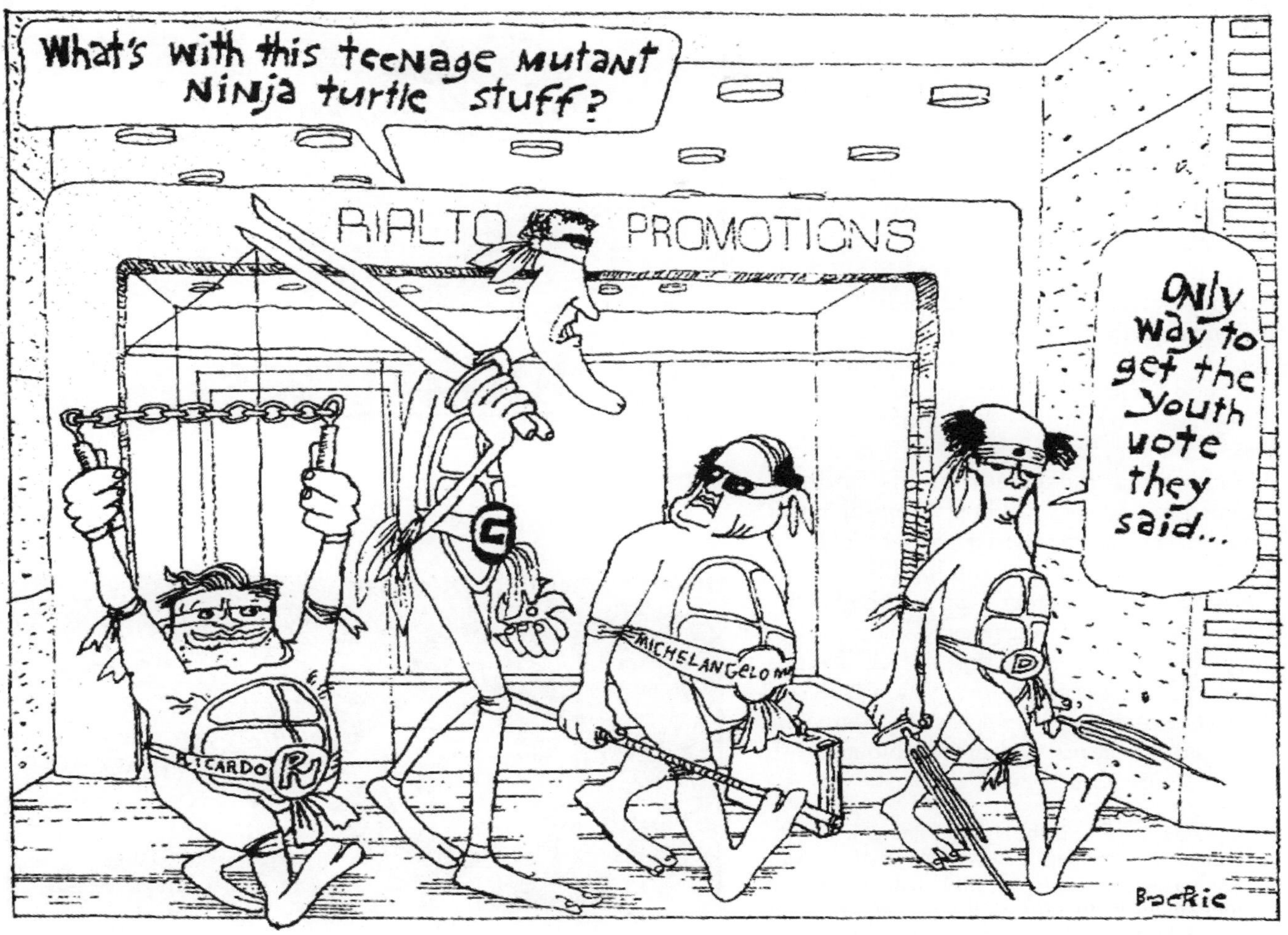

What's with this teenage mutant Ninja turtle stuff?

RIALTO PROMOTIONS

Only way to get the youth vote they said...

RICARDO

MICHELANGELO

Bockie

5

The Ultimate Pragmatist

Jim Bolger, a successful King Country sheep and beef farmer, was a well-seasoned politician – 18 years into the job and an effective minister of labour – when he went to the 1990 election with a comfortable lead in the polls and a 'Decent Society' theme that later proved an embarrassment. There was scant time to enjoy a crushing victory as Bolger was confronted, as Lange had been in 1984, with a financial crisis. In dealing with an insolvent Bank of New Zealand, social spending cuts, the superannuation surcharge backdown and problems with a tetchy Muldoon and temperamental Winston Peters, Jim Bolger demonstrated the extent of his political pragmatism. Flexibility and opportunism, rather than a fixed philosophic viewpoint, were to be his watchwords. Often breathtaking and quite unrepentant shifts of ground or reversals of policy were to help him manoeuvre successfully through one of the most complicated and challenging decades in New Zealand history. National survived the 1993 election, with a single seat majority; the 1996 election, the first under MMP, brought with it a raft of new challenges.

1. Jim Bolger, a little in the Holyoake mould, used his considerable management and negotiating skills while ministers – notably Bill Birch, minister of labour, Ruth Richardson and Jenny Shipley – announced and carried out a number of unpopular decisions. *The Four Horsemen*, Anthony Ellison, *Sunday Star Times*, April 7 1991. ATL: J-044-009
2. Bolger had built his 1990 campaign around a rosy-hued 'Decent Society'. However, the huge Bank of New Zealand bailout meant cuts in social welfare payments to the most needy and abandonment of the promise to remove the superannuation surcharge. *Vote for a Decent Society*, Tom Scott, *Evening Post*, 1992. ATL: A-312-4-025
3. Ruth Richardson, the country's first woman finance minister, and Jenny Shipley, her protégé and social welfare minister, were increasingly unpopular as social spending was cut in response to a ballooning deficit. *"Hullo .... weren t you at ....",* Garrick Tremain, *Otago Daily Times*, 1981. ATL: J-065-073
4. In May 1994, the government committed 250 soldiers to frontline UN duties in Bosnia; closer to home, Bolger had a battle on his hands when, after losing the finance portfolio, Ruth Richardson refused any other cabinet position, resigned from parliament and forced a by-election in August 1994 that could have brought the government down. *"Your country ....er....ummm ....",* Klarc, *NZ Herald*, May 7 1994. ATL: H-102-005
5. The Bolger government made progress in settling Treaty of Waitangi claims but the proposal of a 'fiscal envelope', capping all Treaty of Waitangi claims at $1 billion, was roundly rejected by Maoridom. *"We ran it up the flagpole ....",* Chris Slane, *NZ Listener*, March 1995. ATL: A-317-1-003

1

2

3

4

YOUR COUNTRY...ER
...UMMM...MIGHT NEED
YOU
KLARC

5

SLANE
FISCAL ENVELOPE
WE RAN IT UP
THE FLAGPOLE
AND IT GOT THE
21 GUN SALUTE.

Comings and Goings

Predictably, National had won the 1990 election at a canter. Less predictably, Mike Moore, admitted that the change in Labour leadership had made no difference at all. Moore was used to the ups and downs of politics. He had left school at 15, was soon passionately involved with the Labour Party, and unexpectedly won the Auckland seat of Eden in 1972, at 23 years of age, by far the youngest member of parliament. He lost the seat in 1975, battled cancer, and was back in parliament representing a Christchurch electorate in 1978. He was then a successful and endlessly energetic minister of overseas trade. After the 1990 trouncing, Moore led a seriously depleted Labour opposition with trademark verve and lost the 1993 election by a whisker. But it was two losses and out, Helen Clark quickly replacing him. Prime minister Bolger survived two trying by-elections when Winston Peters took his political ambitions elsewhere in 1993 and Ruth Richardson resigned in the highest possible dudgeon the next year.

1. After easily winning the April 1993 Tauranga by-election as an independent, Peters launched the New Zealand First Party. *"I shall lead this new party ....",* Chris Slane, *NZ Listener*, August 7 1993. ATL: H-103-014
2. Immediately after the November 6 election there was speculation about how long Mike Moore would last. *"I can t, I can t ....",* Tom Scott, *Evening Post,* November 10 1993. ATL: H-113-032
3. Helen Clark's challenge for the Labour leadership shortly after the election had been precipitated by caucus pressure, but the media, encouraged by a bitter Moore, were hostile to the country's first woman political party leader. *"All I ask is for a fair go ....",* Malcolm Walker, *Independent*, April 7 1994. ATL: A-302-136
4. Ruth Richardson's approach to the economy was described, unflatteringly, as 'Rogernomics on steroids'. Subsequently, she was closely associated with the ACT Party, founded by Roger Douglas. *Ruth Quits ....,* Anthony Ellison, *Sunday Star Times*, July 17 1994. ATL: A-313-1-051
5. As the two major parties veered from their traditions, and manifestos, there were an increasing number of defections to form new groupings motivated by policy differences or thwarted personal ambitions. *"So how s about we catch a meal ....",* Frank Greenall, *Dominion*, June 30 1995. ATL: J-065-072
6. Jim Anderton left Labour in 1989, founded New Labour and then, in 1991, built the Alliance coalition that included the Democrats, Mana Motuhake, the Liberals, and the Greens. The umbrella party scored an impressive 18 percent of the popular votes, but only two seats, in 1993, the final first-past-the-post election. The Democrats' Garry Knapp departed in 1995 and the Greens left two years later to contest the 1999 election under their own banner. *Knapp Quits 'Economic Dinosaur Alliance ....,* Jim Hubbard, *Dominion*, November 17 1995. ATL: H-338-058

1

2

3

4

RUTH QUITS...
IT WAS ME ALL ALONG!
ELLISON

5

AYES
SO HOWS ABOUT WE CATCH A MEAL AND A MOVIE, THEN BACK TO MY PLACE FOR A FEW DRINKS AND FORM A NEW PARTY ?!....

6

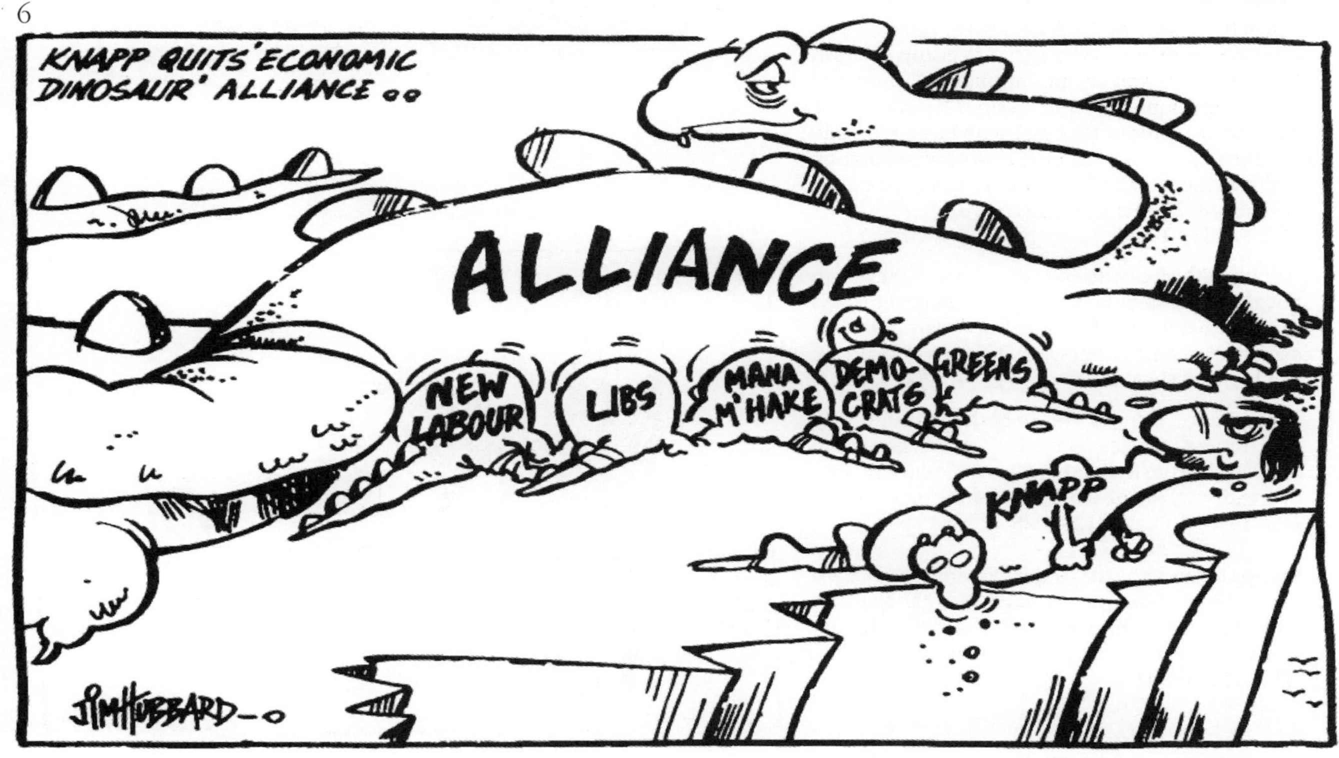
KNAPP QUITS 'ECONOMIC DINOSAUR' ALLIANCE ..
ALLIANCE
NEW LABOUR
LIBS
MANA M'HAKE
DEMO-CRATS
GREENS
KNAPP
JIMHUBBARD

Inside the Winebox

In the 1990s, the 'Winebox Affair' kept Winston Peters' profile high, became a sort of shorthand for 1980s corporate corruption, sullied reputations and made future tax avoidance schemes less likely. In March 1994 Winston Peters succeeded in tabling in parliament 1,860 pages of documents – a cardboard winebox full of them – relating to about 60 Cook Islands banking and financial transactions. Peters alleged they detailed fraud and malpractice by a number of companies and individuals; he later made accusations about the Inland Revenue Department and Serious Fraud Office. Then a TV documentary alleged that European Pacific, a tax haven company chaired by David Richwhite, paid tax in the Cooks, was given Cook Islands tax receipts together with refunds of the tax paid, and then used the receipts to reduce New Zealand taxes, without disclosing the refunds. The experts agreed it was blatant tax avoidance, but not illegal. In September 1994, the government appointed former chief justice Sir Ronald Davison to head a commission of enquiry which sat for 216 days over the next three years. On August 15 1997 his report found no basis to Peters' allegations of fraud and conspiracy by a group of large companies.

1. The inquiry was told that the tax avoidance schemes the Cook Islands' aided and abetted reduced the New Zealand tax take that was, in turn, the source of on-going aid payments to the tiny island nation. *Ambidexterity*, Garrick Tremain, *Otago Daily Times*, May 22 1996. ATL: H-294-035
2. Michelle Boag, Fay Richwhite's PR director, was responsible for covert filming of Winston Peters at the Winebox inquiry, and admitted a charge of contempt against the commission. It was not the best public relations for Fay Richwhite which had acquired, during the inquiry, a growing reputation for 'covertness'. *"Did I hear something backfire?"*, Peter Bromhead, *Dominion*, July 31 1996. ATL: A-314-1-025
3. Although the Cook Islands government refused to budge on its secrecy laws, enough evidence emerged to show that it had played an active part in the tax avoidance schemes. *Hanging Out to Dry*, Malcolm Walker, *Sunday News*, 1996. ATL: H-258-003
4. A number of witnesses, from both companies and government agencies, seemed to catch a nasty strain of amnesia from each other during the commission of inquiry. *"Your Honour ....",* Tom Scott, *Evening Post*, 1996. ATL: A-312-4-026
5. During the inquiry, the evidence from 73 witnesses and lawyers' submissions filled 13,000 pages of transcript. *The Wine Box Papers*, Garrick Tremain, *Otago Daily Times*, December 13 1996. ATL: H-276-002

1

2

3

4

YOUR HONOUR, NOTHING WOULD GIVE ME MORE PLEASURE THAN TO BE SUBJECTED TO SEVERAL DAYS' WORTH OF RIGOROUS CROSS EXAMINATION ON TAX SCAMS...

UNFORTUNATELY, AND BELIEVE ME THIS IS BREAKING MY HEART, SUCH IS MY LOVE, DEEP RESPECT AND AWE FOR COOK ISLANDS' SECRECY LAWS, I MUST DECLINE...

Tom Scott.

5

LIBRARY

THE HISTORY OF CIVILISATION

THE WINE BOX PAPERS

GARRICK TREMAIN

Tails Wag Old Political Dogs

In December 1986, when a royal commission recommended a change in the country's electoral system to Mixed Member Proportional representation (MMP), Labour was preoccupied with revolutionising the economy. Perhaps surprisingly, National decided the 'first past the post' system, which had provided the party with such lengthy periods in office, was inherently unfair and made a commitment to hold two referenda; the second confirmed majority support for MMP. Meanwhile there had been several MP defections: two National MPs formed the Liberal Party in 1991 and the next year joined the Alliance grouping organised by Jim Anderton after he left Labour. After the 1993 election, Ross Meurant formed the Right of Centre Party (ROC), then the Conservative Party briefly before disappearing. Another National MP, Graeme Lee, left to lead the Christian Democrats which later joined with the Christian Heritage Party. In mid-1995, four National and two Labour MPs, plus Peter Dunne, formerly Labour, left their respective camps to form the United Party.

1. The first referendum in September 1992, showed New Zealanders wanted change, with MMP the preferred option. In the second, at the 1993 election, MMP nosed out the status quo. *"Well done! ...",* Chris Slane, *NZ Listener*, October 3 1992. ATL: A-317-1-002
2. During 1993-96, Bolger reached accommodations with several new groupings to maintain his razor-thin majority. *The Grim Face of Power ....,* Frank Greenall, *Dominion*, April 18 1994. ATL: A-300-123
3. As leader of one of the parties with a vested interest in the winner-takes-all system, Bolger was more supportive of change than might have been expected, although he personally favoured an elected second chamber. He later wrote: "On this occasion, principle won out over politics, something that doesn't always happen." *Bedtime Stories with Uncle Jim*, Tom Scott, *Evening Post*, September 8 1993. ATL: H-110-050
4. Despite extensive education programmes, the principles and permutations of the MMP system were not well understood by the electorate in 1993. *"The poll of our readers ....",* David Fletcher, *Dominion*, July 29 1993. ATL: A-317-079
5. There was jockeying for any possible advantage prior to the first MMP election. The minor parties scrutinised everything down to ballot papers to ensure they were not being penalised by the clout the two major parties could bring to bear. *"The minor parties have accused ....",* Garrick Tremain, *Press*, September 22 1995. ATL: J-065-074
6. In 1996, for the first time, small parties could win seats in line with the percentage of votes cast for them nationally. *MMP Explained by Two Ticks*, Klarc, *NZ Herald*, September 7 1996. ATL: A-317-082

1

2

3

4

THE POLL OF OUR READERS ON ELECTORAL REFORM SHOWS THAT 10% WANT FPP AND 18% WANT MMP.
WHAT DO THE OTHER 72% WANT?

SOMEONE TO EXPLAIN IT ALL TO THEM AGAIN.
EDITOR
© D FLETCHER 1993.

5

THE MINOR PARTIES HAVE ACCUSED JIM AND ME OF TRYING TO ALTER THE BALLOT PAPERS TO OUR ADVANTAGE!
SO INSTEAD WE'VE COME UP WITH A VERY FAIR SYSTEM WHERE YOU JUST POP YOUR VOTE INTO THE BALLOT BOX OF THE PARTY OF YOUR CHOICE. FAIR ENOUGH?
GARRICK TREMAIN
ALLIANCE
LABOUR
NATIONAL
NZ FIRST
ROC

6

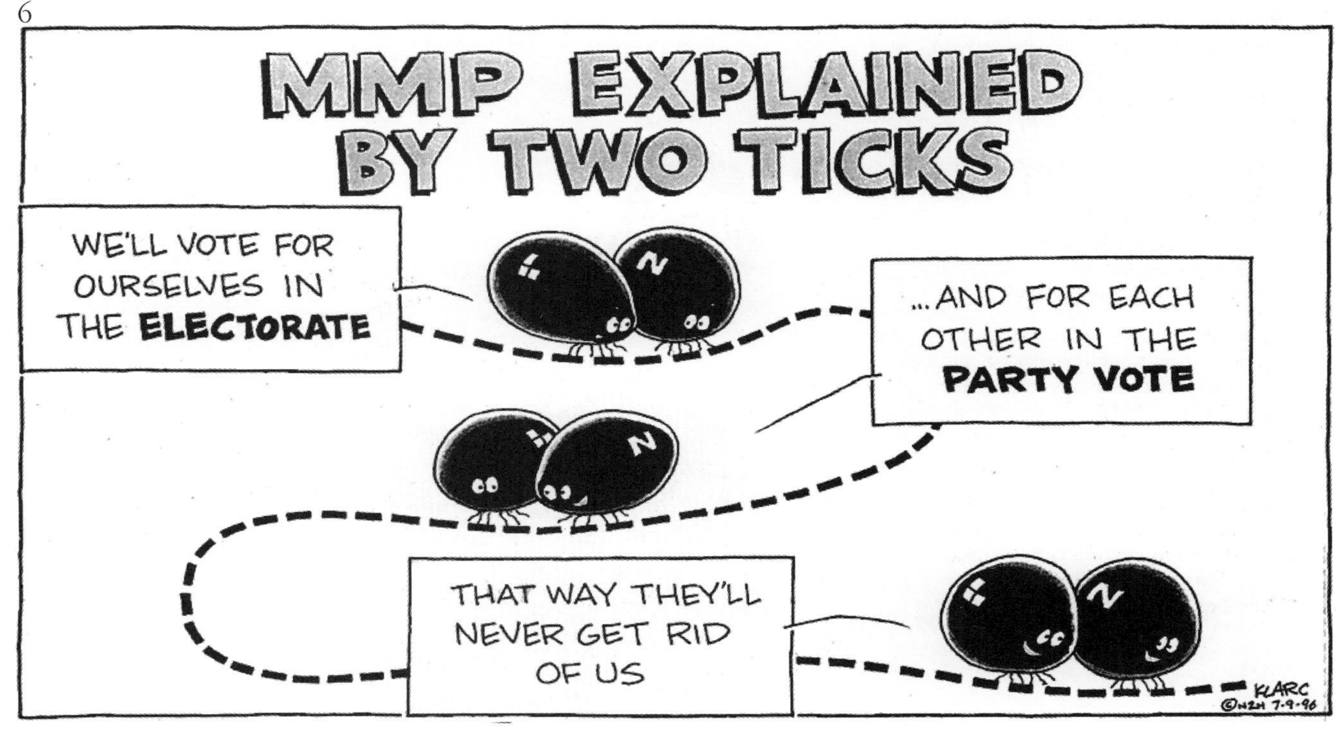
MMP EXPLAINED BY TWO TICKS
WE'LL VOTE FOR OURSELVES IN THE ELECTORATE
...AND FOR EACH OTHER IN THE PARTY VOTE
THAT WAY THEY'LL NEVER GET RID OF US
KLARC
©NZH 7-9-96

Too Close to Call

In retrospect, it's debatable how well either the public or the media understood the new political realities during and after the 1996 election campaign. Certainly, no-one knew better than Jim Bolger the need to keep all coalition options open; he even talked about a 'Great Coalition' with Labour, an idea Helen Clark promptly rejected. National ensured a parliamentary toehold for United's Peter Dunne by not standing a candidate in Ohariu- Belmont. Bolger also took steps to reduce the temptation of National supporters to give their party votes to ACT, fighting its first election, by virtually conceding Wellington Central to Richard Prebble, its new leader. On election night, Labour, and much of the country, believed New Zealand had its first woman prime minister. In fact, Labour had lost much more electoral ground than National, as had potential coalition partners the Alliance and New Zealand First. As it transpired, commentators were too quick to assume that personal animosity between Jim Bolger and Winston Peters would rule out their parties joining forces.

1. The 'worm', supposedly measuring audience responses, added more controversy than illumination to the televised leaders' debates in 1996. Helen Clark was impressive during the election campaign, disguising the fact that Labour's 28 percent of the party vote was its poorest result since 1928. *"I don t know what the others ....",* Tom Scott, *Evening Post*, October 8, 1996. ATL: H-374-085
2. During 1996, the media promoted the idea, still strongly held on election night, that National was seriously disadvantaged by the lack of a likely coalition partner. Bolger's attitude was both flexible and pragmatic: "I am ruling no party in or out". *MMP Alliances*, Malcolm Walker, *Sunday News*, January 28 1996. ATL: A-316-2-022
3. Winston Peters' populist scratching of the electorate's prejudices and fears gave NZ First 17 seats in 1996, more than enough to call the shots during the post-election horse-trading. *"Our definition of xenophobia ?....",* Bob Brockie, *National Business Review*, March 15 1996. ATL: H-451-001
4. The public was increasingly frustrated at the time it took to form a government, and there were mutterings about the wisdom of having changed from FPP to MMP. *"I voted for a firing squad",* Malcolm Evans, *Rural News*, 1996. ATL: H-456-003
5. During the lengthy post-election period he kept National, Labour and the country guessing, the clear winner appeared to be Winston Peters. *The Victory Dais*, Garrick Tremain, *Otago Daily Times*, November 15 1996. ATL: J-065-075

1

2

3

4

A HUNG PARLIAMENT
EVANS.

5

THE VICTORY DAIS
3
1
2
GOO BURBLE BURBLE
GARRICK TREMAIN

The Peters' Principle

For seven long weeks after the October 12 1996 election the final outcome hung in the balance as New Zealand First negotiated with both Labour and National. In the end, to the country's surprise, and anger of many of his party's supporters, Winston Peters signed a detailed coalition agreement with National. Peters had old friends in the National caucus, which had been his political 'home' for a decade; also important, as a conservative male he did not relish the idea of working with and for a woman. He drove a hard bargain, as he also had scores to settle with patronising former colleagues: he was to be deputy prime minister and 'treasurer', delivering the budget and nominally senior to finance minister Birch. Compromises were hammered out over social spending and compulsory superannuation and, in a world in which there were no prizes for coming second, Jim Bolger remained prime minister.

1. After winning Tauranga as an independent earlier in 1993, Winston Peters formed New Zealand First shortly before the election. Generating a barrage of publicity, he retained his Tauranga seat and Tau Henare won Northern Maori. *"Tonight, in front of a capacity crowd….",* Tom Scott, *Evening Post*, April 2 1993. ATL: H-047-002
2. Muldoon had admired Peters' political instincts and ability to command media attention and had talked about him becoming "our first Maori prime minister". There were also similarities between their modus operandi. *"Become a one-man band….",* Peter Bromhead, *Dominion*, June 3 1966. ATL: A-314-1-026
3. The insults traded with some enthusiasm and venom prior to and during the 1996 election campaign were replaced by whiskey-sharing bonhomie during the early months of 1997. *"Y know boy….",* Garrick Tremain, *Otago Daily Times*, February 14 1997. ATL: J-065-076
4. Health minister Bill English found it impossible to work with his NZ First associate minister Neil Kirton, who insisted on airing his alternative views to the media and elsewhere. Peters finally sacked Kirton in August 1997, but there was no provision in the Electoral Act to force recalcitrant MPs to resign from parliament. Nearly a year later Kirton became an independent, depriving the coalition of its majority and forcing an accommodation with Peter Dunne's United Party. *"Get me the Electoral Commission….",* Bob Brockie, *National Business Review*, June 20 1997. ATL: A-314-2-073
5. It was important to Peters personally, and to New Zealand First's standing, that the first budget he presented as treasurer was given 'front-page' coverage. Co-incidentally, the former high commissioner in London had been a National Party president. *"Here we are – ",* Malcolm Evans, *NZ Herald*, June 27 1997. ATL: A-315-5-006

1

2

3

BUS STOP
Y'KNOW BOY...
I CAN REMEMBER
WHEN BOLGER AND
PETERS WERE
DEADLY ENEMIES!!
COALITION
IN HARMONY
SO
CAN
I
GARRICK TREMAIN

4

Get
Me the
electoral
COMMISSION...
NZ FIRST
Brockie

5

HERE WE ARE—
'THE FIRST COALITION
BUDGET WAS PRESENTED
IN PARLIAMENT
YESTERDAY....'
FORMER HIGH COMMISSIONER IN LONDON LOVE TRIANGLE
LOVER LASHES OUR MAN IN LONDON
SAUCY GOINGS AT NZ HIGH COMMISION
NZ'S MAN IN LONDON LOVE AFFAIR
IN LURID LOVE AFFAIR
IN LONDON
NZ'S FORMER HIGH COMMISSIONER ... IN LONDON AFFAIR
LURID LETTER LINKED TO LONDON POST
FORMER HIGH COM IN LONDON LOVE TRYST
ACCORDING TO INFORMED SOURCES

Top Woman

Jim Bolger's grip on the prime ministership weakened during 1997 as embarrassment with New Zealand First increased and the compulsory superannuation referendum, agreed in the coalition talks, was lost. Bolger returned from overseas in early November to find Jenny Shipley had the numbers to replace him and, always the realist, negotiated the most dignified and attractive departure he could. Jenny Shipley had entered parliament, a Ruth Richardson protégé, a decade earlier, her primary teaching and local body politics background giving no hints of her rapid rise through the ranks – six years in cabinet, and the social welfare and health portfolios where toughness and decisiveness earned her loathing and admiration in equal parts. Shipley's 'honeymoon' period as the country's first woman PM lasted some months. Everything, including the polls, went downhill after the coalition foundered in late September 1998, and Shipley's energies were fully engaged keeping her minority government afloat until the next election.

1. As a detail person, Jenny Shipley's coup planning was lengthy and meticulous – her lieutenants gradually built support until a clear majority of caucus favoured a leadership change. *"Meanwhile …"*, Bob Brockie, *National Business Review*, June 20 1997. ATL: H-506-003
2. Bolger accepted the inevitable, his price for going quietly a changeover delay until after an APEC leaders' meeting in Vancouver and a visit to China. *"Why Jim …."*, Tom Scott, *Evening Post*, November 5 1997. ATL: H-448-047
3. The National caucus had supported Shipley with the explicit understanding that she would be more assertive with New Zealand First. *A Marriage of Convenience*, Peter Bromhead, *Dominion*, November 17 1997. ATL: H-725-017
4. Publicly, the coalition leadership of Shipley and Peters seemed to be singing from the same songbook; the new PM enjoyed an eight month calm with National climbing in the polls. Jim Bolger delayed his resignation from parliament (and the subsequent and potentially destabilising by-election) until April 1998. *"Ac-ce-e-entuate the positive"*, Klarc, *NZ Herald*, January 22 1997. ATL: A-317-083
5. The Shipley-Peters coalition made significant changes to immigration policy. Fewer migrants would be allowed in for family or humanitarian reasons; there was an unabashed emphasis on business people, investors, entrepreneurial and skilled immigrants. *"Give me your old …."*, Malcolm Evans, *NZ Herald*, October 14 1988. ATL: A-315-5-008
6. Winston Peters had scuppered any suggestion of the NZ navy acquiring a third frigate. With Peters gone it was briefly on the agenda again. But like the Code of Social and Family Responsibility, it became peripheral to the minority government's struggle to survive. *"Ah! Time for a new frigate"*, Malcolm Walker, *Sunday News*, November 1 1998. ATL: H-526-006

1

2

3

4

AC-CE-E-ENTUATE THE POSITIVE
E-LI-I-IMINATE THE NEGATIVE
...DON'T MESS WITH BY-ELECTIONS IN BETWEEN
OVERSEAS POSTING
©KLARC 22-11-97

5

GIVE ME YOUR TIRED, OLD
WEALTHY POOR, HUDDLED SELECTED
MASSES YEARNING
TO BREATHE FREE
MONEY INTO OUR ECONOMY
NZ IMMIGRATION POLICY
FROM IMPORTING USED CARS TO USED PEOPLE

6

Ah! time for a new frigate...
CODE OF SOCIAL & FAMILY RESPONSIBILITY!
$2,000,000
Malcolm Walker

Lessons Learnt

If Winston Peters did not want to go into coalition with Helen Clark, he was bound to have the same sort of difficulties with Jenny Shipley. The increasingly brittle alliance ended with the sale of Wellington airport in August 1998. Shipley continued with a minority government dependent on several small parties and independents. Helen Clark, a university lecturer in politics in her pre-parliamentary life, observed the problems and pitfalls of coalition government with much more than academic interest. Having survived a May 1996 delegation of senior Labour members asking her to step down, and the party's dismal election showing later in the year, she now made a determined effort to patch up differences with the Jim Anderton-led Alliance Party. The old friends, but more recently bitter antagonists, reached agreement about a post-election coalition. As the polls had been suggesting for months, Clark and Labour won a solid victory at the November 1999 election.

1. Helen Clark's and Labour's fillip in the polls had added ammunition to Jenny Shipley's campaign to unseat Jim Bolger. *Most Preferred PM*, Garrick Tremain, *Press,* June 13 1997. ATL: J-065-077
2. While not entirely fair, Jenny Shipley now had an entrenched reputation as a hard-nosed slasher of social services. The grandly titled 'Code of Social and Family Responsibility' discussion document she released early in 1998 was basically about getting the nation to pull up its collective socks. *"Under our rural housing assistance package ....",* Tom Scott, *Evening Post*, October 9 1999. ATL: H-539-028
3. As the election neared, polls suggested the Greens, a potential Labour ally, needed to win an electorate seat to be sure of parliamentary representation. In the event, they won Coromandel and polled just over 5 percent as well. The cartoonist is making a sly reference to the Greens' cannabis policy and President's Clinton's famous 1992 comment. *"I took a puff, but I did not inhale ....",* Tom Scott, *Evening Post*, October 26 1999. ATL: H-606-018
4. Labour and the Alliance, with 59 seats between them, formed a minority government on their own. The Greens provided the additional security of support on matters of supply. *Trapeze Act*, Malcolm Walker, *Sunday News*, December 12 1999. ATL: A-338-190

1

2

3

HELEN CLARK APPEARS TO SUPPORT COROMANDEL GREEN OVER LABOUR CANDIDATE...

I TOOK A PUFF, BUT I DID NOT INHALE...

4

GREENS

malcolm Walker...

Business Rules

The 1990s were an unsettled sort of decade. As politicians learnt to play the MMP game, there was more political volatility than for over 100 years. And Rogernomics was working its way, with some painful indigestion, through the economic system. The growing disparities of income were dramatised by the bulging fortunes in the *NBR Rich List*. The internet and email fed the culture of instant information, action and constant change and made New Zealand's connectedness to the rest of the world about as complete as physical separation allowed. There were the latest Hollywood movies on DVDs, cheaper travel, and the import flood of famous brand names and cheap bargains from any and everywhere. There was a price tag to practically everything, and big business's acquisitive nose sniffed out opportunities from yachting to rugby. Political correctness thrived as well. From smoking dictates to nursing practice, bureaucratic regulation was often at odds with an increasingly 'open slather' society.

1. In December 1990, Labour's Smoke-free Environments Act ended the sponsorship of sporting events by tobacco companies – and an effective back-door way of maintaining levels of cigarette brand awareness. *"Damned woman ....",* Bob Brockie, *National Business Review*, April 27 1990. ATL: A-314-2-072
2. As minister of health, Helen Clark pushed through legislation that restricted smoking in workplaces, cafes and restaurants and banned it in public transport. *St Helen the Righteous*, Trace Hodgson, *NZ Listener*, April 30 1990. ATL: A-317-3-056
3. The increase in teenage pregnancies from the mid-1980s was masked by a rising proportion of abortions. There was a greater emphasis on 'safe' sex as, among OECD countries, only the United States had a higher teenage birth rate than New Zealand. *Be Prepared*, Eric Heath, *Dominion*, August 1 1990. ATL: A-311-4-026
4. High profile court cases with lawyers in the dock did nothing for the law profession's reputation in the community. *"I wanna see a lawyer! ....",* Eric Heath, *Dominion*, September 4 1992. ATL: B-144-424a
5. The America's Cup, with repetitious monotony virtually guaranteed, was a surprise new spectator sport, courtesy of TV cameramen with strong stomachs. There was often more excitement in the courtroom battles than on the water, but national euphoria in 1995, when New Zealand finally won yachting's most famous competition and international sport's oldest trophy. *"To think I once complained ....",* Tom Scott, *Evening Post*, April 27 1992. ATL: H-002-020

1

2

3

KHANDALLAH
SCOUT
ERIC HEATH

4

I WANNA SEE A LAWYER!
TAKE YOUR PICK!
ERIC HEATH

5

SLAMDUNK HIM ROD!!!!
THROW HIM IN JAIL
AND THROW AWAY
THE KEY!!!!
TO THINK I
ONCE COMPLAINED
ABOUT A FEW
TEST MATCHES
THAT LASTED
80 MINUTES
EACH...

6. By the mid-1990s the professional era had revolutionised New Zealand's national game. A new, free-flowing style of rugby capitivated the fans, but for top players there were now large dollops of money, longer seasons, more matches, stricter training regimes, closer media scrutiny and profitable twilight years overseas. *Lineout*, Klarc, *NZ Herald*, June 9 1993. ATL: H-065-006

7. There were attempts to de-criminalise the use of cannabis for recreational use, with the controversial suggestion that it was basically no different from alcohol. Others, with Tom Scott prominent, saw a much greater, more pervasive danger with cannabis. *This cannabis education resource booklet ....",* Tom Scott, *Evening Post*, March 4 1993. ATL: H-053-004

8. Racism, and separatism, while usually covert, were in evidence, particularly in areas like education. There was 'white' flight, with pakeha parents employing elaborate stratagems to enrol their children in better resourced, higher decile schools; after kohanga reo, some Maori wanted their children in kura kaupapa (Maori language immersion) schools. *".... We shouldn t be seen ....",* Mark Dower, *Dominion*, January 21 1995. ATL: A-317-081

9. While women were making spectacular advances in politics, the public service and some professions, the small group of ageing men who controlled access to the nation's boardrooms were still to be convinced they had the qualities necessary for directorial duties. *"I assume you have no problem ....",* Murray Ball, *The Sisterhood*, 1993. ATL: H-721-007

10. During the 1990s the number of international tourists visiting New Zealand increased by 85 percent. While slick 'clean, green' promotion brought visitors flooding in, locals were being priced out of some of the most popular, traditional holiday haunts. *Excuse me, sir, just a spot check ....",* Trace Hodgson, *Listener*, January 28 1995. ATL: A-317-3-058

6

7

8

9

"I assume you have no problem with me. also being an attentive and loving Mother?"
Murray Ball.
Welcome to QUEENSTOWN
EXCUSE ME, SIR, JUST A SPOT CHECK.. NO NEED TO GET OUT OF THE CAR... DO YOU HAVE A MAJOR CREDIT CARD WITH YOU?
POLICE

10

11. Having lost contact with their tribal roots, some young urban Maori felt a sense of belonging and identity in gangs which the rest of the community found threatening. *Goldie Exhibition*, Malcolm Evans, *NZ Herald*, October 21 1997. ATL: A-315-5-005

12. Such was the power of TV in an increasingly materialistic world, even the commercials made news. One commercial, which broke new ground with the repeated, albeit, creative use of what is now an iconic expletive, survived an outpouring of complaints to sell large numbers of utility vehicles and win multiple awards. *"Bugger",* Jim Hubbard, *Dominion*, March 24 1999. ATL: A-317-080

13. Legislation lowering to 18 the age at which young people could buy alcohol, passed in an August 1999 conscience vote in parliament, inevitably led to a disturbing rise in drinking problems among younger and younger New Zealanders. *"Of course, I m eighteen ....",* Peter Bromhead, *Dominion*, July 30 1999. ATL: A-314-1-027

14. 'Cultural safety' was a new expression in the nursing world and there were louder public grumblings that training had become more academic and prone to PC pressures, while actually taking care of patients, or 'clients' in modern jargon, had been neglected. *"I can quote authoritatively ....",* Jim Hubbard, *Dominion*, June 27 1995. ATL: H-336-109

15. To the young particularly, TV had become such an integral part of everyday life that there were 'withdrawal' problems without the daily dose of the 'drug'. *Bush TV*, Malcolm Evans, *NZ Herald*, January 5 1998. ATL: A-315-5-007

11

12

13

14

I CAN QUOTE AUTHORITATIVELY ON MAORI CREATION MYTHS..

I CAN QUOTE CHAPTER AND VERSE ON THE TREATY..

I CAN HOLD A DISCOURSE ON HOW THE SEALORD DEAL AFFECTS MAORI HEALTH..

BUT THERE ARE ONE OR TWO OTHER MINOR SKILLS IM STRUGGLING WITH

15

WHO'S GOT THE REMOTE REMOTE?

12: 2000-2005

THE PRIME OF HELEN CLARK

Helen Clark and Labour won impressively at the late November 1999 election. With its 49 MPs and the Alliance's 10 in the 120-seat House, and with Jim Anderton as deputy prime minister, the centre-left minority coalition was quickly in place, with an undertaking that the Greens would support the government on confidence and supply.

There was a busy legislative programme, but the dominant political story of the fifth Labour government's first three years was the prime minister herself.

Helen Clark had used her 18 years of political apprenticeship to analyse the ingredients for successful, enduring leadership. They included: a watchful eye on, and regular contact with, all her ministers; a determination to nip problems in the bud; a low tolerance of mistakes and sloppy work by public servants, colleagues and board appointees; and a positive relationship with the media, including regularly programmed radio interviews.

She dealt promptly, and sometimes severely, with a succession of bush fires that might have badly burned her administration. High profile public servants and board appointees left their jobs and she sacked four ministers during Labour's first term. The much-vaunted 'Closing the Gaps' initiative, aimed at lifting up the under-privileged, was quickly 're-focused' when it became an embarrassment.

Jenny Shipley was not an effective opposition leader, and looked even less so as Helen Clark blossomed as prime minister. Ironically, given the way she plotted against Jim Bolger, Shipley came home from an overseas trip in late September 2001 to find her days numbered. Her lack-lustre performance, a minor heart attack a year before and her dismal personal poll ratings underlined the point all too clearly. Barely a week later she made way for her deputy Bill English, with a graciousness that disguised her anger. However, National's new leader made no impression on the government's popularity which was substantially aided by a benign economy that produced record export income, tourist receipts and surpluses.

Labour was intent on holding as wide a swathe of the middle political ground as possible. Clark sought to do this domestically with the government's response to the 2001 royal commission that backed the commercial use of genetically modified products in New Zealand while stressing stringent safely controls. The government allowed GM research, including experimental field trials, to continue while announcing a two-year moratorium on the commercial release of GM organisms.

Internationally, Helen Clark's meeting with President George W Bush in Washington in late March 2002 was a coup that suitably impressed New Zealand editorial writers, trade lobbyists and defence pundits. It was the first time a Labour prime minister had been invited inside the White House since Bill Rowling called on Gerald Ford in 1975.

There was an early 2002 split within the Alliance, in part because of disapproval with government policies, including the despatch of SAS forces to Afghanistan. In an attempt to win the clear parliamentary majority the polls told her was reachable, Clark went to the country four months early, in late July 2002, on the doubtful grounds that the Alliance ruckus made it impossible to advance the government's legislative programme. The public was sceptical and, after 'Corngate' dominated the election campaign – a strategically-released book claiming that the existence of a crop of possibly GE-contaminated corn had been covered up by the government – the coalition parties won only 54 seats. The Progressive Coalition, Jim Anderton's latest political vehicle underwritten by his safe electorate seat, contributed two of them, and the Alliance slid into political oblivion.

If Labour had not done as well as it had hoped, National's election result was disastrous. Still, at an age when many are contemplating retirement, ex-Reserve Bank governor Dr Don Brash was high enough on National's party list to be guaranteed a seat. His first two, unsuccessful forays into politics had been as the National candidate in East Coast Bays in the early 1980s. Later, he was the first major party leader not to hold an electorate seat.

In its second term, Clark's minority administration showed considerable adroitness as it negotiated a different temporary coalition for every legislative measure. Labour's firm grip owed much to Clark's close, highly effective working relationship with Michael Cullen, now deputy PM as well as finance minister.

Clark was securely occupying the centre ground that middle New Zealand is most comfortable with, leaving the opposition parties disconsolate on the periphery. Ironically, her good working relationship with Peter Dunne's United Future, principal winners at the 2002 election, meant her 'centre' now stretched further to the 'right' than before. Through the rest of the year and into 2003, poll after poll reflected this, both for Labour and for Helen Clark as preferred prime minister, before beginning a gentle decline in August.

Despite her 'Helengrad' reputation for aggressive micro-managing, during her second term Clark left her generally competent ministers to get on with their jobs. She was softer on the stragglers as well. Energy minister Pete Hodgson was scrambling during the electricity crisis in 2003, but remained at his desk. Police minister George Hawkins was rattled by claims that speeding tickets were a revenue gathering exercise and, in 2005, by the emergency

111 system fiasco, yet he remained in cabinet through to the election.

Some ministerial difficulties, though, could not be ignored. In February 2004 Lianne Dalziel resigned, caught out misleading the public on an immigration issue. Tariana Turia resigned, and was sacked for good measure, in May 2004 after refusing to support the government's foreshore and seabed legislation, winning the subsequent July by-election and returning to parliament as co-leader of the Maori Party. John Tamihere gave up his ministerial warrants in November, his affairs under investigation on several fronts, and with worse to come. In May 2005 David Benson-Pope took leave from his associate education portfolio when he become personally embroiled in a corporal punishment-in-schools debate.

Internationally, relations with the US took a frostier turn when New Zealand, unlike Australia, was not prepared to support, unsanctioned by the United Nations, the March 2003 invasion of Iraq. While the experts argued about the real value of a free trade deal with the United States, and whether or not New Zealand's anti-nuclear policy was the inhibitor some claimed, in 2004 the government beavered away setting the scene for negotiating a free trade agreement with China, which might have much greater long term significance.

Not all of Labour's initiatives were successful; some were scaled back, aborted or buried. As a signatory to the Kyoto Protocol on global warming, the government planned to tax farmers for the flatulence – or greenhouse gas emissions – produced by their animals, but dropped the scheme after an angry September 2003 deputation of over 1,000 farmers demonstrated at parliament. There was little more enthusiasm for the $15 per ton carbon tax the government planned to begin in April 2007. A massive programme of mergers and closures that began in 2000, intended to eventually affect 1,000 schools, was put on hold in February 2004, when the clamour of concern from parents and teachers reached a politically dangerous pitch, and later scrapped.

The economy went through a temporary trough in 2003, lower commodity prices combining with a strong NZ dollar, but it recovered well, the economic reformers of a decade before claiming it all their doing, with record export highs and record unemployment lows. Others rated highly Michael Cullen's sage and sensible handling of the finance portfolio. He also achieved what was beginning to look impossible, sufficient support in 2001 to launch a superannuation scheme that had a chance of providing adequately for the ballooning number of future superannuitants.

In his 2004 budget Cullen was able to predict large surpluses – a point of later controversy – and strong growth. The economy might be booming, but there were no general handouts; instead, a $221 million package of targeted family assistance and money for Auckland's infrastructure and rail networks.

Labour combined economic frugality with progressive social policies. Predictably the government was accused of 'social engineering' and 'political correctness'. Certainly, the government ignored excessive indulgence on the part of some government agencies and tolerated some of the more risible extremes of PC-behaviour. Labour's social legislation programme included: decriminalisation of prostitution, banning of smoking in bars and public transport, the United Future sponsored Families Commission and, in December 2004, the legalisation of civil unions for same-sex and opposite-sex couples.

National had lagged far behind Labour in the polls ever since the 2002, but was just beginning to show some improvement when, on October 28 2003, Don Brash toppled Bill English in a leadership ballot at a special caucus meeting. Nelson MP Nick Smith was named new deputy leader, immediately went on 'stress leave' and was subsequently replaced by Gerry Brownlee.

The government was caught flat-footed when Brash, in an early 2004 speech, scratched an itch that had been irritating a great many New Zealanders. The hefty media coverage produced a solid turnaround in the polls and National climbed past Labour, staying ahead for about six months. Brash said very little that hadn't already been said by Bill English, but he said it with more conviction: government funding on the basis of need not race; no positive discrimination for Maori; abolition of the Maori seats; Crown ownership of the foreshore and seabed; and accelerated resolution of Treaty of Waitangi claims.

A rattled government paid Brash the ultimate compliment of promptly appointing a co-ordinating minister on race relations to review policies that appeared to give racial preferment. Later in the year Labour's raw nerves showed in its clumsy handling of the foreshore and seabed issue. After the Court of Appeal ruled, in June 2003, that the Maori Land Court had jurisdiction to determine the status of foreshore and seabed, the government announced legislation to reassert Crown ownership and ploughed through the process with the finesse of an out-of-control bulldozer. Considered opinions, including from the Waitangi Tribunal, were ignored, as were most select committee submissions. The impressively large hikoi that marched to parliament was treated with uncharacteristic contempt and the Foreshore and Seabed Bill, and its welter of amendments, was rushed into law in November 2004. The government claimed Maori customary rights – where comfortably ahead for eight or so months, but now National surged ahead again. By the beginning of a lengthy election campaign, the two major parties were neck-to-neck, with the small parties limping along behind.

Labour went into the election with a seemingly unbeatable economic record that even a high NZ dollar and soaring petrol prices couldn't hurt: an average of 4 percent economic growth; 3.7 percent unemployment, the lowest in the western world; record-breaking export receipts; a sustained housing boom – but it came perilously close to losing. After six years running things, Labour was a little careless, clumsy and even arrogant, while two less than edifying traits in the national character – latent racism and "what's in it for me" – were manipulated unblushingly by National.

Aided by the shenanigans of Maori members of parliament and the excesses of Maori education and social service providers, Brash's no-nonsense, if simplistic, formulae for treating all New Zealanders equally was a guaranteed crowd pleaser. National was short on specific policies except in one other area – taxation. Although Brash and his finance spokesman John Key stressed the importance of tax cuts to stimulate both the economy and individual initiative, there was no doubt that a proposal to drop the marginal rate to 19 percent for 85 percent of taxpayers was aimed squarely at that many back pockets.

Labour upstaged, and took some of the gloss from, National's major set-piece election 'king-hit' with its own, more targeted vote buyer. Scrooge Cullen was now Father Christmas, having found the funds to permanently waive all interest on loans of students living in, or coming back to, New Zealand.

On the campaign trail, all the attention was on the two main party leaders with the fortunes of the minor parties, so influential in the three MMP elections to date, little more than diverting sideshows. Clark gave a predictably polished performance but, although he improved, Brash's general gawkiness, regular gaffes and poor grasp of his party's policies raised doubts about whether he was prime ministerial material. In the days before September 17, the political polls had the two main parties locked together, then one or the other grabbing a commanding lead. One thing everyone agreed; it was going to be close.

Much more gripping than the 'reality' programmes that still clog the country's airwaves, the first and continuing returns on election night's TV coverage suggested a substantial National victory; later results, as the big city votes, particularly in South Auckland, were counted, showed Labour narrowing the gap and finally edging one seat ahead. All the small parties survived, most narrowly.

NZ First and United Future were committed to negotiating first with the party with the most votes so, during the next 10 days until the substantial number of special votes were tallied, Helen Clark talked to them and to the Greens and the Maori Party, which took four of the seven Maori seats from Labour. Don Brash held talks too, but with less conviction. When the specials tally reduced National's seats by one, Brash conceded the election.

There was talk of unstable government, but Clark has shown mastery in managing minority administrations, with different levels of support from three other parties from 1999 and four from 2002. Political soothsayers, judging the election decided, were soon predicting Brash's departure – he would be 68 at the next election – and pondering whether Clark would leave before 2008. She might be content to be the first Labour leader to win three elections; on the other hand, the longest serving Labour prime minister, Peter Fraser, was in the job for nearly 10 years.

Expectations that the necessary deals would be done promptly had faded four weeks after the election. What appeared to be a simple enough political equation was muddied by the extraordinary and apparently suicidal willingness of the Maori Party to help National cobble together an unlikely and inherently unstable grouping with enough seats to form a government – a sniff of power seemingly enough for it to also abandon key policy planks.

The commentators have also been generous with advice to the politicians. Helen Clark will need to rethink a range of issues from personal taxation to political correctness and grapple with ideas of nationhood that are inclusive for pakeha and Maori, citysider and country dweller. Don Brash will need to get to know and understand New Zealand, and its history, a great deal better and John Key, the difference between being a successful money trader and a minister of finance in waiting.

A lingering memory of the election is that the profusion of polls and their volatility made New Zealand look faintly ridiculous. They became news themselves as the media, which shamelessly commissioned them, hoped they would, and the wildly fluctuating results had the pollsters scrambling to explain themselves. The most likely cause of such variable results, and a worrying sign for the future, was that only about one third of potential respondents approached were prepared to co-operate.

At the beginning of the 21st century the speed of change affected everything but it has become a coping mechanism, for those who can cope with it at all, to simply get on with their everyday lives. Yet there was no avoiding the staggering fact that the world's body of knowledge is doubling approximately every 18 months and that today's university graduate can expect to have 10 to 12 jobs and four to six careers in his or her working lifetime, with two of those careers not invented yet.

The accelerating speed of everything has produced an impatience about waiting for anything. Neatly symbolic of this was the world's determination, spurred on by marketers and retailers, to celebrate the beginning of the new millennium a year early, at the beginning rather than the end of 2000. By contrast, the 20th century was welcomed, with due decorum, in New Zealand cities and towns on the evening of December 31 1901 with parades, flag, bunting and brass bands.

What happens in New Zealand this century will be what happens elsewhere, modified or coloured to some degree by our size and history. Marshall McLuhan's 'global village' exists, if not the sort he hoped for; the stock market hiccup in New York produces a burp in Wellington; 'McDonaldisation' has changed taste buds internationally; and the kid from Wainuiomata wears a sweat shirt emblazoned with the name of a Washington football team he doesn't know exists.

Too many times in the past our pastoral industries have been written off; they remain, if very different from a century ago, of crucial economic importance. Manufacturing, particularly since New Zealand 'clipped onto' the Australian market, is now significant, but tourism is the new powerhouse sector, with the potential to dwarf the others. During the 1990s international visitor numbers jumped 85 percent; with more than three million overseas tourists. By the beginning of the new century – with the country's population just topping four million – tourism had become New Zealand's leading earner of foreign exchange.

The pressure of visitor numbers will be a growing concern over the next decade. By its very nature tourism will remain largely in New Zealand hands, but in many business sectors – from banking to marketing – New Zealand has become an Australian branch office, as Australia has become an American regional office.

Individuals and groups are responding to the pressures and perplexities of the 21st century in different ways. More successful executives are 'downshifting' long before retirement date, swapping financial for other rewards. Others seek solutions in fundamentalist movements like the Destiny Church; some people have already moved into 'gated communities', the security dimension of conspicuous consumption; others again have adopted the 'new austerity', finding it a satisfying experience to live more frugally – and far-sighted as well.

Maori and Polynesian health remains a major concern while the life expectancy of pakeha New Zealanders continues upwards. Today's middle-aged may contribute, however, a downward blip as the stresses of modern living – and the highest rates of depression for decades – catch up with them. They are also members of the 'sandwich generation', caught between the care of aged parents and children who don't leave home or return after failed relationships.

The speed of change seems, like a giant tsunami, to have undermined the foundations of long-established values systems. It is 'a price for everything' world in which the individual is more important than the team, money is the final arbiter, community volunteering is on the decline, and ignorance is no impediment to airing opinions on talkback radio. There is no immediate economic cost benefit to politeness, civility and consideration. Rudeness and insults are, in fact, a new line in comedy. As teenagers in the 1960s, the 'baby boomers' reinvented the culture; now the population is ageing but the culture remains resolutely adolescent.

Over the years, artists have broken out of old moulds and created fiction, poetry, music, art, dance and fashion design that has mingled tradition with South Pacific experiences to produce work with a distinctive New Zealand flavour that has become increasingly self-assured and admired elsewhere. At the beginning of the 21st century, the creative world is no longer a self-conscious ghetto and its practitioners get on with their work, living here or elsewhere. And, for as long as Peter Jackson's prodigious energy and enthusiasm lasts there is likely to be work for New Zealand film crews and special effects specialists, particularly in 'Wellywood'.

New Zealand continues to get the better of many sporting encounters, the professional era providing some friction along the way. At the 2004 Olympics, on rugby and cricket fields and on golf courses, New Zealand has, to use a metaphor from a sport where exceptional performances are rarer, been 'boxing well above its weight'.

In 2005, New Zealand, along with the rest of the western world, is facing survival challenges it is trying to avoid thinking about. Those who do are branded doomsayers or 'weird'. Politicians and so-called business leaders intone platitudes about 'individual freedom', 'essential growth', 'more prosperity', 'climbing the OECD rankings', seemingly unaware that such concepts are increasingly irrelevant and will not help prepare for the seismic changes to New Zealand life that will certainly affect today's children.

Top of the Pops

Helen Clark grew up in a conservative, long-established Waikato farming family. She discovered radical ideas, the anti-Vietnam and anti-apartheid protest movements and the Labour Party while she studied politics at Auckland University. Her first decade in parliament, after winning Mt Albert in 1981, was often lonely and frustrating as Labour veered sharply to the right. She joined cabinet after the 1987 election and made a sufficient impression to become, at 39, deputy prime minister when David Lange resigned in August 1989. She became Labour leader following the 1993 election, and after a rocky period in May 1996, when senior colleagues asked her to stand down, performed well at that year's election. Shrugging off Jenny Shipley and National's unsubtle attacks about her lack of children and unconventional marriage, Clark won the 1999 election comprehensively. Some new prime ministers struggle and others cope; she blossomed in the role.

1. Persuaded, during the 1990s, that style and substance were not incompatible, Helen Clark got grooming advice, her clothes from leading fashion designers and help with television technique. As PM, her media accessibility resulted in the sort of 'personality' spreads in women's magazines normally the preserve of TV stars. None of which hurt Labour's poll ratings. *"Relax, my son ....",* Tom Scott, *Evening Post*, February 29 2000. ATL: H-606-088
2. Labour kept its election pledge to end the logging of indigenous forests on the West Coast despite the vociferous protests of local communities and mayors. The forests, milled by Timberlands West Coast, were added to the conservation estate and a large economic development package helped compensate for job losses. *"We seem to have run out ....",* Malcolm Walker, *Sunday News*, May 7 2000. ATL: A-316-2-021
3. No prime minister had been so dominant since Muldoon, so there was a certain inevitability about columns of newsprint searching for similarities. The cartoons were usually more perceptive. *Why Helen is not ....,* Tom Scott, *Evening Post*, August 10 2000. ATL: H-618-059
4. With the Court of Appeal about to pronounce on the foreshore and seabed, Tariana Turia's refusal to toe the government's line on the issue and Brash's "drift towards racial separatism" speech at Orewa still reverberating in the polls, Helen Clark was under considerable pressure. *"Apart from that ...",* Bob Brockie, *National Business Review*, May 7 2004. ATL: A-314-2-075
5. Despite the popular perception that Helen Clark pulled all the strings, Margaret Wilson, the parliamentary speaker appointed in Jonathan Hunt's place, was a strong-minded ex-law professor. *"And when I speak ...",* Rod Emmerson, *NZ Herald*, March 3 2005. ATL: J-065-080

1

2

3

WHY HELEN IS NOT ANOTHER MULDOON
☐ MULDOON RANG EDITORS HE DIDN'T LIKE LATE AT NIGHT.
HELEN RINGS REPORTERS SHE DOES LIKE LATE AT NIGHT.
☐ MULDOON WAS BLINDLY LOYAL TO EVERY NO-HOPER IN CABINET.
HELEN PUBLICLY REBUKES COMPETENT MINISTERS FOR ANY FAILINGS.
☐ HELEN INTERFERES IN EVERY PORTFOLIO.
MULDOON DIDN'T LET ANYONE ELSE HAVE A PORTFOLIO.

4

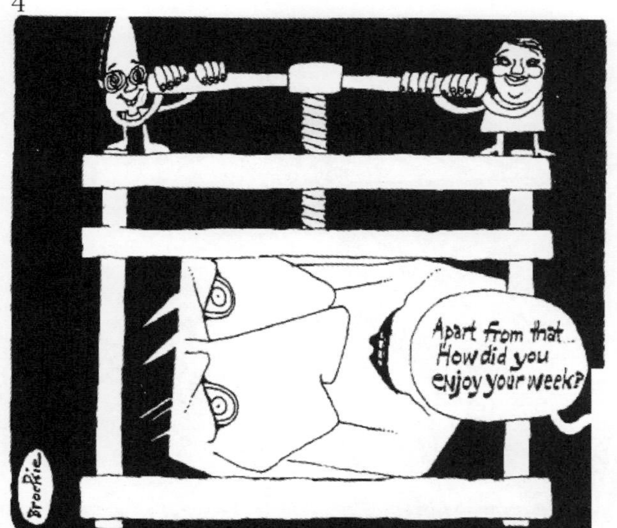

Apart from that... How did you enjoy your week?
Brockie

5

....AND WHEN I SPEAK IT WILL BE WITH ONE UNMISTAKABLE VOICE
WILSON REPLACES HUNT AS SPEAKER
WILSON

Busy in the Beehive

Helen Clark, the shy, uncertain opposition leader of 1994 was now, at the beginning of the new century, in control of Labour's agenda and respected by her generally capable cabinet. A swag of legislation was passed – dealing with ACC, hospital services, industrial relations, student loans, the bulk funding of schools, defence, shop trading hours, energy conservation, and the logging of indigenous West Coast timber. Clark had long since abandoned the heady leftist enthusiasms of her university days; there were still ideals and aspirations, but they were more 'corporatist' in tone, with the state, employers and trade unions working co-operatively to modernise and diversify the New Zealand economy in tandem with measures to minimise economic and social difficulties. There was even the occasional political coup to savour, like the 2002 appointment of former National prime minister Jim Bolger to the chairmanship of NZ Post and its new Kiwibank subsidiary, after he sold the Bank of New Zealand to Australians in 1992.

1

2

1. Badly bruised by the 1991 Employment Contracts Act, the union movement welcomed the Employment Relations Act that came into force in October 2000. The legislation gave unions a key part to play in employment relationships. *"Yep ....I m still a contender!"*, Anthony Ellison, *Sunday Star Times*, March 19 2000. ATL: H-609-003
2. Some saw a republican 'agenda' in the abolition of knight and damehoods in 2000 and then, in 2003, a new Supreme Court as the country's court of final appeal, in place of the London-based judicial committee of the Privy Council. *"I thought they were jesting ...."*, Jim Hubbard, *Dominion*, April 12 2000. ATL: J-065-078
3. Helen Clark took the unusual step of becoming minister for arts, culture and heritage, and provided an early, unprecedented injection of $80 million into the arts sector. Her interest and support has continued. *Arts Minister*, Jim Hubbard, *Dominion*, May 19 2000. ATL: A-350-044
4. The Pathways to Arts and Cultural Employment (PACE) scheme, or 'artists-on-the-dole' as it was dubbed, was introduced in November 2001 to help job seekers develop careers in the arts and creative industries. Critics said there were hopeful tattooist-body piercers and stuffed-toy makers on its books; in June 2003, the government claimed that with help from the scheme over 1,200 beneficiaries had found work, mostly long-term. *"You do realize ...."*, Garrick Tremain, *Otago Daily Times*, March 14 2002. ATL: H-668-023

3

GOVT
ARTS
$86.8
MILL'ON

4

YOU DO REALISE THAT WHEN YOU'RE A GAINFULLY EMPLOYED BALLERINA YOU NO LONGER GET THE ARTISTS' DOLE?
WINZ
TREMAIN

Taking the Flak

The difficulties governments face on a daily basis are sometimes predictable, sometimes completely unexpected, like TV3s GM crop release 'ambush' midway through the 2002 election campaign. On the other hand, Labour knew it would get both barrels from the defence establishment, and the usual bevy of ageing gold braid, when it announced, in March 2000, the cancellation of the $700 million agreement to buy 28 F-16 fighter jets from the United States to replace 19 ageing Skyhawks. The government could, though, feel more aggrieved that some of its agencies had adopted with such enthusiasm some of the worst excesses of the private sector. And the government might have also expected the building industry to be sufficiently checks and balances conscious not to have the 'leaky building' problem dripping messily on the minister's desk.

1. PM Clark said cancellation of the F-16 agreement would allow for more logical and coherent defence planning; opposition leader Shipley said it spelt the end of the country's ability to defend itself in the air – the Wanaka Warbirds excepted. *"Thank God for the Spitfire ….",* Peter Bromhead, *Dominion*, March 22 2000. ATL: A-314-1-028
2. PM Clark is the country's prime 'tall poppy' candidate. 'Scandals' that would barely rate a mention elsewhere are opportunities for outpourings of righteous moral indignation. Signing an abstract painting she had commissioned for a charity auction in 1999 became, with encouragement from opponents, the symbol of Machiavellian perfidy. *"Do you think it s a fake?",* Chicane, *Southland Times*, April 15 2002. ATL: H-703-008
3. In a pre-recorded interview with Helen Clark on July 9 2002, TV3's John Campbell, without revealing his sources, accused the government of covering up the release and planting of genetically modified corn the previous summer. The next day Nicky Hager's *Seeds of Distrust* was launched and the interview aired. It was just 17 days before the election. *".... And so it came to pass ....",* Jim Hubbard, *Hawke s Bay Today*, July 16 2002. ATL: H-756-016
4. Several government departments, but most notably Work and Income (WINZ), headed by Christine Rankin, spent large amounts of taxpayer's money on consciousness raising, bonding and self-congratulatory functions and conferences, sometimes flying to out-of-the-way luxury locations. *"So …. How have our bookings ….",* Malcolm Evans, *NZ Herald*, February 29 2000. ATL: H-643-015
5. Poor design, sloppy construction and wrong materials contributed to the 'leaky building syndrome' and the possibility of rotting and leaks in half the country's houses less than 10 years old. *"Incontinence knickers ….",* Tom Scott, *Dominion Post,* October 9 2002. ATL: H-734-040

1

2

3

4

SO... HOW HAVE OUR BOOKINGS BEEN AFFECTED BY THE BIG CRACKDOWN ON STATE-OWNED ENTERPRISES SPENDING HUGE SUMS OF PUBLIC MONEY ON MEETINGS AT RITZY RESORTS?

WE WONT KNOW TILL AFTER THEY'VE FLOWN IN FOR THE 3-DAY CONFERENCE THEY'VE ARRANGED TO DISCUSS IT!

Evans

5

INCONTINENCE KNICKERS, CHEAPER THAN PINK BATTS WILL ABSORB WATER FOR TWO YEARS BEFORE THE FLOOR ROTS, BY WHICH TIME WE'LL BE IN THE SOUTH OF FRANCE...

Ins and Outs

Some observers saw Clark's public criticism of her own ministers – she sacked four of them during Labour's first term – as domineering, autocratic and insensitive; others approved of her 'hands on' style and her formidable ability to identify and fix problems before they got out of hand. Later, she was more forgiving of John Tamihere before it became impossible for him to remain in cabinet. There were other 'ins and outs' elsewhere on the parliamentary spectrum. The Alliance imploded in early 2002, the faction representing the party's governing body 'expelling' seven of its 10 MPs for backing the government's 'right-wing' agenda. Bill English made no impression on Clark's popularity, so National replaced him with the even less charismatic Don Brash. When Richard Prebble stepped down from the leadership of ACT, a majority of his colleagues contested the position.

1. During 2000-01 four ministers were sacked or resigned. Dover Samuels faced allegations of sexual misconduct; Marian Hobbs and Phillida Bunkle were investigated for allowances claims; Ruth Dyson failed a breath test while driving. All, with the exception of Bunkle, were later reinstated. *"I couldn t stand to see....",* Chris Slane, *NZ Listener*, March 10 2001. ATL: H:-676-010
2. Jim Anderton continued as deputy PM after his 'expulsion'. Both factions continued to operate under the 'Alliance' name, meeting in separate caucuses and planning for the next election as opposing parties. Had any left the Alliance 'offically' they would have been forced out of parliament, caught by the previous year's Electoral Integrity Act that followed a string of defections from the minor parties. *"Jump, Jimbo, jump!",* Chris Slane, *NZ Listener*, March 30 2002. ATL: H-724-041
3. At the 2002 election, National's pitiful 20.9 percent of the party vote translated into 27 seats and a fight to retain its position as the official parliamentary opposition. Despite rumours, it was not until October 2003 that Don Brash took the highly unusual, and risky, course of publicly challenging Bill English. Brash won a caucus vote at the end of October. *"Look! The plotters and ....",* Jim Hubbard, *Hawke s Bay Today*, April 8 2003. ATL: H-756-028
4. Following Richard Prebble's surprise resignation from the ACT leadership in late April 2004, 'perk buster' Rodney Hide won the poll of party members. *"Is it just me ....?",* Tom Scott, *Dominion Post*, June 25 2004. ATL: A-312-4-024
5. Tamihere's career as a cabinet minister looked shaky after allegations about his business dealings before entering parliament. The end came after an interview in the April 2005 issue of a current affairs monthly in which, among other things, he insulted a number of colleagues from the prime minister down. *"This Tamihere Chappie ....",* Bob Brockie, *National Business Review*, April 15 2005. ATL: A-314-2-078

1

2

3

4

IS IT JUST ME, OR IS RODNEY LESS FUN NOW THAT HE'S LEADER OF ACT..?
STAY ON MESSAGE
REMAIN DIGNIFIED AT ALL TIMES

5

Take Your Partners

Helen Clark took the risk, on a flimsy pretext, of seeking a second prime ministerial term at a time when personal and party poll numbers suggested she and Labour might win enough seats to govern with only Jim Anderson's newly-minted Progressive Coalition. This appealed as the Greens, who had supported the government on confidence and supply during its first term, had made it clear they had an immoveable 'bottom line' – no support for a government that lifted the moratorium on the commercial release of genetically modified organisms in October 2003. Clark did not hide her displeasure then or during the subsequent election campaign when Hager's book was 'released', its own burst of GM contamination clouding public confidence. While the Greens claimed no knowledge of the book, they suffered in the government-led backlash. After the election Helen Clark, with fewer seats at her disposal than before, was obliged to dance a tune or two of Peter Dunne's making.

1. They might have made history as the country's first two women prime ministers but Helen Clark and Jenny Shipley had very little else in common. Shipley's poor performance against Clark in the House was one of the reasons her colleagues replaced her later in the year. *Mud Wrestling, Round 2*, Tom Scott, *Evening Post*, March 22 2001. ATL: H-648-037
2. The Greens, who had worked well with Labour since the 1999 election, did not pull any punches in attacking the government's decision to allow, after a moratorium period, the commercial release of genetically modified organisms. *"Greens should stay ...."* Chris Slane, *NZ Listener*, June 8 2002. ATL: H-724-043
3. Labour was so far ahead in the polls, with Bill English no more effective an opposition leader than Jenny Shipley, that Clark decided to go to the country early. The election campaign, though, did not go exactly to plan. *"You re well ahead in the polls ....",* Tom Scott, *Evening Post,* July 2 2002. ATL: H-674-129
4. The GM 'cover-up' furore rekindled public suspicions about giving one party too much power. With no surge in seats on election night, and the Alliance's collapse, Clark was in a more difficult position than before. But this time relations with the Greens (9 seats) had fractured to the point that she came to an accommodation with Peter Dunne's United Future (8 seats). *"Dirty dancing",* Bob Brockie, *National Business Review*, August 9 2002. ATL: DX-003-070

1

2

3

YOU'RE WELL AHEAD IN THE POLLS GIRL, YOU MUSTN'T APPEAR ARROGANT..

CAN I SAY AT THE OUTSET, WHAT AN HONOUR, WHAT A PRIVILEGE IT IS...

THIS IS GOOD. STAY HUMBLE GIRL, YOU CAN DO IT...

FOR YOU TO HAVE ME AS YOUR PRIME MINISTER!

OOPS...

TOM SCOTT

4

THE MMP CLUB

DIRTY DANCING...

Brockie

A Brash Alternative

Dr Donald Brash was an unlikely party leader: nearing 65 when he got the job; a political novice; a numbers nerd; a poor performer in the House; quiet, owlish and old-fashioned. Brash grew up a liberal, his father a prominent church minister, and became a market economy convert during post-graduate studies. He was a pioneering merchant banker in New Zealand and ran the NZ Kiwifruit Authority before becoming, for 14 years, the governor of the Reserve Bank, and guardian of the interest rate. It is hard to know whether his black and white ideas about New Zealand society and history are genuinely held or simply opportunist. Either way, the view that everyone in the country, Maori and non-Maori, should be treated equally struck a chord with many New Zealanders who felt the same, but had been inhibited by the strong whiff of political correctness in the air, and sent National soaring up the polls, and into contention again. National's horror of sinking to third party status was averted, at least for the present.

1. The Reserve Bank governor's primary role, since the reforms of the 1980s, has been to establish and maintain price stability or low inflation. *Housekeeping at the Reserve Bank*, Malcolm Walker, *Sunday News*, August 3 2000. ATL: A-350-088
2. Now that he was opposition leader, journalists took much more interest in his private life than ever before. Don Brash blurred cause and effect as he discussed the end of his first marriage and relationship with his new wife-to-be. *"At least I m still ....",* Chris Slane, *NZ Listener*, March 27 2004. ATL: H-754-005
3. Shortly after his Orewa speech, Brash fired the sole Maori in his caucus, Georgina Te Heu Heu, from the Maori Affairs spokesperson role because she found some of his comments unacceptable. *"Within days of calling ....",* Tom Scott, *Dominion Post*, February 4 2004. ATL: A-312-4-028
4. Don Brash showed his political naivety with unguarded comments about changes he would like to make to the country's anti-nuclear law at a subsequently reported meeting with US politicians. Given the country's collective view on the subject, it was a stick Labour was able to beat him with regularly during the election campaign. *"While it s true ....",* Tom Scott, *Dominion Post*, June 24 2004. ATL: A-312-4-023
5. Brash's use of the b...... word generated more mirth than apprehension. Asked why he had not given more tit-for-tat at the first televised debate against Helen Clark he confessed he found it inherently difficult to shout down a woman. *"Stand well back, everyone ...."* Tom Scott, *Dominion Post*, May 26 2005. ATL: DX-025-119

1

2

3

WITHIN DAYS OF CALLING FOR AN END TO PREFERENTIAL TREATMENT BASED ON RACE, I AM ABLE TO ANNOUNCE THAT OUR LONE MAORI MP IS NO LONGER OUR SPOKESPERSON FOR MAORI AFFAIRS...
THAT TASK WILL BE FILLED BY A PAKEHA MALE FROM CHRISTCHURCH...

4

WHILE IT'S TRUE WE SAID THE ANTI-NUKE LAW WOULD BE GONE BY LUNCHTIME WHEN WE CAME TO OFFICE, WE WERE VERY CAREFUL NOT TO SPECIFY WHICH CENTURY...
NUKE SHIP BAN STAYS, SAY NATS

5

STAND WELL BACK, EVERYONE. NATIONAL ARE ABOUT TO UNLEASH DON BRASH! NO SUDDEN MOVEMENTS AND NO FEAR. HE CAN SMELL FEAR. IT COULD BRING OUT THE MONGREL IN HIM AND HE'S FIERCE ENOUGH AS IT IS...
MICHAEL CULLEN TALKS BALONEY!

High and Not so Dry

There were issues with Waitangi Day observances, Maori TV, the Pipi Foundation, and Te Wananga o Aotearoa, but it was the foreshore and seabed debate that dominated attention. In 1997, several top of the South Island iwi, concerned about their customary interests – rights and practices prior to the Treaty of Waitangi but guaranteed by it – asked the Maori Land Court to determine whether particular areas of foreshore and seabed were Maori customary land. When the Maori Land Court decided it had jurisdiction to investigate the issue, the attorney-general and others appealed and, eventually, the High Court found in favour of the appellants. In July 2003, the iwi went to the Court of Appeal which, a year later, said the Maori Land Court was able to determine the status of foreshore and seabed, and that the Crown did not own it. Aware of the iconic status of 'the beach' in the New Zealand 'psyche', and eyes firmly fixed on the political polls, the government was decisive rather than considered.

1. Traditionally, women did not have speaking rights on marae, but a special dispensation was sought for Helen Clark during Waitangi Day ceremonies in 2000 – and turned down. *"Now can I speak ....",* James Waerea, *NZ Truth*, May 2000. ATL: H-617-008
2. In 2002, Clark said she would return to Waitangi for the first time since 1998, when activist Titewhai Harawira reduced her to tears as she tried to speak on the lower marae. Harawira threatened protest action again but, in fact, escorted Clark at Waitangi. *"Who is the tall broad ...?",* Tom Scott, *Dominion Post*, February 6 2002. ATL: H-674-030
3. Despite a checkered history of funding, personnel and programming crises, Maori Television began broadcasting in March 2004 – a state sector organisation dedicated to promoting language and culture, and actively supported by Maori affairs minister Parekura Horomia. *"We re making progress ....",* Garrick Tremain, *Otago Daily Times*, December 2 2002. ATL: H-690-001
4. Helen Clark described the Court of Appeal's foreshore and seabed ruling as "very narrow and technical". She said the government would legislate, if necessary, to preserve the status quo, claiming such decisions were the preserve of government policy not the courts. *Surf s Up*, Malcolm Evans, *NZ Herald*, July 14 2003. ATL: DX-002-303
5. While Clark said legislation would remove any doubt that the coastline was held by the Crown for all New Zealanders, there was considerable confusion when the government also said Maori customary rights were still preserved. *"As far as the seashore ....",* Jim Hubbard, *Hawke s Bay Today*, August 19 2003. ATL: H-756-041
6. Maori were angry they were being denied the right to test foreshore and seabed claims before the Maori Land Court. It was never the intention, as widely feared, to restrict access to beaches. *"Hands off Maori land!",* Chris Slane, *NZ Listener*, January 10 2004. ATL: H-754-002

1

2

3

4

SURF'S UP!

5

AS FAR AS THE SEASHORE ISSUE IS CONCERNED, GOVT. HAS DRAWN A LINE IN THE SAND!

6

SLANE
HANDS OFF MAORI LAND!
FORESHORE IS OUR SHORE FOR SURE
MAORI PROPERTY!
OUR PLACE
YOU'RE NOT THE BOSS OF US, HELEN!
BUT DO COME IN.

Better Bribes

Labour should have won the 2005 election easily. The economy was in election landslide shape; Helen Clark was a flinty, effective campaigner and Don Brash an at times bumbling political neophyte. Yet National had sensed the mood out in the electorates much better: the country was booming and people wanted their cut, and they wanted it now; there was a growing frustration and anger about what was perceived as race rather than needs based social spending. National and Labour dominated the campaign. If the personal tax cuts were a massive election bribe, Labour had dollops of money tucked away to concentrate the minds of special interest groups. The minor parties were left floundering, having to actually promote policies, many of them good and worthy. Labour's focus, and certainly its advertising, wasn't as good, but it did court possible coalition partners and associates while National gave no succour to potential parliamentary helpmates.

1. What Michael Cullen presented in May 2005 did not read like an election year budget, its derisory amounts of tax relief too far in the future to interest anyone. The public, equating the much publicised surpluses with money in the bank, resented his parsimony. *"You get the rest ....",* Peter Bromhead, *Dominion Post*, May 20 2005. ATL: A-314-1-030
2. Broad hints about more generous and immediate tax cuts and regular repetition of that successful mantra about treating all New Zealanders the same, guaranteed a positive reception for National. *National Poll Dancer*, Rod Emmerson, *NZ Herald*, June 28 2005. ATL: DCDL-0000141
3. The Greens survived the election in reasonable shape but ACT, written off by most commentators, kept a toehold only after Rodney Hide's Houdini-like effort in the Epsom electorate. *"Fair Go ....",* Rod Emmerson, *NZ Herald*, July 29 2005. ATL: DCDL-0000144
4. For whatever reason, Winston Peters' support dropped during election year. He lost his Tauranga seat after 22 years, and brought fewer MPs to Wellington. *"For those of you ....",* Tom Scott, *Dominion Post*, June 18 2005. ATL: DX-025-135
5. The Maori Party's Turiana Turia refused to condemn police-state rule in Zimbabwe and claimed Donna Awatere Huata was the victim of a racist legal system. Yet her party was 2005's biggest winner. *At least we re all on the same planet ....",* Bob Brockie, *National Business Review*, September 2 2005. ATL: A-314-2-080
6. The special vote count changed little, except National's loss of a seat gave Clark more palatable options, including her preferred minority administration position. *The New Political Dynamic*, Bob Brockie, *National Business Review*, October 7 2005. ATL: A-314-2-081

1

2

3

4

FOR THOSE OF YOU WHO CAN, AND DON'T RISK IT IF YOU CAN'T, HOW ABOUT A STANDING OVATION FOR OUR HERO AND SAVIOUR, WINSTON PETERS!!
STRUTH, FROM THE LOOK OF THEM I HOPE HELEN CALLS AN ELECTION SOONER, RATHER THAN LATER...
TOM SCOTT

5

At least we're all on the same planet...
MR SENSIBLE
ELECTIONS
Brockie

6

CRACK!!
THE NEW POLITICAL DYNAMIC
THE PROMISED LAND
Labour
GREENS
UNITED
JIM
NGA MAORI
Brockie...

Life Goes On ....

For many, in New Zealand and everywhere else, the 1990s ended with anxiety that the Y2K or millennium bug was going to do terrible things to computers and other essential adjuncts of modern-day life. As it turned out, Y2K may well be modern marketing man's proudest achievement: the invention of a new product that has to be dealt with within a short, finite period; to service it, the creation of a world-wide industry, that earns billions of dollars; and then huge global relief, rather than court cases and furious litigants, with the discovery that it had never existed in the first place. So life went on .... drug worries, sex scandals, sporting ups and downs, women at the top and on the street legally, fractured families and fundamentalist faiths ....

1. The world celebrated the dawning of the new millennium at the end of 1999, the purists insisting it was a year too soon. *"You ve got the ...",* James Waerea, *New Truth,* December 22 1999. ATL: A-214-130
2. There were drug-related suspensions of nearly 1,500 students from New Zealand schools in 2002. Since then, random drug testing at schools has proved more successful than suspensions. *Drug testing in school ....,* Peter Bromhead, *Dominion,* June 26 2000. ATL:A-314-1-029
3. For a range of reasons, petrol prices rose spectacularly during the first years of the decade, with the very real possibility that the era of 'cheap' petroleum was over. *The Modern Version ....,* Chicane, *Southland Times,* 2000. ATL: H-641-013
4. Professional sportsmen, like other fathers, get time off work for the birth of their children. But baby-minding 'at work' might be more problematical. *"Being there for the birth ....",* Jim Hubbard, *Dominion,* June 6 2000. ATL: J-065-079
5. Women were increasingly prominent in public life. Early in the decade, New Zealand had a woman prime minister, opposition leader, attorney general, chief justice, and governor-general – all at the same time. *"You re too late ...",* David Henshaw, *Jock s Country Life,* 2001. ATL: J-052-010
6. The Prostitution Reform Act, passed by parliament in June 2003, decriminalised prostitution, introduced measures to protect the health and safety of sex workers and their clients and prohibited anyone under 18 working as a prostitute. *"What should we do ....?",* Tom Scott, *Dominion Post,* March 28 2003. ATL: H-734-144

1

2

3

4

BEING THERE FOR THE BIRTH WAS ONE THING, BUT THE BABYSITTING IS PLAYING HAVOC WITH OUR INTERCHANGE...

5

"You're too late, the voting papers are posted . . . an' you voted for 3 feminists and the sitting lady mayor!"

6

7. Russell Coutts skippered New Zealand's *Black Magic* to win the America's Cup in 1995 and helmed the successful defence in *Team New Zealand* in 1999-2000. When he won again in 2003, this time sailing for the Swiss challenger *Alinghi*, for many New Zealanders distress at his move to a competitor overshadowed his remarkable sailing achievement. *Cuckoo Clock*, Malcolm Evans, *NZ Herald*, March 3 2003. ATL: DX-002-214
8. Faith in the police diminished for a number of reasons, none more damaging than allegations of sexual attacks on vulnerable women. *"Hello, hello …?"*, Tom Scott, *Dominion Post*, February 19 2004. ATL: A-312-4-027
9. The number of New Zealanders getting married halved between the late 1970s and 2000, and those marrying were doing so later and increasingly having children in their mid to late-30s. Divorces – with violence one of the factors – are also rising steadily. *Engagement …*, Chris Slane, *NZ Listener*, October 2 2004. ATL: H-754-021
10. Apart from some tragedies involving inadequate 111 emergency responses, the international call centre is a metaphor for the determination of companies to cut costs regardless of the frustration it causes customers. *A story of our troubled times,* Bob Brockie, *National Business Review*, November 26 2004. ATL: A-314-2-077
11. The Destiny Church, which raised shivers and hackles during its black-shirted 'Enough is Enough' Civil Union Act protest march through Wellington in August 2004, was refused permission to march across the Auckland Harbour Bridge in February 2005. *"Pastor Brian ….",* Garrick Tremain, *Otago Daily Times*, January 31 2005. ATL: DX-022-168
12. Restructuring, particularly in government agencies, was endemic in the 1990s and continues, if at a slower pace, in the new century. The dislocation to people rarely seems to be weighed against possible operational improvements. *"Oh, that reminds me ….",* Klarc, *NZ Listener*, September 29 2001. ATL: H-756-043

7

8

9

10

A STORY OF OUR TROUBLED TIMES

Thank Christ! A phone box!

PHONE

111!! HELP! I've been assassinated! Bludgeoned!

YES SIR... YOUR NAME PLEASE...

IS THAT WITH OR WITHOUT A 'W'?

For Chrissake! I'm bleeding to death!

ERM... ERM...

WHERE ARE YOU SIR?

Main street Auckland

IS THAT AUCKLAND AUSTRALIA?

AUCKLAND CANADA?

AUCKLAND UK?

AUCKLAND USA?

AAAAARGH!

HE HUNG UP!

111 CALL CENTRE CALCUTTA

Brockie

11

12

OH, THAT REMINDS ME, LEWIS. THERE'S ANOTHER ROUND OF RESTRUCTURING COMING UP.

KLARC

INDEX

The New Zealand Cartoon Archive was launched on April 1 1992 as a partnership between the New Zealand Cartoon Archive Trust and the Alexander Turnbull Library, Wellington, New Zealand. In 2005 it was fully absorbed into the Alexander Turnbull Library. Its primary role is to collect and make publicly available New Zealand editorial cartoons. The collection includes over 25,000 cartoons, originals and copies that have been donated by cartoonists, their families, newspaper and other publishers and the general public. It is a valuable resource for the general public, academics, history and social studies teachers, students and researchers of articles, books and TV programmes. The collection is indexed on the National Library's 'TAPUHI' http://tapuhi.natlib.govt.nz website and the Archive now has several hundred cartoon images on the National Library's 'Timeframes' http://timeframes.natlib.govt.nz website. Copies of cartoons can be viewed at Turnbull Library Pictures on the ground floor of the New Zealand National Library, Molesworth Street, Wellington. For further information about researching and ordering copies of cartoons, and on the aims and background of the New Zealand Cartoon Archive, visit the website http://www.cartoons.org.nz or contact the Cartoon Archive Librarian at the Alexander Turnbull Library.

ALEXANDER TURNBULL LIBRARY
NATIONAL LIBRARY OF NEW ZEALAND
Te Puna Mātauranga o Aotearoa